Treading Water

Tracey Wickham
with Peter Meares

EasyRead Large

Copyright Page from the Original Book

Addresses for companies within the Random House Group can be found at www.randomhouse.com.au/offices

National Library of Australia

Cataloguing-in-Publication Entry

Wickham, Tracey and Meares, Peter.
Treading water: my life in and out of the pool.

ISBN 9781 74166 951 0 (pbk).

797.21092

Wickham, Tracey, 1962–.
Women swimmers – Australia – Biography.

Other Authors/Contributors: Meares, Peter.

Cover design and front cover image by Elizabeth Allnutt
Cover inset images by the International Swimming Hall of Fame,
    Newspix and Getty Images
Internal design and typesetting by Midland Typesetters, Australia
Printed in Australia by Griffin Press, an accredited ISO AS/NZS 14001:2004 Environmental
    Management System printer

10 9 8 7 6 5 4 3 2 1

MIX
Paper from
responsible sources
FSC
www.fsc.org   FSC™ C009448

The paper this book is printed on is certified by the © 1996 Forest Stewardship Council A.C. (FSC). Griffin Press holds FSC chain of custody SGS-COC-005088. FSC promotes environmentally responsible, socially beneficial and economically viable management of the world's forests.

ReadHowYouWant partners with publishers to provide books for ALL Kinds of Readers. For more information about Becoming A (RHYW) Registered Reader and to find more titles in your preferred format, visit:
www.readhowyouwant.com

TABLE OF CONTENTS

To my beautiful angel, Hannah Lee, my little Hannah Banana.

You are always in my heart.

PROLOGUE

It was to be the race of my life: the final of the women's 400-metre freestyle at the World Aquatics Championships in Berlin, August 1978. Every female world record holder was in the field, including little old me, fifteen-year-old Tracey Wickham from Brisbane. Although I was considered one of the favourites on the strength of my double gold and 800-metre world record at the Edmonton Commonwealth Games in Canada three weeks earlier, the odds were up against me.

I'd had tendonitis in my left shoulder for some time and it flared up again while training in Berlin. As a precaution, my coach withdrew me from the 100-metre butterfly and even talked about painkilling injections. In reality, he had overdramatised the shoulder problem as a publicity stunt and the media fell for it. I reckoned all I needed was adrenalin to get back on track, and there was plenty of that at the World Championships.

It was midsummer, but the night was unseasonably cold and the wind whistled through my thin nylon green-and-gold Speedo tracksuit as the eight finalists marched into the outdoor arena. It was the same pool that was used for the 1936 Berlin Olympics and had only eight lanes, unlike the standard ten used today. This would pose problems for swimmers in the outside lanes, of which I was one, with splash off the walls ricocheting into waves and creating a backwash.

Beside me in lane two, almost blotting out the light, was the giant East German Barbara Krause, the world 100-metre freestyle record holder. She was rugged up in a full-length, fur-lined overcoat and looked every bit of her daunting, musclebound 190 centimetres. And there was I: a skinny kid, standing 164 centimetres and weighing only 50 kilograms. I became more determined to fight.

Shivering, I watched the Amazon as she took off her coat and tracksuit. She had hair under her arms that you could plait and the hairiest dark legs I have ever seen. As we would later learn, this – along with the Adam's apples and acne sported by the East Germans – was a dead giveaway that anabolic steroids were being used. Not that I blamed the swimmers themselves, they were told they were taking vitamins. It was the officials and politicians who were the cheats.

I cursed myself for being so dumb and cruising in my heat, which made me the second slowest qualifier and put me in the outside lane. Although I had won the heat easily, I'd clocked only 4:14 and my coach Bill Sweetenham erupted afterwards, saying I'd miss the final. As it turned out I nearly did, scraping in ahead of just one contestant, a little-known Dutch girl who would start in lane eight. I was in lane one, next to Krause, and my plan was to stick with her over the first half of the race. She was a sprinter and would lose energy whereas I, as my old coach John Rigby put it, was the first long-distance female swimmer in history who could negative split (that is, finish the back half of the race faster than the front half).

In many ways, Krause was the least of my worries. In lane three was the in-form American, Kim Linehan, who had set a new 400-metre world record at 4:07.66 at the US National Titles just two weeks earlier. In four, as fastest qualifier, was my Aussie teammate and former 800-metre world record holder, Michelle Ford. In lane five was Annelies Maas from the Netherlands, a finalist at the 1976 Montreal Olympics. World 200-metre freestyle record holder American Cynthia Woodhead was in six. I knew 'Sippy' well, having raced her over the nine months I was stationed in the US the previous year. A middle-distance sprinter with a strong kick, she was the big worry. She had broken Krause's world record for the 200-metre freestyle with a sizzling 1:58.53 two days earlier.

Whoever won tonight would surely break the world record: this was the hottest field ever assembled. Never before or since have the world record holders for every freestyle event from the 100 to 1500 metres met in the one race.

Australian swimming was in the doldrums in those days. At the 1976 Montreal Olympics, Australian Stephen Holland won a solitary bronze medal in the 1500-metre freestyle and in West Berlin, Max Metzker was the only Aussie outside Michelle and me to even make a final. Australia desperately needed a win, and

I was more than ready to meet the expectations. Norman 'Nugget' May was in Berlin, commentating for ABC TV and as excitable as ever about my prospects:

Tracey won the 800 in Edmonton [1978 Commonwealth Games] in a phenomenal 8:24.62, taking almost 6 seconds off her own world record. Michelle Ford was only a second behind, so she's a chance here too. Tracey swam 4:08.45 in Edmonton and, although she's been suffering some shoulder problems lately, she's a real fighter. So watch out for her in lane one!

There was a false start before the first gun. Michelle Ford went in and I decided that if it was good enough for her, it was good enough for me, and went in as well. But I was eighty percent sure it was a wrong move. Michelle was renowned for 'false starting' and, while nowadays you would be disqualified, back then two false starts were allowed. If someone broke on the third, they were automatically out, even if they hadn't gone in the first two times. Most of the time swimmers would false start to psych each other out. I just wanted to get in, race and leave.

The starting gun went again, and we were off. As soon as I hit the water I knew I had problems. After just two strokes I was almost a body length behind Krause (a whole 2 metres), who had a wash like an outboard motor. Not only did I have to contend with the churning white water, I also had no idea what the rest of the field were doing on the other side of the pool because I couldn't see over or under the Amazon. Krause was going like a bat out of hell, clocking 59.74 seconds for the first 100 metres. However, she started to die off in the third lap and by the fourth lap, halfway through the race, I finally passed her.

What a difference! Suddenly, as I turned at the wall, I was in beautiful smooth water and could see the rest of the field in my peripheral vision. I thought to myself, 'Right, this is a 200-metre sprint now.' I went flat strap.

The time for the first 200 was right on 2:04, they've gone out very fast. Linehan the American leads Wickham and then the other American, Woodhead. Remember, Tracey's capable of finishing the back half faster than the first, so there's a chance of a world record, but she's got to beat these Americans first.

At 300 metres, 'Sippy' Woodhead was in the lead but only just, by 0.01 seconds. Linehan was right behind me but the rest of the field were far gone with 100 metres left in the race. We three world record holders fought it out over the last two laps. Strangely enough, I didn't feel tired. My adrenalin was pumped. Coming to the final turn I felt supremely confident. I wanted to win it for Stephen Holland, who'd been shamefully criticised by the media when he 'let down' Australia by 'only' winning bronze at Montreal. Steve, who broke thirteen world records in his career, was a brilliant turner and had let me in on his secret: 'You have to start pushing off the wall before you touch it with your feet. Use your arms to flip your body over.'

I never forgot those words and so there I was, making one of the fastest turns ever. Sure enough, I came up in front. I felt like I had wings and I was just flying over the water. It was a surprise to everyone, including the television producer from the States who had focused on the Americans in the centre lanes and ignored me out in lane one. He had to quickly cut to me in the last 15 metres.

With 25 metres to go, Tracey Wickham is in front. You can't see her I know, but trust me, she's ahead of the Americans and they won't catch her.

I touched the wall and turned around to look at the electronic scoreboard. Next to my name were two asterisks flashing, meaning a world record. I'd done it!

Gold for Australia! Tracey Wickham, this little dynamo from Brisbane is the world champion!

That last 100 metres was timed at 59 seconds, the fastest of the race. Her upbeat tempo never slackened and she hit the wall two strokes in front of Woodhead in 4:06.28, a new world record. She swam the last 200 metres in 2:02.17, much faster than the first 200 and took 1.38 seconds off Linehan's mark. That's her fourth world record in six months.

I said it at Edmonton and I'll say it again. I've seen all the great Australian distance swimmers for the past quarter of a century and this girl Tracey Wickham is as good as anyone we've ever produced. That was one of her greatest swims. What a performance!

I was overcome with emotion. I swam 10 metres down the pool and Michelle, who finished fifth, came over to congratulate me. She gave me a big hug and I burst into tears. I only cried twice in my career after a race, this first time because I suddenly realised the enormity of what I'd achieved. I'd done it the hard way, with no sponsorship and no fanfare – just natural ability, family support and hard work.

No one in my family could afford to be in Berlin, but my Aussie teammates cheered their heads off and, funnily enough, the German crowd was really generous. Before the race, when I was introduced, I waved and they started yelling out, 'Tracey, Tracey.' The majority of them came from the west of Germany and loved anyone who beat the detested East Germans. I suppose they were also partly on my side because they wanted someone to beat the dominant Americans. It felt nice all the same.

Despite the drama in the press about my shoulder problem, I barely felt it during the race. Years later, at my wedding, 'Nugget' May presented me with a terrific framed caricature. It showed me sitting in a wheelchair with my shoulder in a sling and the next picture had me on the victory dais with the gold medal around my neck. I went on to win the 800 metres at those World Championships too and was the only

Australian to win gold at the meet. The paper ran a photo with the caption: 'Tracey: our one-girl team'.

I've swum plenty of great races, but the memory of that 400 metres will stay with me until I die. Greg Lalor, the onetime head of the Queensland Amateur Swimming Association, says it was: 'the best swim ever by any Queenslander. She even swam the second 200 metres of that race in 2:02, faster than the Australian record for that distance!'

My 400-metre record was to stand for almost a decade until it was finally broken by American Janet Evans in December 1987. It had been a world record in itself: the longest-standing world swimming record in history. It was the greatest swim of my career.

PART 1

BIRTH OF A CHAMPION

'THAT SOLOMON'S CRAWL'

BY HANNAH CIOBO, DAUGHTER OF TRACEY WICKHAM

You see me here, an old and frail man in the twilight of my time. I sit here by the Roviana Lagoon, where my life began and where it starts to fade. I practically grew up in this lagoon, swimming and diving in our island way. The water and the reef were my home. I will soon fade away and no longer will the waves on the reef sing their songs to me. I see the fish and the creatures of the deep. The spirits whisper to me and give me strength to tell my story so that, one day, my name may be remembered.

Part of me belonged to the white race. My father, Frank Wickham, was an Englishman. He took me and my brother from the Solomons and brought me to a large island to the South West, with great cities and harbours, where no reefs held back the waves from golden beaches. I came to this land, Australia, still a child.

I was homesick for my lagoon. I missed my mother, the sea. I missed the scent of coral and the thunder of waves on the reef, so I went to Bronte Pool. Friends were nagging me to go in a swimming race. I dived in and won, leaving people open-mouthed at my speed. I swam in my island style, crawling across the water. Nobody had ever seen such a stroke. I created a sensation. One coach said, 'Wickham's six-beat kick reminds me of an outboard motor.'

After that race I started competing in more events and relays against other swimmers, setting world records which stood for many years. Alick Wickham became a famous name. My Solomon's crawl became known as the Australian crawl. Today the entire world calls it freestyle and it is the fastest swimming stroke known. But people forget its birth and nobody remembers my name.

As the years passed, I made a living by becoming a trick diver and swimmer in carnivals throughout Australia. I could beat all comers in all the techniques known. I could run 100 yards underwater, beating swimmers on the surface. People thought I had drowned, but were left in amazement when I bobbed to the surface.

My diving feats became legendary. I was thirty-two when I was offered two hundred pounds to dive from a 100-foot tower into the Yarra River in Melbourne. But I was tricked: the tower was on a cliff 106 feet high, so it was twice the height. I put judgement aside and leapt into space, wearing three costumes. I made *a huge splash. The fall left me naked and in a coma for a week. Never again would I be so foolish.*

My islands called to me and I returned in my later years. When the Japanese invaded during World War II, my brother and I became coastwatchers, protecting our nation from behind enemy lines. One day, we helped change the course of history. We assisted an Australian coastwatchers' rescue of Lieutenant John F. Kennedy.

As I sit here telling my story, I breathe in my home air: the air of the islands. My life is coming to its end. The spirits of the reef tell me I will not be forgotten. For there will be another who carries my genes that will remind new generations of Alick Wickham, who gave the world the Solomon's crawl. The waters whisper. They see above me a shooting star that will come from that Great Land to the South West. A burst of light, a golden star, will light up the sky again with our name, for a moment in time.

1

I was born to swim. It's in my blood. In fact, my ancestor Alick Wickham is credited with introducing the Australian crawl to the world. Alick hailed from the Solomon Islands and came to Australia as a seven-year-old boy. His father, Frank, was an English sailor who had been shipwrecked in the Solomons and married a local girl. When his father took him to Sydney, young Alick went to the old Fort Street School and loved to frolic with his classmates at Bronte Beach. One day in 1898, at the urging of his friends, he entered an under-tens race at the Bronte sea-baths. He won by a mile, using the style he had learned back home in the Roviana Lagoon. He astonished onlookers with his speed and unusual stroke. Watching the race, prominent swimming coach George Farmer exclaimed, 'Look at that kid crawling!' The description stuck and the Australian crawl was born.

While the crawl was gaining popularity, Aus tralia had found its first Olympic swimming gold medallist in Freddie Lane, who won the 200-metre freestyle in Paris in 1900. At that time, the sport of swimming was undergoing fundamental changes and Lane's style was known as the 'Trudgen'. First invented by Englishman John Trudgen, it was effectively the forerunner of the modern butterfly stroke. It involved a scissor-like kick with alternate arm sweeps out of the water while swimming on the left side. Alick

Wickham's style revolutionised the sport of swimming, turning the swimmer face down so they appeared to 'crawl' across the surface. It was much faster.

Alick went on to win many races, including the Australian 50-yard freestyle championship, for which he set a new world record in 1910. His style was refined by swimming teacher 'Professor' Fred Cavill and three of his sons, Syd, Arthur and Dick. It was passed on to Frank Beaurepaire and Fanny Durack, who each won Olympic medals for freestyle before World War I. Soon the whole world was copying the crawl and Australia's dominance of freestyle swimming had begun.

The features of Alick's own personal style were his hightempo, rhythmic stroke and his powerful kick, much like my own swimming style. He was also a magnificent diver, surfer and spearfisherman. In recognition of his aquatic feats, Alick's name can be found in the Sport Australia Hall of Fame, right next to that of his descendant, me.

There are still Wickhams in the Solomon Islands. I was lucky enough to meet some of these faraway relatives a few years ago and wondered how I missed out on their beautiful olive skin. Auburn hair and freckles aren't the ideal combination for a swimmer, but that was the way the dice rolled.

My mother came from strong English stock. Her great, great, great-grandfather, Samuel Rothery Colborne, was a blacksmith at St Bees in Cumberland, on the west coast of England. As the poet Henry Wadsworth Longfellow has written:

> The smith a mighty man is he
> With large and sinewy hands
> And the muscles of his brawny arms
> Are strong as iron bands.

This blacksmith physique has been passed down through the generations and the Colbornes are a tough lot. Samuel's son, Joseph, emigrated to Charters Towers in Australia during the gold rush. There he had a son named Samuel, who in turn had a son named Samuel, the father of my grandfather, Dave Colborne.

Dave's mother's family had also emigrated from England. My great, great-grandfather, John Cracknell, was a cabin boy from the age of eleven and was swept overboard on the North Sea. His large canvas pants filled up with air and became buoyant, so he stayed afloat until rescue came. He went on to become a Master Mariner and was the Commodore of the Tyne River. His daughter, Ann, joined the Carmelite nuns before leaving to marry and come to Australia with her husband Walter. He was an explosives expert in the Queensland Charters Towers mines during the 1870s gold rush, but died from a fall when attempting to climb a mine shaft. He didn't want to wait for the cart to take him up. 'Impatience killed him', said the report of his death.

His daughter, Clara Jane, was left fatherless and quit school at the age of twelve. She married into the Colbornes at eighteen and became a nurse and ultimately matron of her own hospital where she cared for 'fallen women' and teenage mothers at Shafston Avenue in Brisbane. In 1950, she made a pilgrimage to Jerusalem and Rome and brought back holy water and rosaries blessed by the Pope for my mother, Elaine.

My Grampa Dave was Clara's only child. Athletic and strong, Dave was tall, with fair hair and clear blue eyes. He was educated at St Joseph's Nudgee College in Brisbane. It's always been said there are two religions at that school: Catholicism and rugby. Nudgee College is regarded as the greatest rugby nursery in Queensland, with the boys in the blue-and-white butcher's stripes winning more Greater Public School rugby premierships than any other team. Matches against GPS archrivals, Gregory Terrace, regularly draw crowds of over ten thousand and if you make the First XV you are regarded by fellow students as a demigod.

At Nudgee, Grampa Dave won the Senior Cup for being the best all-round athlete. For three years he played on the wing in the First XIII (in those days they played rugby league) and represented the school in cricket, athletics, boxing, swimming and lifesaving. Grampa was a great swimmer, but he was haunted by a tragedy in the late 1930s. He was staying at Mermaid Beach on the Gold Coast when he saw a man swept out to sea. Dave dived down to grab the body by the hair and nearly died bringing him back to shore. Unfortunately, the poor man, who was on his honeymoon, had drowned.

In 1924, Dave's second year in the First XIII, Nudgee played Toowoomba Grammar for the GPS premiership and was awarded a penalty in front of the posts. The scores were level – six–all – and fulltime was approaching. The next move was vital. Dave was the team's goal kicker and so renowned for his skills that the Nudgee supporters had already begun to celebrate their victory. In he came with his left foot kick ... and missed! He never got over it.

The premiership was shared, but despite that blot on his copybook, Dave was regarded by Brothers' rugby legend, Jack Ross, as the greatest all-round athlete ever to go through Nudgee. That assessment came fifty years after Dave had left the school, so he beat out alumni like Wallabies Mark Loane and Paul McLean, rugby league internationals Kevin Ryan and Mick Veivers, surfer Peter Drouyn and many other fine sportsmen.

He was a truly great athlete, however one of the Christian Brothers at Nudgee used to put him down intellectually, saying, 'Remember, Colborne, brains and brawn don't mix.' Dave set out to prove that they could. He enrolled in dentistry at the University of Queensland and, not being naturally academic, made sure to concentrate on his studies. He graduated, but entered the workforce during the Great Depression.

There were no jobs and few had money, so he and a friend set themselves up as roving dentists and travelled through the bush, fixing teeth in return for room and board. Eventually he returned to Brisbane, where he lived in a room under the hospital and set up a practice in Ipswich. On a trip to Burleigh Heads, he met Heather Goldsworthy, who captured his heart. He used to bribe her sister Joy into telling him Heather's movements and, soon enough, they were married.

During my career and early days, Grampa Dave was my greatest supporter. With Dad often away in the US, Mum struggled to raise all three girls, my sisters Kelly and Julie and me, on her own. Even though we were battlers, we ate well thanks to Dave. We loved him so much.

After state or national championships, I would always have a week or a few days off with him down the coast, just hanging around the beach. He would take me fishing out in the tinny at 4am and we'd eat cold pies and sit on the river for a few hours. He did all the work, baiting the lines and casting the rods, but he always let me pull in the fish.

Grampa attended all my meets and even some that I wasn't swimming in, just to keep an eye on the competition. I can still see him now, sitting up at the finish end of the Valley Pool with his old-fashioned stopwatch in hand, peering over his reading glasses at the swimmers before marking down places and times. In a way, I think I made up for the sports career he wasn't able to have because of the Depression.

***

My paternal grandfather, Bill Wickham, who I call Pop, was born in Ipswich in 1909, the youngest of thirteen children. He was a clerk for the Queensland Railways and then learned shorthand and was so skilled he could read it upside down. He applied for a temporary job as a stenographer to the General Manager of Mount Isa Mines Limited (MIM), Julius Kruttschnitt, an American mining engineer from Louisiana. Moving to Mount Isa, Pop became Kruttschnitt's right-hand man and, in later years, the executor of his estate. He was the first person to render forty-five years service with MIM and never took a day of sick leave in all that time. A great one for sport, Pop and his mate Sam Cumming laid the first turf wicket in the town. He was a handy spin bowler and batsman and competed in athletics and golf.

One day in town, Pop met his future wife, a young girl named Mary Veronica who everyone called Mim, in honour of the Mount Isa Mines where her father was foreman. Mim suffered from asthma and had a very bad mishap as a young girl when her father accidentally dropped a car battery on her. Notorious for liking things her own way, she was a meticulous homemaker and did everything by hand. In those days, Mount Isa had no electric irons or washing machines or even refrigerators, with vegetables arriving once a week from Townsville by non-refrigerated train.

Mim was also a great gambler. All her married life, she paid for her own clothes and accessories with winnings from punting on horses and cards. She was also a good tennis player and golfer. She gave birth to my father, Roger, the second of five children, in Mount Isa in 1941. When he was eleven, he caught cattle blight, which in those days was incurable. The doctors told the family he would go blind. 'We'll see about that!' replied Mim and, with loving care, set about treating her son herself. In ten days, Roger was cured.

Roger became a student at Nudgee College in Brisbane and the star of the First XV. Pop wanted to take him on a trip to the 1956 Melbourne Olympics, but the school refused to let him go. Perhaps winning the GPS rugby premiership was more important than the Olympics to the Nudgee College administration. Pop took Dad anyway and on their return installed him at Nudgee's arch-rival school, Gregory Terrace. Dad played for the First XV and went on to become captain of the swimming team, breaking many GPS records.

Dad spent all his spare time on the Gold Coast surfing and hanging around with his mates. While at school, he joined Kirra Surf Club and excelled in surf lifesaving competitions. In 1959 he won the Australian Junior Belt and Kenny Wiles, a surf lifesaving legend, won the Senior Belt. It was a meet to remember for Kirra Club, as no club before or since has ever snagged both titles.

Dad was 185 centimetres tall and lean, with very strong legs. He had calves like Popeye and, like Alick Wickham, had a powerful kick. I've always been a daddy's girl. We even look alike: auburn hair, freckles and strong calves. Whenever I stood on the pool blocks, Dad's contemporaries swore it was Roger standing there, and now my son Daniel has inherited the same physique. If you put us side by side, we look like three peas in a pod. The Wickham gene lives on.

If there was one quality in particular that I inherited, it was the Wickham legs. Throughout my career I had a powerful, two-beat kick (meaning one kick with each leg per stroke), which was as fast as most people's six-beat. Holding onto a kickboard, I could just about keep up with an average swimmer using both arms and legs. Even today, in my late forties, I have very defined calves, just like Dad.

***

My mum Elaine Colborne, Dave Colborne's daughter, grew up on the Queensland beaches and was a strong swimmer. She loved the sea, but preferred tennis and piano. In her own words:

I was born in 1940 at my grandmother's private hospital, St Clair, at Kangaroo Point in Brisbane. I had two younger sisters and we were educated at St Mary's in Ipswich, All Hallows and then were boarders at Star of the Sea Catholic Convent at Southport. I did well at school but had to miss a lot of classes to look after our mother who was sick.

For the last year of her life she was bedridden and I used to cook, clean and carry her to the bathroom. She died at the end of my sub-senior year and after I matriculated I went out and got a job as a secretary instead of going on to university, against the wishes of my father, who always wanted me to study. Ironically, fifty years later, I'm now into the second year of an arts degree at the University of Queensland.

Holidays with my sisters, Denise and Narelle, were spent hanging around the beach at Surfers Paradise with boys mainly from Nudgee or Terrace. Rock and roll had arrived in Australia and we used to go to dances at the local church hall, wearing rope petticoats and huge circular skirts that flared out when we turned. The bikini had just been invented and I bought one from Paula Stafford's swimwear shop at Surfers Paradise. It was blue on one side and white on the other. Our father forbade us from wearing any type of two-piece, but my sister Denise secretly wore one and had her photo printed in the paper, leaping off a sand hill. Not only was she was in big trouble, she even had an explicit phone call from a pervert.

At the beach one day I met Roger Wickham, a good-looking, dark-haired Terrace boy who was a star swimmer at school and a keen surf lifesaver.

The strapping bronzed lifesaver and the petite blonde were a match made in heaven, it seemed. They began going out together and eighteen months later, things got serious. Mum fell pregnant with me very quickly and did not want an abortion. Although my parents weren't sure how 'in love' they were, they got married because it was the right thing to do in those days. They were very young: Mum was twenty-one years old and Dad was only twenty.

The wedding was in May 1962, with Mum twelve weeks pregnant, and I was born six months later in Rosebud, Victoria on November 24. Over the next two-and-a-half years I would have two sisters in my life, Kelly and Julie. That meant Mum had three girls under the age of the three to raise.

Dad had always dreamed of studying law in America and had been offered a few scholarships but, feeling the responsibility of his newfound family duties, he joined the army. With Dad being on assignment so often, the marriage soon soured. Mum struggled:

Roger was away often, either on army duty or somewhere in the United States, where he spends most of his time these days. He was always chasing a dream, trying to make millions of dollars. Even though his children idolised him, he was never at home much to see them grow up. He doesn't realise what he missed, especially with Tracey. She was something very special.

So I effectively raised my three girls on my own. We struggled financially as I got nothing from Roger. I had to support a family on a secretary's wage. If it wasn't for my father, Dave Colborne, bringing us food each week and assisting financially, we would have starved. His efforts enabled Tracey to become a world-class swimmer.

I didn't feed her anything special, just plain, healthy food. I knew she had a sweet tooth and loved ice-cream, Mars Bars and cream buns, but with the amount of training she did, that didn't matter. She just burned off all the calories.

I remember one time we were so broke that I hesitated before buying a twenty-cent Delicious apple. Believe it or not, but that was a significant amount of money to me in those days. Eventually, I bought one for Tracey, as she needed it. Kelly and Julie had to miss out.

2

When I was born, Dad was posted to the Portsea Barracks in Victoria and we lived there for twelve months. He was then transferred to Woodside in South Australia and was promoted to captain. My sisters Kelly and Julie were born in Woodside and then the whole family moved when Dad was transferred to Malaysia, where we lived for two years.

Dad loves telling his story about me and my sisters before the big move:

Tracey had a large dose of that protective streak probably common to most children when it comes to younger sib lings. In mid-1965, my battalion, 4th Battalion, Royal Australian Regiment, was preparing to embark for a two-year tour of duty in Malaysia, as part of the 28th Commonwealth Infantry Brigade, based in Malacca. Part of these preparations required all family members to be inoculated against typhoid, malaria and other tropical diseases.

The Regimental Medical Officer (RMO) was Captain Daryl Salmon, a gentle, bespectacled 2-metre behemoth. Well, he must have seemed that way to a two-and-a-half year old 76-centimetre tyke. Tracey had short hair, a deep voice and was dressed in brown corduroy overalls with a shirt and green sweater. At first glance it was easy to mistake her for a boy, which Daryl did.

'And how are you, my boy?' he asked.

This brought the immediate low baritone response, 'I'm not a boy! I'm a girl!'

'Oh! I see. Well, my humble apologies, Miss,' said a severely-chastened Daryl.

Next up to get her injections was Kelly, who was then about fourteen months. She had watched Tracey glowering at Daryl as she received her injections, but when Kelly was placed on the examination table and saw the needle at close range, her bottom lip hit the table and she immediately began crying. Not whimpering, crying – real, from-the-belly crying. That was enough for Tracey. She immediately reached up to her full height and whacked Daryl as hard as she could on his knee, blurting out, 'Don't you hurt my widdle sister!'

Daryl was pleased to see the last of the Wickham family.

In Malacca, we lived in a no-frills army house in a cul-de-sac, right next to the ocean. There were about twenty houses on our street, which was really just a dirt track. It was incredibly hot but airconditioning was unheard-of in those days, so my sisters and I used to lie on the tiled bathroom floor to cool off. Malacca was a whole new world, and Dad was surprised at how quickly we picked up the new way of life:

We had three Chinese amahs, Ah Eng, Ah Choo and Ah Eng's elderly relative not long down from China, whom we called Aunty. Julie was only a few months old at the time, so Aunty forever had Julie in her arms cooing and speaking Hokkien to her. Eng spoke English, Mandarin and Malay while Choo spoke no English. Both Eng and Choo, however, spoke to Tracey and Kelly in Chinese. Once when I returned from a six-month tour of active duty in Borneo, Eng was excited to show me something. '*Tuan,*' she said. 'Watch this!' She then rattled off a burst of Chinese to Tracey and Kelly and they immediately scurried upstairs. I smiled and asked Eng, 'What did you tell them?' She replied, 'I tell them, Daddy home. Quick! Go upstairs and have bath.'

Ah Eng used to bathe us in a big galvanised iron tub. Nobody ever worried about security, so I used to run in and out of our neighbours' houses, up and down the dusty street and on the rocks by the sea. I was a naturally strong child. Even as a baby of seven weeks, I could raise myself out of the bassinet solely on the strength of my arms. When I was three, I used to love climbing the poles under our house and hanging, suspended by one arm. Ah Eng would shriek in horror, thinking I might fall and hurt myself, but I would slide down to the ground with a big grin on my face. I was a tough little bugger.

As the oldest sister, I was fiercely protective of Kelly and Julie despite there being only thirty months between our ages. As Dad recalls:

Not long after we had settled in to Jalan Tay Boon Seng in Malacca, I had cause one afternoon to rebuke Kelly for something. The bottom lip immediately dropped as always and charging to the rescue came the cavalry, her big sister, who immediately flung her protective arm around Kelly and glared up at me and said, 'You always pick on the little people!' She had managed to discard 'widdle' by then. I had not known until then, that there was a species which lived in my house called the 'Little People' but I never forgot it afterwards.

Another time, an English boy from a neighbouring house deliberately broke Kelly's favourite plastic cup. Kelly burst into tears, so I quickly ran next door and gave the boy, who was a good 30 centimetres taller than me, a left hook flush on the nose. He started bawling but I had no pity. I just said, 'You can't do that to my sister.'

Grampa Dave Colborne, who was visiting, saw the whole thing and had to bite his lip to stop laughing. Years later, whenever anyone asked about my aggressive nature, he would tell the story.

***

There were monkeys everywhere in the trees in Malacca. I'm a real pet lover and wanted to cuddle them but we had strict instructions not to go near the creatures. One day we chased a whole troop of monkeys but they turned on us. We screamed and ran.

There was also a creek which fed into the sea and we spent many happy hours there trying to catch tadpoles with jam jars. One day, I fell on the slippery rocks and into the creek. My stomach hurt and, to my horror, I saw that my jar had broken and a jagged fragment of glass had punctured my abdomen. I ran home crying and Mum laid me on the dining-room table and removed the glass shard. She then took me to hospital, where the doctor inserted several stitches. I still have the scar today.

Another incident from those days is planted in my mind because it was the first indication of how at home I would be in the water. I used to clamber over the rocks by the ocean and, despite warnings from my parents, would climb onto one especially big rock when the tide allowed me to reach it. Always competitive, I scrambled up the smooth, slippery surface and reached the top, where I threw out my arms and looked scornfully down at my sisters on the water's edge, chanting: 'I'm the king of the castle and you're the dirty rascals.'

Suddenly I lost my balance and fell forward, pitching into the deep water, which was well over my head. I plunged down with my arms and legs outstretched like a starfish. Strangely, I didn't feel panic, even though I couldn't swim. I felt serene and could see the sandy bottom and even a few fish darting between the rocks. It was quiet and beautiful and I was in my element. Suddenly, I felt a strong arm grabbing me and pulling me upwards. Mum had seen what had happened, rushed to the rock on the water's edge and came to my rescue. When we arrived home I got a smack on the backside from Dad, but I was happy because I had somehow managed to open my eyes under the water, even though I was drowning. It was a rude introduction to the underwater world but I loved it.

In 1998, I returned to Malacca to see where I used to live. I was calling the swimming with 'Nugget' May at the Commonwealth Games for the ABC in Kuala Lumpur. We were there for ten days, so on a day off I made the two-hour drive with my girlfriend, Linda, down to my old stamping ground. Thirty years on, the road had been sealed and most of the houses had been rebuilt. Ours was still standing but clearly nobody lived there anymore. I could see through the windows and was shocked at how small Ah Eng's room was.

The street was barely recognisable but, by the shore, the big rock was still there, the same as always. The memories came flooding back. I took plenty of photos to show my own kids. It was a really moving experience.

3

I was a born achiever, but it was swimming that was in my blood. At school I was a pretty good centre or goal assist on the netball court. I wasn't bad at piano either, scoring ninety-six percent in my practical exam and eighty-seven percent for theory in my first few years. I loved ballet as well and won a two-year ballet scholarship, my natural strength proving a huge asset. I reached the toe-shoes stage before the demands of swim training led me to quit. I have always been a competitor, as Mum knows:

> Tracey could have chosen many different paths, especially in the sporting field. She excelled in whatever sport she tried, but she had to be the fastest and the best. She always got the reddest face in the netball team, because she wanted to play every position at once. She hit the hardest tennis ball and played only fast tunes on the piano.

In tennis, I had a strong left-handed backhand and for a while I imagined myself becoming another Evonne Goolagong. After I returned from the 1978 Commonwealth Games, my tennis coach, the famous Davis Cup player Mal Anderson, told Dad I could make it to Wimbledon if I really set my mind to it. But that would mean giving up swimming and there was something about the dedication required to become a top swimmer that appealed to me. Pity, really: think of the money I might have made on the court. But when I set my mind to anything, no matter how tough, I do it. And I set my mind to swimming.

I first learned to swim when I was three years old, taught by Mum in Malaysia. As she remembers:

> I gave Tracey her first swimming lesson, at the age of three. It was dog-paddle, because she flatly refused to put her head underwater, but she had a huge kick.

I would paddle up and down the pool with Mum holding my hands, wearing my floaties and thrashing as hard as I could with a perfect natural six-beat kick. Grampa Dave said, right then and there, 'She's going to be good. Look at that kick!'

In 1968, when I was five, we returned to Queensland. We lived in a rented house at The Grange while Dad was at Enoggera Barracks. He would jump out of helicopters during training and I used to be able to hear the chopper blades from the primary school. At lunchtime I would look up in the sky and watch the army at work.

I was enrolled in Year One at Our Lady of the Assumption. I'll never forget my first day at school. It was May and the other kids had been there since February. I didn't know a soul and was very shy. What made it worse was that everyone had a school uniform except me. I stood out like a sore thumb. When I was introduced to the class they all chanted, 'Good morning, Tracey. God bless you.'

I burst into tears. I've always been emotional. I cry in romantic or sentimental movies or when an animal is in distress. I remember Mum taking me to see *Benji,* the Disney movie about a loveable dog. When Benji got lost and was limping along by himself, I bawled my eyes out.

'Mum, Benji's all alone. He's lost and they'll never find him.'

I've always been a real softie, although my swimming rivals won't believe it.

***

In 1970, the family moved again, this time to Stafford, north of Brisbane. I felt like a gypsy during my childhood because we moved around so much. This time, Dad had left for the Vietnam War. At the time, I couldn't understand why the war had happened and why he had to go. I just wanted to be with my dad. To this day, I have never really spoken to him about what happened there, what he witnessed or what he had to do to survive. I know it was a terrible war and the veterans never got the respect and thanks they deserved. When Dad visited us during army leave, he would make sure to wear civilian clothes when getting off the plane. He knew that if he was in his uniform, he would have been jeered at and spat on. Disgusting. In my mind, I never felt prouder to be Roger Wickham's daughter than when I marched with him in Melbourne on Anzac Day 2000.

Dad still keeps up with his friends from that war, and still rides with the Vietnam Vets Motorcycle Club here and in the United States.

While Dad was in Vietnam, he wrote to us every day. I used to race down to the letterbox to get his letters which Mum would read out to us. When we got a letter telling us he'd be coming home for good in a few weeks, we couldn't wait. The next day after reading the letter, Mum picked me and my sisters up from school. We pulled into the driveway and I ran out to open the garage door. It began opening all by itself. I was petrified, thinking there must have been a thief inside trying to get out, but it was Dad, home early. Shocked and happy, we all jumped on him, holding on to his legs and hugging and kissing our long-lost father.

***

In 1971, I was eight years old and entered the 50-metre freestyle in the local zone competition. I was a last-minute replacement for a sick contestant and had never been in a 50-metre pool before, just the standard suburban 25 metres. At the zone competition, I was supposed to dive in at the deep end off very high blocks, or so they looked to me. I dived off the lower ledge instead with Mum by my side. I came fourth, clocking around 54 seconds, and enjoyed it. There was one problem: I didn't like losing. I told Mum I wanted to win that race next year.

'Okay, darling,' she said. 'We'll have to get you some lessons.'

The next year I won the zone, then swam in the interzone 50-metre freestyle and 50-metre back-stroke. At that stage my best stroke was backstroke and I won. Bill Willis, a Queensland selector, came looking for Mum in the stands and told her I had just broken a record held by the state champion, Berna-dine McCawley. 'You've got to keep her going,' he said.

Mum booked me and my sisters in with John Rig-by's swim school at Everton Hills, where I was fortu-nate to come under the guidance of the great stroke technician, Peter Diamond. I was so lucky. It was a superb new indoor heated complex, the first of its kind in Brisbane, and I had a fantastic coach in Peter.

I can vividly recall my first lesson with Robyn Rigby, John's wife, before moving up to training with Peter. Wearing a little red-and-white bikini bottom, I was told to swim across the pool, a distance of about 12 metres, lying on my back with a kickboard on my stomach to help me float. Determined to beat the other kids, I ploughed ahead, thrashing as hard as I could with my arms and legs. I got there first all right, but had veered completely off course and swum diagonally to the far corner!

It was at John Rigby's that I also met one of my long-time friends, Michael Bohl. He was a top swim-mer who would become the Australian Coach of the Year in 2008. He currently coaches Olympic gold medallist Stephanie Rice, but when we first met we were nine years old. As Michael remembers:

> Tracey was a skinny, undersized little thing, with masses of freckles. But could she swim fast! We were both lucky enough to be taught by Peter Diamond, so we got a good grounding in the sport. Tracey and I have been friends now for nearly forty years.

Another man with fond memories of the early days is Greg Lalor. Greg was known as 'Mr Swimming' and was the Executive Chairman of the Queensland Amateur Swimming Association for twenty-seven years from 1973 to 2000. He worked from a little office above the kiosk at the Valley Pool, sometimes labouring for up to a hundred hours a week without ever receiving a cent. As he reminisces: 'I can remember Tracey coming around when she was about eight, with her two sisters and their little white dog. She was a nice little girl and she never changed.'

My sisters also started swimming around this time. Kelly, the middle sister, had a lot of talent but in the end preferred ballet and rollerskating. She was a huge support to my swimming, though, and as my career ramped up Kelly used to have the task of organising dinner while Mum drove Julie and me home from training. Her specialty was tuna mornay and it was delicious.

Julie, my youngest sister, was also a talented swimmer and made state and national age championships, but must have hated being compared to my times. She retired from swimming to concentrate on finishing Year Twelve. She became a nurse, which had always been her dream since the age of five.

***

In 1972, Mum took us to watch the Australian Olympic swim team train at Scarborough Pool, thirty minutes north of Brisbane. It was there I saw Shane Gould for the first time. That year, she would go on to win three gold medals at the Munich Olympics, and eventually would hold every women's freestyle world record from the 100 to 1500 metres. She was my idol and I had made up my mind.

'Mum, I want to go to the Olympics and swim like Shane Gould.'

'Okay, darling. It will be a lot of hard work, you know. But I'll take you to training if you really want.'

Seeing Shane gave me a tremendous incentive to swim. I wanted to wear an Australian tracksuit and togs, just like my hero. Four years later I got my wish. If only everything in life was so simple.

When I was in Year Six we moved again to a new brick house with a large cement carport on Leeside Street, Aspley, and I went to the local school: Our Lady of the Angels at Wavell Heights. After school and on weekends, I would hit tennis balls against the wall of the carport for hours and played netball for the school and Norths Netball Club, which won the grand final several years in a row.

But swimming was always number one and, as a kid, backstroke was my favourite. I liked to watch everything going on around me, instead of just the black line on the bottom of the pool. One day, I called my mother over to the side of the pool and yelled, 'Mum, watch this!' I dived in and started to swim butterfly.

She couldn't believe it. 'Who taught you to do that?'

No one had. I had been watching the other swimmers and mimicked their stroke, picking it up in an instant despite the difficult coordination involved with the arms and legs. It soon took over as my favourite.

I continued my training at John Rigby's. Peter Diamond, my coach, had spotted my talent and told Mum, 'If she wants to, Tracey can go a long way, maybe even to the Olympics.' Boy, Mum didn't realise what she was getting herself into! Three afternoons a week I was at the pool, thriving on Peter's coaching, even when it went from being fun to just hard work. I loved training almost as much as racing because I could hang out there with other kids and make friends.

Peter was fastidious about technique and his backstroke mantra sticks in my mind:

Thumb up ... turn hand over ... little finger in ... brush your ear ... arm in ... bend your elbow ... push right back down your side ... hips up, chest up high ... and keep kicking.

I give most of the credit for my success in swimming to him. He taught me the art of the perfect stroke right from the very start. In my mind, we were a great team. Peter thought so too. He loved my give-it-all attitude:

Tracey was always very determined and competitive. She was extremely strong for her age and the only swimmer in our squad who could beat her was Paul Moorfoot, who was two years older. She had a burning hunger to be a champion.

One evening, I bawled her out for not training properly. She said her throat was sore (we later found out it was tonsillitis) and I told her to go home. She refused and I lost my temper.

'Okay, if you don't want to be a champion, just sit around here and do nothing.'

As I was cleaning up to close, I heard shouting and went to see what the commotion was. There was Tracey, on her own, looking miserable. She'd had an argument with her mum about going home and had stubbornly stayed behind.

'Mr D,' she said, 'do you really think I don't want to be a champion?'

That was just one example of her phenomenal work ethic. When I told her to take a break between seasons and only do a couple of swims to keep in touch with the water, she would do the couple on the first Monday of the break and then ask if it was all right to come again. I would tell her mum to try and make her have a break, but you know Tracey.

I set my first state age record in an under-elevens 200-metre individual medley race at Rigby's pool. I had to stand on the blocks and pose for a photo in the local paper, the *Northside News.* I felt proud but a bit shy, as all my mates sitting in the stands were ragging me and making me laugh. Peter Diamond had me autograph a copy of the photo for him and said, 'You'd better get used to it, because there'll be a lot more of these in the future.'

More than thirty years later, Peter presented me with the very same autographed photo on the national television program, *This Is Your Life.* He had been carrying it around in his diary for all those years. There I was, a skinny kid in a nylon costume with a skirt on the front and a ribbon tied at the back to stop the straps slipping off my shoulders, a far cry from the supersuits of today.

I have never forgotten what Peter did for me and I am so glad he was my first coach. He was my launching pad and created my powerful stroke. I can still picture him walking up and down the side of the pool with his megaphone, calling out to us to correct this or that with our arms and legs. He was awesome.

4

I began to grow accustomed to posing for photographs and being interviewed. In 1974, when I was eleven, my photo appeared on the front page of the Brisbane *Telegraph* after I had broken my twenty-fifth state age record in five months.

That same year I went to the Australian Age Championships in Hobart as second reserve for the under-twelves 200-metre backstroke. It was freezing at the outdoor pool, but I didn't care because my hero, Shane Gould, was going to be there. I was doing laps in the warm-up pool and kept an eagle-eye on the front gate, waiting for her arrival. There was a sudden commotion and people began swarming around the far end of the pool. The Golden Girl was here!

I grabbed a towel and waited in line for ages to get Shane's autograph. It was so cold my bare feet were numb and started sticking to the concrete. I was excited to meet her, but too shy to tell Shane I had swum the 100-metre butterfly at the State Age Titles that month in 1:10.5, which was 9.6 seconds faster than she had swum at my age.

Shane signed her name for me and drew a fish below her autograph. I loved her so much that for the rest of my career, I signed with a fish too (see below). The only difference was that my fish pointed the other way because I'm left-handed. I still have her autograph to this day.

I was thirteen years old and in Year Eight when I moved to All Hallows, a Catholic girls' school in Brisbane, near the Story Bridge. The teachers there were supportive and understood how important my swim training was, especially in the later years. Quite often, I wouldn't get my assignments done and Sister Harndy would say to our Year Ten class, 'Stand up those who haven't done their homework.'

I would rise, slowly, from my silky oak desk in the back corner. Usually around six others in our class of twenty-five would also stand. Sister Harndy would look at me and say, 'Oh, you sit down, Tracey, I know you've been training hard. Just try and do what you can when you have the time.'

The other girls would shoot me death looks, but they soon forgave me. Everyone knew I was training my butt off and wouldn't get home until 7pm each night. Then there was barely enough time to help cook and eat before I crashed into bed at 8.30pm, ready to rise at 4.30am to cook a breakfast of bacon, eggs, tomatoes, toast and cereal to take with me to the pool for gruelling before-school training.

Not only were the teachers kind, but the principal, Sister Anne Hetherington, was a sports nut. Being away a lot of the time with training or meets, I was often behind in my studies, but Sister Hetherington always smoothed things over for me. I'd also get in trouble for having arguments with teachers over the fact that my socks weren't pulled up or I wasn't wearing a hat when I left school. But how could I run all the way to the pool with a hat on? Sister Hetherington understood. We often had little chats over a cup of tea in her office as she quizzed me on my exploits in the pool. I rewarded her by swimming my guts out for the school.

When I was thirteen, I set a new state age record for the open 100-metre freestyle, clocking 59.8 at the Catholic Secondary Schools meet. I was the youngest ever Queensland schoolgirl to break the minute. I also won the 50-metre freestyle and 50-metre butterfly in record time and swam in four relays. At the presentation afterwards, over a thousand schoolgirls chanted:

> She is our champion.
> Tracey Wickham, our girl!
> All Hallows got Tracey Wickham! Ha! Ha! Ha!

That was the most moving moment of my young life and, throughout my whole career, it would be the school competitions that gave me the biggest buzz. The school kids really got behind their champions.

In my three and a half years at All Hallows, I was never beaten in the inter-school competition. I was in the Blue House and was entered in every stroke in my age group and the open events. For example, I would swim the fifteen-years 50-metre butterfly and then run straight back to the start to swim for the open'fly.

All that training made me hungry and I ate like a horse. I was lucky that I never seemed to put on weight because I burnt it all off in the pool. To ward off the hunger pangs, Mum used to pop four hard-boiled eggs in my lunchbox each day, so I'd wander around the school, munching on them between classes.

While school and swimming were under control, things back home weren't going as smoothly. It felt as though Dad had never really come back from Vietnam. He was deeply affected by the experience of war and seemed closer to his mates than his family. He left the army and got a job as an insurance repre-sentative with National Mutual. Although he was smart and capable, he couldn't settle and soon quit. He tried network marketing and real estate but neither of those lasted very long either.

In 1975, he tried his hand at politics and nearly made the big-time. He won pre-selection for the fledgling Progress Party, but when it came to drawing up the ballot, he arrived five minutes late with his nomination papers at the electoral office. That meant he was ineligible to stand and the dream was over. The local newspaper published a photo of him looking very despondent, holding the too-late forms. It was a shame, because he would have made a really good politician.

For me at least, 1975 was going great guns. I broke dozens of state age records and progressed to John Rigby's elite squad. They trained at the Fortitude Valley Pool, just five minutes from All Hallows. Plenty of world records had been set at Fortitude Valley since it opened in 1927, by legends like Murray Rose, David Theile, Dawn Fraser and Stephen Holland.

I loved that pool, although it looked old-fashioned with its dark brick façade and grubby change-rooms. There were no modern gym facilities, just rusty old iron bars built over dirt and rubber straps we used to stretch with. But there was a sunny grassed area next to the pool and an intimate feel, with the little grandstand right up close to the pool deck with only a metre between them. Best of all, the pool just felt *fast* to me and it's where I set my first world record. Maybe it had something to do with the fact that it was on Wickham Street!

John was a great coach and we were very close. He has always championed my skill in the pool:

> Tracey had this incredible will to win, whatever she did. Even though she was so tiny, she developed a stroke that suited her anatomy perfectly. She was high in the water, a straight line through the hips, and used little apparent effort. She wasn't a bay cruiser, she was a hydrofoil!

> Tracey soon became the fastest girl at the pool, despite being two years younger than some

others, and woe betide anyone who dared get in front of her at training. She was the best swimmer I ever had, male or female, and I was once National Team Coach. I think she had the all-round ability of Mark Spitz or Michael Phelps, but in those days scheduling didn't allow you to swim many different events. The Australian Championships at that time lasted only three days, so Tracey had to concentrate on her best events, the middle-distance freestyle races. However, I've no doubt that she could have been a world-class butterfly swimmer. You just have to look at her record: as she grew up she broke every age record in 'fly as well as freestyle.

One particular race I swam in 1975 sticks in my mind. I was twelve years old and was overtaken in the last 75 metres of a butterfly race at the National Age Championships in Adelaide. It was the 200 metres and I had only ever swum about three of those races in my life, so was very 'green' as far as tactics were concerned. As soon as I dived in, I began swimming flat out. At the halfway point I was a body length in front of Karen Van de Graaf from Queensland, but by the second-last lap my arms started to feel heavy and I hit the athlete's infamous 'brick wall'. On that final turn, Karen touched the wall just ahead of me and by the end of the race finished two body lengths in front. I was barely able to muster up enough energy to make it to the end. I was exhausted and embarrassed. It was the worst moment of my young life and I vowed that never again would I let anyone pass me once I got in front.

And they didn't. I've never told people this before, but it was from that day forward that I became an expert in negative splitting. This meant I would take it easy in the first half and then mow the opposition down in the second. I would pretend to myself that I had just dived in fresh and would bolt to the finish. My bad experience at the age of twelve had taught me well and I never wanted to be left without fuel in the tank ever again.

In November 1975, my coach John Rigby switched me to endurance freestyle training despite my love for backstroke and butterfly. He explained that although I had a talent for the form strokes, I had an extraordinary ability for endurance events. He wanted me to start training for the Australian Titles, which were to be held in Sydney three months later. Those titles would also serve as the trials for the Montreal Olympics.

I was daunted at the thought of swimming against the big guns. I was a small-statured thirteen-year-old and nobody, not even I, thought little Tracey Wickham had a chance at such an elite level. John said it would be good experience to race against the major players, girls three or four years older than me. So I churned out the laps: 8–10 kilometres a session, twice a day. A typical session would look something like this:

- 1500-metre freestyle warm-up
- 8x400-metre freestyle on 4 minutes 45 seconds

- 30x50-metre kicking – freestyle and'fly every 60 seconds
- 3x500-metre pulls (with feet tied together)
- 20x50-metre sprints, with a jump-out at each end, on 60 seconds
- 500-metre warm-down
- 20 minutes practice of turns (two or three times a week)

One of my favourite training sessions at Valley saw me swimming 30x200-metre freestyle on 2:40 minutes and averaging all of them under 2:08, with the last ten sets all under 2:02. It was exhausting, but I was flying on top of the water.

In later years, heavy training schedules like this would be criticised. Even the great Shane Gould, who won five medals at the 1972 Munich Olympics, thinks I overtrained:

> Tracey swam some incredible times. She was a pocket rocket, like Libby Trickett or Janet Evans. In that time they thought more was better and she was a training demon. But I think she may have done too much. You need balance in your life.

For me though, while the training was hard, I loved it. I loved being the best I could be. At last I was ready for Sydney and the 1976 Olympic Trials.

5

North Sydney Olympic Pool was a stunning venue for the National Swimming Championships and Olympic Trials held in February 1976. An outdoor saltwater pool, it was built under the Sydney Harbour Bridge and sits right on the water, next to Luna Park. Being so close to the bridge, the rattling roar of the trains took some getting used to.

To a thirteen-year-old kid from Queensland it was a scary experience, but after all the hard work I'd done, I felt up for the challenge. That was despite the fact that it would be only the third or so time I had raced the 400-and 800-metre freestyle. At least nothing was expected of me, so I wasn't too nervous, just very excited and aiming for a personal best. My main goal was to try to get autographs and photos of the star swimmers.

It was summer and pleasantly warm, and a big, noisy crowd was creating a thrilling atmosphere. Queensland's Stephen Holland was the drawcard, hoping to break his own 1500-metre freestyle world record and perhaps even the 800 record as well. I was in awe of him.

My first event, an open 400-metre freestyle heat, was scheduled for the first session and I swam within my limits, not exerting too much energy. As usual, from the very start I swam at the head of the pack, raced against myself and finished a comfortable winner. When I looked up at the clock, I had swum 4:24.10, a whopping 6 seconds better than my personal best! It wasn't anywhere near the American Shirley Babashoff's world record of 4:14.76 but, for my age, it was phenomenal. I was the fifth fastest overall qualifier for the 400-metre final.

The final was held that evening and I was in lucky lane two. I don't know why I call it 'lucky', but I just love it and never feel any pressure to win when I'm there. I was the dark horse, 'green' and unknown in distance races, even to myself. I was daunted as we filed out onto the pool deck. I was by far the youngest at thirteen years and three months, not to mention the smallest at 40 kilograms. I wasn't even 150 centimetres tall.

All the big names were there: Commonwealth record holder Sonya Gray, the sensational New South Wales champion Jenny Turrall, who held the 800-metre world record the year before, Michelle Ford, Rosemary Milgate and Narelle Moras, holder of the 1500-metre world record. I had no tactic, apart from trying to stay with them and give my best.

Dad watched the whole thing on television on a four-hour delay because he had to stay in Brisbane and look after my sisters. He remembers the race vividly:

> I arrived home from work, gave Kelly and Julie their dinner, knocked the top off a beer and settled in to watch the 400 metres.

The race got underway with Tracey in lane two. Norman 'Nugget' May was broadcasting the event and Forbes Carlile, the famous Australian coach of that and an earlier era, was providing the expert commentary. Early in the eight-lap race, 'Nugget' mentioned that 'young Tracey Wickham from Queensland' was showing the way from Jenny Turrall, the Australian and Commonwealth 400-metre champion. Forbes responded that Tracey was a high-rating stroker and it was not unusual for high-rating strokers to take an early lead. However, Forbes pointed out, Jenny Turrall, the champion in lane four, would, at the appropriate time in the race, forge to the lead.

As the race continued and Tracey clung to her early lead which was now a mid-race lead, 'Nugget' kept saying 'young Tracey Wickham from Queensland out there in lane two, still maintains her lead' and Forbes kept responding that the champion and her New South Wales compatriot, Sonya Gray, would make their moves shortly. With two laps to go and Tracey still in front, 'Nugget' reminded Forbes that the champion would need to make her move shortly if she was going to beat 'young Tracey Wickham from Queensland'. Well the champion never made her move or, if she did, it simply wasn't good enough. 'Young Tracey Wickham from Queensland' at thirteen years of age became the Australian 400-metre champion, in a time that was 4 seconds faster than Jenny's gold medal time at the Commonwealth Games in Christchurch. A totally gutsy swim. Not a soul predicted it or could have, except maybe one and she never let on.

I won in a time of 4:18, an incredible 6 seconds off the personal best I set that morning, a total 12 seconds off what I was swimming before the meet. I was the Australian Open 400-metre Freestyle Champion and had beaten my opponents by over a second. I put my hand over my mouth. All I could think was: 'What just happened? I just beat my heroes! Am I supposed to do that? Ooh, ahh, I don't think those girls are going to like that a thirteen-year-old beat them.'

Mum, Grampa Dave and my paternal grandmother, Mim, were in the stands and sat still, totally in shock. Then they started going crazy, jumping up and down and waving to me, yelling their heads off. Back home in Brisbane, Dad was doing cartwheels in the living room. He went nuts, racing around the house yelling, 'Kids, wake up! Tracey's winning. Quick, quick!' But Julie and Kelly were deep asleep and missed the whole thing.

When I rang Dad later that evening, I couldn't contain my joy and exhilaration and there were lots of happy tears, at both ends of the phone. Of course, I had known the outcome before it was broadcast on delay to Dad, but I hadn't wanted to tell him so it could be a surprise. It was great to hear him yelling down the phone in excitement.

Greg Lalor, the Executive Chairman of the Queensland Amateur Swimming Association, remembers the aftermath of my record-thrashing swim. Despite my success, I was the same old Tracey:

> The next morning I went down to breakfast at the North Sydney Travelodge and asked one of our officials, Enid Morrison, where the team manageress, Lorraine Short, was. As it turns out, she was woken early by Tracey, who wanted someone to take her to mass. She was still a shy young kid.

Two days after my 400 win, I also placed third in the 800-metre freestyle and beat my personal best by almost 30 seconds. On the last day of the trials, the national swimming officials had a special meeting. It was standard practice for the first three place-getters to go to the Olympics, but I was so young that several officials had their doubts. How could a thirteen-year-old manage being away from home for three months? Fortunately, they gave me a chance and I would become the youngest Australian ever sent to an Olympic Games. Meanwhile, it was back to school in Brisbane the next day.

At All Hallows, I was welcomed with huge fanfare. Everyone was excited to have a future Olympian in their own school. A group of girls visited each classroom and collected enough money from all the students to buy me a camera, suitcase and travelling alarm clock to take to the Olympics. I was presented with my gifts at a special farewell assembly.

In June 1976, I flew to Perth for a pre-Olympic training camp. Mum had to work, so my grandmother Mim came as my chaperone. We stayed at a motel unit just across the road from the Beatty Park Pool. Everything should have been perfect, but I felt miserable. I missed home, Mum, my sisters and my dog. The camp lasted what seemed an eternity: seven weeks.

After Perth we flew to Melbourne, where the whole Olympic team came together. While I stayed with Mim, the other swimmers were billeted with local families and had no chaperones. With a total lack of supervision, many ran wild.

The day before we flew to Montreal, I walked into the break-up party and was shocked. It was supposed to be a harmless barbecue at a motel near where I was staying, but it was obvious that everyone had been drinking, and not just the fruit punch. This was despite the fact that most of the team were underage. There didn't seem to be any coaches or managers around, so it was on for young and old.

One of the fifteen-year-old swimmers was so drunk she lay on her back in a skimpy bikini next to the pool, yelling out, 'Somebody come and fuck me. Somebody please fuck me.'

I was stunned. I didn't even know what those words meant, until I told John Rigby the next day and he explained. I thought being picked to represent your country at the Olympics was the ultimate honour and you would be expected to give your best in training and competition. But it was apparent that to some, selection was simply a means of having a free holiday away from their parents. Where were the managers? Where were the coaches?

Those really were the bad old days of Australian swimming and our standing in the international scene reflected this. At Montreal we would not win a single gold medal – in fact, our only medal was Steve Holland's bronze in the 1500 metres – and it's not hard to work out why. The swimmers were out of control and ate everything in sight. It was a shambles.

I ran out of the party and straight back to my grandmother. I was so grateful to have Mim there to keep me company. She always made the best gravy for my steaks and we often played cards at night. She was a dab hand but I won plenty of games of gin rummy (no doubt she let me win on purpose). Like all my family, Mim loved watching me compete at various championships and would come to most of my swim meets in Brisbane.

∗∗∗

When we flew out of Melbourne for Montreal in July 1976, I was more excited about my mum visiting me than about the fact I was flying on a special team jumbo jet halfway around the world to go to the Olympics. Mum came down from Brisbane the night before I left and we went together to the airport on the team bus, which made me feel a whole lot better. I didn't get too emotional when I filed through customs because I thought I'd be able to give her a hug and a kiss later on. I'd never flown overseas before and was too young to realise that after you go through customs, that's it. When they told us that we wouldn't see our relatives until we came home after the Olympics, I burst into tears. After so many weeks away from Mum, the thought of another month was devastating.

The only person who could calm me down was another little girl, not much older than me. She was from Thailand but trained with us in Perth, so it was funny that I was the one who was emotional when she was much further from home. A few paparazzi took a photo of us as she put her arm around me while I wept. The next day, the photograph was published in papers all over the country. We became good friends, and even caught up in Kuala Lumpur at the 1998 Commonwealth Games.

After we'd gone through customs, there was an official farewell for the team, with a marching band, balloons and flags as we crossed the tarmac to the plane. Fans and family were gathered behind barriers the whole way. I spotted Mum, crying and calling out to me and barging to the front of the crowd. I ran up to the barrier and we hugged and kissed and she said she would call me every day I was away. I began to feel better and actually started looking forward to the trip.

When I got on the plane my spirits sank again. The whole team was hung-over and a complete disgrace. A sixteen-year-old swimmer, who I had beaten in the 400-metre trials, was put in the seat next to me. She seemed about to vomit. She tried sitting up but felt too ill, so she slumped down on the floor, moaning. She lay there the whole time during takeoff and somehow the hostesses didn't see her. After a few minutes, her moans died down and she passed out.

6

At Montreal, I was keen to get stuck into training but my form was beginning to slide downhill. Until that moment, every time I jumped in the pool I seemed to get faster, but not here. It was a bit of a mystery, but certainly one part of the problem was the fact that my coach, John Rigby, was not on the team. While he had come to the Perth training camp, the authorities had decided they didn't 'need' him at Montreal. I felt that decision was unfair and insulting to John.

The worst part of the whole trip was the accommodation. Twelve of us were crammed into a two-bedroom apartment with one bathroom. There was nowhere to sit except on your bed, since the lounge-room was full of bunks, and not much to do but eat and read. I wasn't very sociable at that age anyway and I was too timid to chat to athletes from other countries.

The food was terrific, I must admit, so out of sheer boredom we would often wander over to the dining hall for an ice-cream or some other snack. You could have as much as you liked and some girls began to stack on more weight. One girl was so huge, she would wait until all the team were in the pool training before she hopped into the water. She was too embarrassed to stand with the others on the pool deck. It was ridiculous to see how much the team ballooned. Not me though, you can't fatten thorough-breds. I always had that skinny, muscular build.

The 1976 Australian Olympic team in Montreal numbered a hundred and eighty-four, but we didn't win a single gold medal for the first time in forty years and the fourth time in our nation's history. It was pathetic and reflected the poor Australian team management at the time. Dad remembers sitting up in the stands at Montreal, when I paid him a visit:

Out of nowhere, Tracey appeared, dressed in jeans and an Australian tracksuit top. Just a thirteen-year-old whip of a girl with auburn hair, freckles and a friendly smile, seemingly unaware of the wonder that she was there at all, especially as a competitor. She sat down on the stairs next to my seat. She had spotted me among the huge crowd from the other side of the pool.

We had watched all the swimmers from the various countries on display. Many had heavy cotton bathrobes over their tracksuits but I noticed the Australians didn't have them, so I asked Tracey why. She said they did have them, but they were only for the team managers and officials, not for the competitors. I couldn't believe it. Talk about negligence. It may have been coincidental but Montreal was the worst performance by an Australian team in decades.

Everyone swam poorly, including myself. The team coaches tapered my training right down so I was barely swimming any distance in the weeks leading up to the race. A year or so later I would learn that I needed to train hard right up until a few days before racing to be in my peak form for competition. By the time I stepped on the blocks at the 1976 Olympics, I was unfit and knew there was no way I'd swim my best. I'd lost condition and was sluggish in the water.

There was one exception on our poor Australian team: our superstar, Stephen Holland. By the time the eighteen-year-old from Brisbane arrived at Montreal, he had broken thirteen world records. He didn't just shave fractions off them, he shattered them, sometimes taking as much as 10 seconds off the mark. Twice he set double world records in a single race meet for the 800 and 1500 metres. He was awesome to watch, always far out in front which, as I know from experience, is a tough gig when you're there by yourself with only the clock for competition.

Stephen finished fifth in the 400 metres in Montreal, but that distance wasn't his speciality. There was no 800-metre competition at the Olympics for men, only for women, so Steve's focus was on the 1500. His two main rivals were the Americans, Bobby Hackett and Brian Goodell. They cleverly double-teamed poor old Steve. Hackett led for the first half of the race and although Holland overhauled him at 900, with 200 to go he was in trouble. Sure enough, Goodell and then Hackett passed him. All three of them broke the world record, including Steve, who had beat his personal best by 4 seconds. Nevertheless, he had to be content with bronze, not gold.

This wasn't good enough for the Australian media. They flayed him. Channel 7's Ron Casey even asked, 'How does it feel to let down Australia?' Casey should be ashamed. Steve went from hero to zero in one swim and after the Olympics retired to work as an apprentice carpenter for fifty-five dollars a week. For my own part, I didn't do anywhere near as well as Steve and finished fifth in my 800-metre and third in my 400-metre heat. Well outside my personal bests.

Outside of swimming, the entire Australian team won only one silver medal (men's hockey) and four bronze medals (yachting and equestrian). Poor show, but every cloud has a silver lining. This disaster led to an inquiry and ultimately the formation of the Australian Institute of Sport in the 1980s. Since those dark days, Australia has punched above its weight at every Olympics, but all I can remember enjoying at that meet was playing with my yo-yo around the pool and eating the dining hall ice-creams. I had a lot to learn about training and competition.

Following Montreal, Swimming Sectional Manager Jack Howson, in his review of the team's performance, recommended that no swimmer under fourteen should be selected in future. I was just too young, he said. Nevertheless, six years later at the 1982 Brisbane Commonwealth Games, Dimity Douglas swam the 200-metre breaststroke at the age of twelve while Danielle Somerville-Kimlin, aged thirteen, came third in the 800-metre freestyle trials. To me, it was pretty clear that age itself wasn't the problem with the

Montreal swim team. That was just a smokescreen. After all, I had swum better than most of my elders. The real problems were the lack of funding and the abysmal team management.

***

Montreal 1976 will also be remembered for the infamous domination of the East German female swimmers. While they failed to win a single gold medal at the 1972 Munich Olympics, here they won eleven out of thirteen events and fared even better at the 1980 Moscow Olympics, averaging two out of three medals per event.

As a thirteen-year-old kid in Montreal, I was in awe of the East German sprint queen, Kornelia Ender, who that year became the first female swimmer to win four gold medals at one Olympic meet. I remember being too shy to approach her when I saw her on a bus travelling to the pool, sitting next to her boyfriend, Roland Matthes, the defending Olympic champion and world record holder for both backstroke events. I was star-struck and would have loved to get their autographs, but I just smiled at them. They smiled back. It was a thrill.

Later, after the fall of the Berlin Wall in 1989, we would learn that East German gold came at a terrible price. Kornelia Ender and her teammates retired and revealed that they had been given anabolic steroid injections from the age of thirteen and were never told what they contained. They just supposed they were vitamins. These injections made the athletes extraordinarily muscular and strong, but had debilitating side effects such as sterility, liver cancer and organ damage.

The world was shocked. Why wasn't the cheating discovered earlier? While the Olympic Committee had introduced drug testing in 1972, it was very expensive so they would only do a few random tests. The East Germans had little trouble beating the system. Testing failed to advance until the 1988 Seoul Olympics, when the Canadian sprinter, Ben Johnson, was found to be positive to steroids and was stripped of his 100-metre gold medal.

Aside from risking the swimmers' health, the East German drug-taking was grossly unfair to all other competitors. At Montreal, American champion Shirley Babashoff would have won an unprecedented five gold medals had it not been for her drug-boosted East German rivals beating her to gold every time. I always wondered what Shirley did with those silver medals. Would she have hung them up or thrown them to the back of a drawer? I know what I would have done – I would have chucked them in the Brisbane River!

After the fall of the Berlin Wall, it was also revealed that the reason the East Germans left one of their best female swimmers, Barbara Krause, out of their 1976 Montreal team was because the team doctors had miscalculated her steroid doses and she would have failed the drugs test. She came back, drugged, for Moscow 1980, where she won the freestyle sprint double in world record time. At least I can say that I beat her, steroids and all, at the 1978 Berlin World Championships. Shirley would have been tickled pink!

At last, in 2000, Lothar Kipke, the head doctor of the East German Swimming Federation from 1975 to 1985, was convicted of causing bodily harm to fifty-eight swimmers, mostly young girls who were now barren. He received a fine and a fifteen-month suspended gaol sentence, joining several other convicted East German officials. Nevertheless, nothing can make up for the damage caused by that nation to the entire sport of swimming during those decades of the 1970s and 1980s.

***

In August 1976, after four weeks in Montreal, the whole Olympic team headed back to Australia. On the return flight we stopped over in Bahrain and had to sit in the airport for two hours. Everyone was tired and desperate to get home. Finally, we boarded the jumbo for our last leg back to Australia but, when we were all seated and the flight attendants about to close the doors, I realised my handbag, wallet and passport were all still inside the terminal.

I panicked and started to cry. I ran over to the women's swim team manager, Evelyn Dill-Macky, who was like my second mum on the trip. She informed the flight attendants and a bus came to take us from the plane to the terminal. I thought for sure my bag would have been stolen, but when I raced to where I had been sitting, there it was along with all my precious items. I was so lucky, but also so embarrassed as Mrs Dill-Macky and I reboarded the plane. I ended up delaying take-off by at least half an hour. That was a lesson worth learning from my first time overseas: never leave your belongings out of your sight. I sunk in my seat and was very quiet on the way back to Australia.

7

I spent the rest of 1976 in routine heavy training with John Rigby and continued competitive racing, setting more and more personal bests. By February 1977, I had set a new Australian open record for the 1500-metre freestyle of 16:43 in Hobart at the National Championships. My success didn't faze me though, as Dad remembers:

> I was sitting at the Valley Pool in Brisbane with a friend one night, watching as various swimmers entered. Many were dressed in Australian team tracksuits with Australian team swim bags. When Tracey walked through the entrance, she was dressed in jeans and t-shirt, sneakers and a nondescript tracksuit jacket. Her old swim bag hung over her left shoulder. I pointed her out to my friend and said, 'If you didn't know who she was, you would never know who she was.'

Things were all pretty normal, considering, but yet again, life was about to change dramatically. Dad had always had a fascination with America and met plenty of Yanks during his time in Vietnam. Now he was convinced he needed to try his luck in the Land of Opportunity and, of course, there would be plenty of opportunities for me to better my swimming in the US. In April 1977, we packed up the whole family, sold everything down to the last knife and fork, and moved to California.

A month before we left for the States, Mum seemed devastated one afternoon when she picked me up from the pool. I'll never forget the look on her face. I noticed a card from the vet on the dashboard and knew it must have been something to do with our pet corgi.

'What's wrong with Susie?' I asked.

Mum wouldn't say anything at first, but finally she started crying and blurted out, 'She was run over, Tracey.'

I began to tear up. 'Is she okay?'

'No, darling, she didn't make it.'

I cried my eyes out all the way home and for days after. In hindsight, though, it was for the best as we couldn't have taken Susie overseas and she would have missed us if we had left her behind. When we got to California we bought a fluffy white poodle and called her Tammy. Home just isn't the same without a dog.

When we arrived in America, Dad was able to get me in with one of the best swimming coaches in the world, Mark Schubert, who didn't need much convincing after seeing my swim times. Mark, currently Head Coach of USA Swimming, has been on every US Olympic swim team since 1980 and has had thirty-eight of his own swimmers compete. He's trained people like the Olympic swimmers Brian Goodell, Shirley Babashoff and Cynthia 'Sippy' Woodhead. In 1977, his squad was based at Mission Viejo, south of Anaheim, where he drove a Porsche with

'SWIMUSA' numberplates. I joined the squad at Easter.

It was an incredible experience and I trained alongside five world record holders. While I was there, one of the American girls, Alice Browne, set a new 1500-metre freestyle world record of 16:24.60. It made me realise how much hard work I needed to do. I began to improve my times, inspired by the master coach and his elite disciples. From Mark I learned the valuable lesson that, to be the best, you have to work harder than everyone else. However, the drive to do that can only come from within.

The Mission Viejo swimming complex was owned by an oil company which ran the town and no expense had been spared in its construction. From what I could tell, every town in the area had its own pool, gymnasium and squash courts. No wonder America always does so well at the Olympics, I thought.

While Mum and Dad were busy trying to find jobs and a home I was billeted, along with my swimming friend from New Zealand, Monique Rodahl, with a family in Mission Viejo. The family had three children and three old English sheepdogs. My room was a small converted office next to the kitchen and I was kept awake by the very noisy dishwasher. I rarely got a proper night's sleep.

Mark Schubert would come by our billet and pick us up in his minibus around 5am each morning. We would train flat out for two hours, then come back in the afternoon and do it again after school. He was a tough coach but knew what he was doing. I thrived on the work and enjoyed mingling socially with most of the squad. This helped when later I swam against them at various international competitions. I wasn't intimidated by their reputations because they were all people I knew.

Culturally, the transition from Queensland to California was a shock. The American girls all looked like Farrah Fawcett, wore plenty of make-up and seemed obsessed with boys. By contrast, I was a shy fourteen-year-old from a strict Catholic school in Brisbane where you got into trouble if you forgot your hat. Compared to the glamour girls, I looked more like a ten-year-old boy, with short, chlorine-bleached hair, masses of freckles and no boobs. I felt completely out of place in my Queensland outfit of shorts, t-shirt and runners.

I went to school at Mission Viejo High. Australia wasn't at all well-known in those days. The kids didn't even know where it was on the map, but they were intrigued. They wanted to know if kangaroos ran wild down the streets of Sydney and if we hunted with spears for food. 'Say something in Australian,' they would ask and I would answer, 'I am saying something Australian!' They didn't even know we spoke English down under.

I still remember my first day there. After class, I went to the toilet, where the bad girls were busy preening themselves and smoking. As I walked in, they looked incredibly guilty. They're smoking dope,

I thought. So this is America! I ran out, confused, and rang Mum straightaway. I cried into the phone, 'Get me out of here. I hate it. Please come and get me.' We were both emotional. I wanted to leave there and then, but I knew that I had to stay and train.

The girls at the pool weren't much comfort, and there were a few who were totally obsessed with sex. They were extremely promiscuous and always trying to attract the bestlooking boys. One statuesque fifteen-year-old blonde used to stand in the water at the shallow end and flash her privates as boys swam by. Hardly conducive to good training! I like a bit of fun as much as the next person but, to me, swimming was my business and I was focused.

***

After a few months at Mission Viejo, Mark Schubert announced that I, and nineteen other swimmers, had been selected to go on a two-week reconnaissance trip to Moscow. The US government was sending our swim club over because it was thought we would all be there for the 1980 Moscow Olympics. Little did anyone suspect that boycotts and other problems would intervene and not one of us would ever go.

We were officially farewelled by President Jimmy Carter at the White House. As we were shown through the Oval Office, I 'souvenired' a few sheets of the President's notepaper from his desk.

Communist Russia was incredible. Security was tight, sometimes ludicrously so, but that's communism for you. For example, you were not allowed to take photos of train stations or post offices. Moscow looked impressive, especially the stately buildings in Red Square, but the people were very poor. It seemed as though everyone drove a tiny car, and they were all the same make and model. For some reason, they were not allowed to wash their cars, which were covered in grime. Shop shelves were bare and the only things we saw that we even wanted to buy were the Babushka dolls. There was a strange smell everywhere.

Before we left, we packed lollies, chewing gum and blue jeans to take with us. At a Los Angeles baseball stadium flea market, we bought the jeans for a dollar a pair and cut-offs for fifty cents. We sold them on the Russian black market for roubles equivalent to ten dollars and five dollars respectively. The problem was, we had to spend all our roubles in Moscow and couldn't take them with us. There was nothing to spend them on! We ended up giving away a lot of our jeans and lollies because we felt so sorry for the poor Russians.

***

Mum and Dad eventually managed to rent a house in Mission Viejo, close to the town's magnificent training centre and I was able to move in. We had virtually no furniture of our own, so we hired everything, from the fridge to our beds.

Dad had set up a meat pie business, but it was struggling. It seemed that Americans liked the idea of fruit in pies, but that was it. Dad thought the meat pie could be the hotdog of the future, but he couldn't raise any money or get major companies to back the idea. Undaunted, he set out to do it on his own and prove to the guys with the cash that the Yanks were going to love the Aussie favourite.

In the kitchen of our rented house, he started baking pies in a small oven and sold them through the *Penny Trader* (something akin to our *Trading Post).* Mim flew over to help but it wasn't easy having her there. I love my grandmother, but she and Mum just didn't get on. She was certainly a help in the kitchen, though. Sales increased and the smell of cooking meat filled the house. The pies became so popular that Dad and Mim sometimes worked right through the night. People began showing up on the doorstep to collect their orders, but still no major company would back the concept and we were struggling financially.

Mum had found a job as a secretary, which was illegal since she didn't have a green card, but the money wasn't enough. I couldn't afford to eat properly as good meat and fruit and veg were expensive. I was 7 kilograms overweight, which was reflected in my slower times in training. You can't break records on donuts and Burger King.

The final straw came from the Amateur Swimming Union of Australia. They rang to tell us that I would not be picked for the next Commonwealth Games if I didn't swim in the forthcoming Australian Championships in February 1978. It was typical of their inflexible attitude, but I was happy to go back home. After nine months in America, Mum and I flew to Brisbane in December 1977, and Julie would join us two weeks later. Dad wanted to stay in California and achieve what we considered an impossible dream. He still loved Mum, but not enough to come home and give up his vision. Kelly wanted to stay in the States because, among other reasons, she liked not having to wear a uniform to school. Eventually, after a lot of persuasion from Mum, she ended up joining us in Brisbane for the beginning of the school year.

All my cousins were waiting to meet Mum and me at the airport. I hugged and kissed them all. I remember Grampa Dave was standing back from the crowd, waiting his turn. He stood there crying, tears rolling down his face. He was just so thrilled to have us home. He thought that when we left to go and live in the States he would never see us again. I gave him the biggest hug and kissed him heaps.

We were stone-broke but glad to be back. Grampa drove us to a unit he rented in Toombul, which was furnished with a fridge, beds, a lounge suite and a television set. He was a champion and always looked after me.

***

An unfortunate incident took place a couple of weeks after we had moved into Toombul. We had brought a suitcase of Mim's clothes back with us from the States, because Mim expected to only be visiting California for a month's holiday, not the twelve months she ended up staying. We were meant to drop the clothes off at her house, but in all the excitement of coming home and moving into a new unit, we forgot. Soon enough, my aunt (one of Mim's daughters) came to pick it up.

Julie and I were sunbaking downstairs when we heard raised voices, then a scream. Mum, in our top-floor unit, yelled out, 'Tracey, she slapped me in the face!'

By the time I got upstairs, my aunt had left, taking the suitcase with her. She had accused Grampa Dave of being a thief and then hit Mum in the face without warning. We found out later that Mim had painted Mum as a scarlet woman and blamed her entirely for the break-up with Dad.

Furious that someone had hurt my mother, I raced down the stairs three at a time. I was too late, and my aunt's car was driving off as I got to the car park. I chucked a few stones at the back of the Peugeot, but missed. I have seen that woman once or twice since then and I keep promising myself that she'll get back what she did to Mum. One day, I'm going to belt her with a left hook. Nobody hurts my mother. Nobody.

There was a huge rift between the two families after that. When Mim came back, poor old Pop, my paternal grandfather, had to sneak out when he wanted to watch me swim. Dad would ring me whenever Mim left the house for a few hours, and I would race over and spend some time with Pop. He was a great fan and would always offer advice regarding my swimming. He thought I should concentrate on butterfly, because he felt that I could break the world record. I adored him.

PART 2

THE BEST YEAR OF MY LIFE

8

Gee, it was great to be home. Lying in the sun on the grass by the Valley Pool and chatting with my mates was heaven. After feeling lonely and homesick in California, I felt completely at home in Brisbane. Sadly, my old coach John Rigby had given up his lease at the pool just before I went to Montreal. His wife Robyn had cancer, they had three young children and were trying to run three pools, as well as coach.

I was devastated, but John Rigby believed it was for the best as his replacement, Bill Sweetenham, was just what I needed. Says John:

> I don't think Tracey ever forgave me for leaving. When the team departed for the Olympics, I went to the airport and she and her mum tried to talk me into coming back. I don't think she was aware of the seriousness of Robyn's condition and my mind was made up. It actually turned out for the better, as Bill was a hard taskmaster and took her to a new level. The more he pushed her, the better she liked it.

Twenty-six-year-old Bill Sweetenham from Mount Isa was now the head of the squad and was the first coach to be professionally appointed by the Queensland Amateur Swimming Association. These days, Bill is an international swim coach legend, but if you ask him he'll tell you his claim to fame was coaching learn-to-swim in Mount Isa, where his first family were the Rafters – as in Pat Rafter, the tennis superstar. 'So,' says Bill, 'if you want to make a good tennis player, just get me to teach him how to swim!'

Bill sure knew how to make a champion swimmer and loved experimenting:

> This was before the days of biomechanical analysis, so I used to con Channel 7's sports producer Kel Geddes to send a cameraman down to film Tracey. We used to use a rubber ducky as a camera platform, which was fairly primitive, but in slow motion I got what I wanted, and Channel 7 got an exclusive interview.

I was very lucky to have Bill, and I could say the luck went both ways, as Bill is happy to admit:

> Thanks to Peter Diamond, her first stroke development coach, Tracey had a magnificent stroke, the like of which I have not seen since. Tracey's balance and rhythm were perfect: she rode high in the water, elbow close to the surface underwater and high out of the water, with a straight line to her fingertips. From full extension, she had the earliest application of force in the stroke that I have ever seen.
>
> So rhythmical was her stroke, she had an uncanny ability to swim to instructions, to within a

fraction of a second each lap. She used to count strokes, so she knew that fifty-two strokes over 50 metres equated to a time of thirty seconds, for example.

What's more, her capacity for hard work seemed limitless. I've only ever encountered one other athlete who had the same hunger for training: Australian Olympic hurdles gold medallist, Debbie Flintoff-King. With these girls you had to rein them in, not whip them on.

With these attributes, linked to her fitness and strong two-beat kick, I could get Tracey to negative split. She was the first female swimmer to have this ability and it made her a coach's dream.

Bill knew his stuff and soon I was shedding the few extra kilos I had gained in the States. My goal was the nationals which would be held at the Valley Pool in February 1978. In those days we trained hard, really hard. They do about one-third as much nowadays. The old adage was, 'If you want to get better, do more.' Others got stale and burnt out, but I seemed to thrive on it. The harder Bill worked me, the more I wanted to do. Bill has fond memories of those days:

We had terrific morale in that Valley squad. It showed at state titles, when we would win upwards of sixty gold medals every year. Afterwards, I rewarded the squad by taking them all, along with their parents, to the Waterloo Hotel for a slap-up dinner. Lionel Hogg Snr, the editor of the

Brisbane *Telegraph,* was a generous sponsor and helped us out financially. Occasionally we would go to the best restaurant in town, Gino Merlo's Milano, for a big celebration, with lots of cake and ice-cream. I tried to make it as egalitarian as possible but there was no disguising the fact that Tracey was the star. Nights like this made not only Tracey but the whole squad feel pretty special.

I also liked to reward hard work. So, whenever she was about to go for a record or had a major meet coming up, I spoiled her by having her check into Lennons, one of the city's luxury hotels, the night before. As she was a high-profile sports star I used to be able to negotiate a good deal with the manager, so it didn't cost too much. She not only got a good night's sleep but she also felt a bit special. It was all about attitude.

And I, in turn, would reward Bill by working my guts out. I used to run down from All Hallows to get to training early, so I could sneak in a kilometre or so before the others got there.

Sometimes I would buy a cream bun or a Mars Bar, if I had any money, and eat it on the way. I loved to sit on the grass by the pool, drying off as the others arrived, knowing I had extra miles in the tank. Over a week those kilometres added up to one whole training session. I never felt that training was a grind and I tried to make each session faster than the one before.

Despite my enthusiasm, Bill would still find coaching such a young, headstrong swimmer difficult at times. Luckily for him, there was help at hand:

> My greatest ally in my relationship with Tracey was her grandfather, Dave Colborne. Not only was he always around, keeping tabs on lap times and other heat winners, but more importantly, he had a great calming effect on her. I knew if I had a problem I only had to tell Dave and he would have a word with her.

While training was tough, the squad had a lot of fun with each other. One incident that still makes me chuckle concerned Joe King, the veteran swimming coach. Joe was a netball coach before he turned his hand to swimming and had success in both sports. His swimming club, Leander, used to do some sessions at the Valley Pool in the winter, alongside our Commercial Club (the oldest established swimming club in Brisbane). I was swimming my last few laps late one afternoon, idly watching old Joe pulling in some lane ropes. Suddenly, he was tugged off balance and fell into the pool at the deep end. To my amazement and mirth, Joe began floundering about. He yelled for help and was pulled like a drowned rat from the pool. We all cracked up laughing. After thirty years of teaching others how to swim, Joe couldn't manage a single stroke himself!

I really enjoyed the company of the Valley squad, especially the boys. Guys like Adam Sambrook, Gary Watson and Stephen Fry were, and still are, my great friends. Michael Bohl is particularly special to me. These days he is happily married with two kids but I used to have a teenage crush on Michael. It was nothing serious, of course, given that I was thirteen at the time. I told his dad, George, a police sergeant and our team masseur, that I was in love with his son. George replied, laughing, 'Oh, Trace, how could you love a thing like that?'

Funnily enough, I didn't get on so well with the girls. The way Bill Sweetenham sees it, the girls found it hard to hack the competition and didn't really understand where I was coming from:

In training, Tracey was relentless. She'd mow down anyone who got in her way. And I mean that literally. If a girl was in the same lane and didn't move over to allow Tracey to pass, she'd tap the girl's leg and, if she still didn't stop, would pull her leg back and sometimes swear profusely as she swam past.

But she was there to train, not to socialise. So some of the other girls interpreted this as arrogance and the old greeneyed monster, jealousy, came into it too. Tracey got all the media exposure and the others felt they were snubbed.

Her family was quite poor and she sometimes had to pay her pool entry in one-and two-cent coins. So some of the squad thought she was a skinflint. Far from it, she was generous to her mates.

When I came back from Montreal we didn't have a lot of money, so I wore my green-and-gold Australian togs to training. I was given eight pairs of these togs for the Olympics, so it made sense to wear them. There was never any idea of showing off in my mind, but some of the girls thought differently.

One such girl used to be one of my best friends ever since I took up swimming and beat me regularly in the early days. But when I got selected for the Olympics and she didn't, things changed. One day at training she was gossiping by the pool, unaware that Mum was in earshot. She said, 'Tracey always wears her Aussie togs. Did you know she uses green-and-gold toothpaste too?'

All the girls fell about giggling, but Mum was not amused. She was the shy type, but when she got really upset she would show it. She had heard other hurtful things before and this was the last straw. I was waiting in the marshalling area for a race and saw Mum gesticulating and arguing with another lady. I was confused. On the way home, Mum told me what had transpired. She had confronted my ex-best friend's mother and had a piece of her for backstabbing me. Things were never quite the same between that girl and me after that. Still, these days we're quite friendly and catch up at our swim squad reunion from time to time.

***

This wasn't an easy time for Mum. A single mother now, she scrimped and saved to keep our family going. She was a tower of strength. Working as a secretary, she barely made enough money to feed and clothe us. Some weeks she would be down to a few coins before payday and would agonise over whether to buy an apple for my lunchbox. Regular bills like electricity and rates were major crises in our lives. If it hadn't been for Grampa Dave, we wouldn't have survived. He would show up regularly at our door with a box of fruit and vegetables or some fish he had caught from lines he threw out into the river behind his unit on the Gold Coast. An athlete himself, he knew how important nutrition was and always insisted I had a healthy, balanced diet.

School had also become too much of an expense for Mum. She told Sister Hetherington, the principal of All Hallows, that we just couldn't afford the fees and that the three of us, my sisters and I, would have to go to Brisbane State High School. Sister Hetherington wouldn't hear a word of it and immediately offered me a special scholarship. There was no way she was going to lose the Wickhams just because we had no money.

Greg Lalor, the kind chairman of the Queensland Amateur Swimming Association, waived pool entry and coaching fees and would often give me a lift to training or meets during the school holidays when Mum was at work. With everyone helping us, I was

happy and motivated, determined to repay their generosity with my best efforts in the pool.

9

Four weeks after I returned from the States, I raced Michelle Ford in a special event called the KB Games, sponsored by the Kent Brewery. I was still about 2 kilos overweight and only eighty percent fit. Michelle beat me in the 800 metres and set a new world record time of 8:31.30. It was the only world record she ever broke and one of only three times she beat me. That was all the motivation I needed. I had to get back on top.

Bill Sweetenham was thrilled with my progress. After nine weeks in the pool I returned to my normal weight and broke the world 1500-metre record five times in training. As Michael Bohl, my fellow squad swimmer, remembers:

> It was incredible, breaking that world record so many times in the old Valley Pool, with the old-fashioned cork lane ropes, the chop from other swimmers and high walls that created more turbulence. She was phenomenal.

'Let's make this official,' Bill told me. 'Let's have a crack at this world record in public.'

The florid, fair-haired Bill was no fool. He knew how to get publicity. He contacted a few major sports journalists, like Wayne Smith from the *Telegraph* and Frank O'Callaghan from Channel 7, and offered exclusive rights to the record attempt. The deal was, if I broke the world mark, they could have the story, but if I didn't, nothing would be reported.

On Tuesday night, 8 February 1978, I set out to break my first official world record. To say I was nervous would be an understatement. I had taken the day off school and went to Bill's place to rest before the event. It was a typically hot and humid Brisbane summer day and I was so wound up I couldn't sleep, even with a fan blowing on me.

Finally, Bill arrived home to take me to the pool and told me his race plan. As he remembers:

> I had a system worked out to let her know how she was going: three different coloured towels, which I would wave to let her know if she was on pace. This was strictly illegal of course, but Percy Cerutty used the same system with that great miler Herb Elliott to win the 1500 metres at the Rome Olympics in 1960. Anyway it worked like a charm.

At the pool, we had the requisite electronic timing of three officials with stopwatches, as well as lane ropes and about forty swimmers from Commercial Club and their parents in the stands. No one knew why they were there as the whole business was a well-kept secret. The only outsider who found out was Laurie Lawrence, who would later become my coach. The public had not been invited but the adrenalin flowing through my body made me feel as though this was an Olympic final.

Wayne Smith remembers the scene well:

It was a funny sight, all these people hanging around and only one person swimming. The rules required a stopwatch on every lane, so there were eight officials there, seven of them with empty lanes.

When I dived in to warm up, the water was so hot it felt like soup. My body felt lethargic and I was terribly nervous. I had chosen lucky lane two, the lane in which I qualified for the Montreal Olympics, and I was to swim on my own, mainly because nobody else wanted to do thirty laps of the 50-metre pool. This made the attempt all the more difficult, as an opponent not only gives you a sense of pace, but charges you with a bit more aggression.

The gun went and straightaway I felt sluggish. Sure enough, after the second lap, there was a red towel: too slow. I picked up my pace and, after eight laps, there it was, the blue towel. However, at the halfway mark, there was another red towel. Shit! Too slow! I was just mastering the negative split at this new distance, but I was confident I could do it. With 400 metres to go I was bang on world record pace, which was Alice Browne's 16:24.60 at Mission Viejo.

I could hear Laurie Lawrence screaming something at me, waving his arms as he stood next to Bill. I knew that I was in with a chance. Up in the stands, Mum was frozen and couldn't bear to look. She could never watch those last few laps in the big races, even when I swam world records. It was too nerveracking. But Grampa Dave was checking his stopwatch and getting excited. My stomach started churning, looking at the crowd jumping up and down.

I really picked it up over the last couple of laps and flew. I put my head down and gave it everything. Finally, I touched the wall, anticipating the applause that would come with a world record. Had I done it? The crowd was silent. It was eerie. At last, the loud-speaker blared out, 'Tracey Wickham has swum the 1500 metres in 16:14.93. A new world record!'

The kids from Commercial Club went berserk. I had slashed nearly 10 seconds from Browne's mark. It was pandemonium. They ran to congratulate me, some swimmers jumping in and nearly drowning me as I clung, exhausted, to the side of the pool.

Grampa Dave was ecstatic and rang Dad in California from a public phone to tell him the news. The *Courier-Mail* photographer spotted him and took a photo which appeared in the paper the next morning. Dave's huge grin told the whole story.

Eventually I clambered out of the pool and Lorraine Short, a QASA official, wrapped me in a towel and took me to Bill, who organised the media. I was interviewed by O'Callaghan from Channel 7 and it was on the news the following night. I was a celebrity and I loved it. But, from that day forward, I was public property. My life was a headline.

Bill Sweetenham was stoked with my success, but he didn't want me to get complacent:

> I had a trick to motivate Tracey after she had set her solo world record. I bought a huge bunch

of flowers and had them delivered the very next morning to Tracey at the pool. There was a note attached which read, 'Congratulations, but you won't have it so easy next time. Michelle.'

No wonder Tracey gave her arch-rival a scathing look the next time they mounted the blocks! She wouldn't find out until months later that it was me who had sent them.

∗∗

Two weeks later I was back at the Valley Pool for the 1978 Australian Championships, which doubled as the selection trials for the Commonwealth Games in Canada that August. I was entered in the 400 metres and 800 metres and was dead keen to avenge my recent defeat by Michelle Ford. Our rivalry went back as far as the 1975 Australian Age Championships, when we were both just twelve. Then, I had beaten her in the 400 metres, but three years later, under coach John Rodgers, she was in the best form of her life. She had beaten me at the KB Games and many were tipping her to repeat the performance.

The media seized on the rivalry and built it up, with a photo spread of the two of us that compared our records and statistics like two prize-fighters. Next to the solidly built Michelle I looked like a stick insect, since she was 5 centimetres taller and around 8 kilograms heavier.

This really was a duel in the pool and there was plenty of pressure. The papers had been reporting the findings of Bob Treffene, a medical physicist who in the past had predicted with astonishing accuracy the times I would swim, including my world record. He used heart rate measurements and blood count tests to formulate his predictions. This time, he forecast that I would break the 800-metre record easily, clocking 8:25.00, 6.3 seconds better than Michelle's mark. In theory it sounded great, but could I pull it off in reality?

Boosted by a specialised coaching session from the great Stephen Holland on my turns, I was confident of winning, despite my sore shoulder. It had forced me to cut back on my normal training and even on my warm-up.

The 800 metres was my first race and I was in lane five, with Michelle on my left in four. As the gun went, we got away to a good start. I was determined not to let Michelle get in front at any stage. The crowd were making a heap of noise, which struck me as peculiar. Why were they cheering now? We still had fifteen laps to go! I turned to breathe at the 75-metre mark and spotted Michelle, but when I turned back to breathe on that side again a few seconds later, she had disappeared. Where had she gone? Did she get a cramp? I was too absorbed in my technique to really worry.

Suddenly, something grabbed my leg. I stopped and looked up to see the race had stopped and nobody else was swimming. Officials were running around looking flustered and the crowd was booing. What the hell was going on? I perched on the lane rope, confused and upset, and yelled at an official. It turned out that there had been a malfunction with the electronic timing and the false-start rope was dropped. But we had all swum so fast it couldn't get to us in time. Those cheers I thought I heard from the crowd had been them yelling at us to stop. I was livid.

The next day, the *Courier-Mail* published a photo of the incident. There was no mistaking my mood at the time: the camera had caught me just as I was shaping my mouth to say a charming four-letter word! After the false start, the officials postponed our race and put the men's 400-metre individual medley on instead. At least it gave us time to cool down and get our breath back.

When the women's 800 metres was finally underway again, I was fuelled by anger and started like a demon. Once more, I was determined that nobody would pass me and I thrashed the water in my usual up-tempo style. I never saw anyone else and was content to swim my own race.

Bill and I had agreed that I would aim to go through the halfway stage in 4:12, but I clocked 4:17. I wasn't thinking about the time and was just trying to concentrate on keeping a body length clear of Michelle. After all, I thought, she was the world record holder and if I beat her the time would be close to a record anyway.

Bill was worried, but I pulled it together and mastered a negative split to come home faster in 4:13. I didn't know the exact times as I touched the wall, all I knew was that I had won. I looked up at my training partner, Michael Bohl, by the blocks and mouthed to him, 'What was the time?'

He was grinning like a Cheshire cat as he replied, 'Eight minutes, 30 seconds. You did it. You bloody beauty!'

My official time was 8:30.53, which was 0.77 seconds inside Michelle's world record. I was stunned. Two world records in two weeks! I swam back up the pool and ducked under the water, allowing the full impact to sink in. At only fifteen, I was a dual world record holder, the Australian 800-metre champion, and I was off to Canada. Bloody beauty all right!

The next day, I raced in the 400 metres and pulled off another win with 4:09.39. It was the second fastest swim on record, just outside East German Petra Thümer's mark of 4:08.91. It was also the Commonwealth record, 3.86 seconds inside Michelle Ford's time, and I had done it with painful tendonitis in my left shoulder. I couldn't be beaten.

***

There was another major drama at the nationals that year, which took place on the last night of the competition during the men's 1500 metres. The boys had swum nine laps, with Max Metzker in front, when the officials began blowing their whistles and waving their arms for the race to stop. Not again, I thought. The crowd started booing. My Aunty Denise, Mum's sister, got so worked up, she threw her shoes at the men in white while yelling expletives and shouting, 'Can't you guys get it right? The poor swimmers!'

But it wasn't a false start, it was a bomb scare. Someone had rung up Greg Lalor in the QASA office and said they had planted a bomb in the pool complex, although it turned out to be a hoax. The race was called off and the whole building had to be evacuated, with everyone filing out into the street.

As luck would have it, a sudden storm hit, complete with thunder, lightning and hail. I still had to do an interview about my records with *Telegraph* journalist Wayne Smith, so we sat outside in a bus shelter. The rain came sideways into the shelter and poor old Wayne got soaked, his notes a soggy mess.

10

Not many people can say that their best year came at the age of fifteen, but it did for me. The days of 1978 were a high watermark in my swimming career. Sadly, I would learn that the higher you climb, the further you have to fall.

Following my success at the nationals, in March I was selected for the Australian team for the annual Coca-Cola International swim trip to London, Japan and Germany. In those days, the Coca-Cola was our only chance to swim overseas apart from the major championships, unlike today when swimmers have the chance for international trips just about every month. My studies at All Hallows were put on hold since swimming took priority. I had been falling behind anyway, with all the time I had been away for meets, so it didn't seem to matter that I went overseas for another three weeks. Year Ten could wait.

Australia had always done well at the Coca-Cola International, and won the previous three point-score trophies. This year was no different: we blitzed'em. Our young team won nine of the twenty-four events and amassed fifty-three points, well ahead of the forty-strong British team with twenty-nine, East Germany with twenty-five and Canada with nineteen.

The biggest surprise in London was my last-minute entry into the 100-metre butterfly. It isn't unheard-of for freestylers like me to be good butterfliers or even backstrokers and my dad, Roger, thinks I could have been an all-round champion:

There has never been the slightest doubt in my mind that had Tracey concentrated on back-stroke, she would have been a world record holder. If she had concentrated on butterfly, she would have been Madame Butterfly. Somebody else would have had to step down. In my humble opinion, if she had concentrated on medley, the world record book would show a different name. Joe King, incontestably the doyen of Australian butterfly coaches in the 1960s, 1970s and 1980s, said that Tracey Wickham was the greatest butter-flier he had seen since Mark Spitz. He did not say she was the greatest 'female' butterflier. He had good reason to hold that opinion.

At the 1978 Coca-Cola International meet in London, Terry Buck, the Australian team coach, came to Tracey and asked if she would stand in for Linda Hanel in the 100 metre butterfly because she was sick. Tracey being Tracey immediately agreed to the request.

It was a sight to see her on the blocks. The towering East Germans looked like the South African Springbok rugby second row, with Tracey a pint-sized midget next to them. But this skinny fifteen-year-old girl, weighing under 50 kilograms dripping wet, a nobody freestyler on the world stage, who had never trained for this event, streeted the best butterfliers in the world in their toughest event. She pummelled the East Germans and won.

After the race, the East German coaches came over to the stands where Tracey and her mother were sitting and respectfully asked if they could talk with Tracey for a minute. They could not understand how so much power could be packed into such a small frame. All their modelling told them that BIG meant power. Of course BIG also meant drag. This is what separated Tracey from the other top swimmers of her time.

She had an incredible natural power-to-weight ratio, coupled of course with the will to win. Not for nothing did Dawn Fraser remark that Tracey Wickham had the most devastating killer instinct in Australian sport. Tracey had no fat, which meant minimal drag. When women begin developing into a pear shape, it means too much drag and not enough power. The East Germans knew there was only one way to reshape the pear: testosterone and steroids. But every action has an equal and opposite reaction. They needed truck loads of razors. Beards on girls are unbecoming, unless you're East German I guess.

The 100-metre butterfly was a triumphant win. The report in the *Times* read:

The heroine of the meet was the pixie-like dual record holder, Tracey Wickham ... She won't be sixteen until November and she's a real favourite with English swimming spectators. As she left the pool for the victory ceremony this afternoon she was besieged by autograph hunters.

It was a grand success, but Michelle Ford, my old rival, had managed to get the better of me and won the 400-metre and 800-metre freestyle, as well as the 200-metre butterfly. This only added fuel to my competitive fire.

**

In preparation for the Commonwealth Games in Edmonton, Canada, the Amateur Swimming Union of Australia sent the entire team to Hawaii for a training camp in July. We would stay there for a month and then fly directly to Edmonton. This was okay in principle, given that it was midwinter back home and a warm summer in Hawaii, but the union failed to factor in the bad attitudes and wild behaviour of many of its young swimmers.

I wasn't overjoyed with the decision because it meant I would be away from home even longer. I needed my support system: Mum, my sisters and my own warm bed. I was never a great traveller and always seemed to get the flu when I went away. I probably contracted it on the planes themselves.

I was sharing a room with Sydney backstroker Lisa Forrest, and we got on well, but the other girls on the team were not so easy to deal with or as dedicated to their sport. I have always been a light sleeper, especially in a strange bed, but it was made worse when one night two girls started skylarking around our dormitories. It was their first time on the Australian team and they were running up and down the corridor, in and out of bedrooms, slamming doors, screaming and giggling.

Fair enough, you might say, this is what teenage girls tend to do from time to time. But it wasn't fair enough when you were preparing for the Commonwealth Games. I was training harder than anyone: 16–18 kilometres each day, every day. Up at 5am, down to the pool by 5.30am, a rest at midday and then back at the pool for another session between 3.30pm and 6pm. It was gruelling.

I tried to tell the skylarkers to shut up and go to bed, but they ignored me. I got up in my pyjamas with a pillow tucked under my arm and went in search of the team supervisors. I searched high and low but none were to be found. Where were the coaches and managers? Eventually I found them, having a quiet drink on the rooftop of the building. It looked as though they were hiding out from the noisy swimmers.

'Do you know what's going on down there?' I yelled. 'How can I get any sleep with that bloody racket? After all the training I've done I don't want to stuff it up. If you don't stop it I'm on the next plane home!'

I was the only world record holder in the team and training as hard as anyone, so they knew I was right. After that night, all was quiet. I was offered a room of my own and I slept like a log.

Later that month, our Hawaiian training camp manager, Berry Rickards, was quoted by the press as saying: 'This training camp has been better than expected and the team will show the benefits of it in Edmonton.' To call it 'better than expected' was laughable, as these comments came off the back of a major swim scandal in Hawaii.

For some of the boys, a month on the island, surrounded by good-looking local girls, was too much temptation. There was plenty of temptation for the girls on the swim team, too, and four days after we arrived in Hawaii, a couple of them snuck out with three of the swim team boys for a night on the town. One of the girls, about a year older than me and new to the team, asked me to join them but I refused. I warned her that if they were caught, they'd be sent home.

Sure enough, they were caught and the whole team was carpeted. We were pulled out of bed at 2am when the boys returned to their dorms and read the riot act. The three boys – team captain Mark Tonelli, Joe Dixon and Mark Kerry – were all sent home. The Australian media had a field day. Tonelli was a close friend of mine and used to call me 'Wilbur Worm' because I was so small and skinny. I felt really sorry for him and was shocked that the girls involved had all escaped punishment. They weren't even publicly named, despite one of them being a very high-profile sprinter from Queensland. It just seemed unfair. I tried to speak out about it at a press conference when we returned home, but the team officials shut me down.

I have one good memory from Hawaii, however. When the movie *Grease* came out, the whole team went along to watch it. I'm normally an action movie girl, but I fell in love with the musical and bought the VHS as soon as it came out. These days, I own two *Grease* DVDs, just in case one goes missing. My kids grew up watching, singing and dancing to it every week and my son Daniel knows every word and all of John Travolta's dance moves. He used to play Danny to my daughter Hannah's Sandy. We all loved that movie, it's a classic.

11

Edmonton is hardly a metropolis. It sits on the Saskatchewan River, on the Alberta plains and usually plays third fiddle to Vancouver and Calgary on the western side of Canada. But in 1978, it was the venue for the 11th Commonwealth Games and the Canadians really turned it on. The weather was superb, the hospitality warm and the atmosphere friendly. Unlike the Olympics in Montreal, there was no political grandstanding or overzealous security. The Commonwealth Games are like a kid brother of the Olympics, smaller and a lot more fun.

I did have a bad experience on the flight over from Hawaii, however. As we sat on the plane and the lights went down, the boy I was sitting next to, a fellow team member, started trying to kiss and fondle me while I was asleep. Confused and frightened, I got up and found another seat but couldn't sleep as I was too scared to shut my eyes. What a start to my Commonwealth dream! Did Shane Gould have to put up with this?

One thing I can certainly boast about is the fact that I never, ever messed about with boys on the trips away. I was serious about my sport and they respected that, for the most part.

***

Edmonton was another bad meet for Australia and it seemed that Hawaii had only contributed to our suntans. Our whole team, not just the swimmers, performed below expectation. Our return of twenty-four gold medals was the second-worst result ever from Australia and we were thrashed by Canada. Even in the pool, where our nation had ruled supreme since World War II, we were humbled by them. Led by Graham Smith, who became the first swimmer in history to win six gold medals at a Commonwealth Games, the hosts dominated. Well, almost.

I was under a lot of pressure. My coach, Bill Sweetenham, had decided that I was capable of two world records. The basis for his bold forecast was a 400-metre trial I swam in Hawaii in a time of 4:10.60, just 1.69 outside the world record of Petra Thümer of East Germany. What's more, I managed the time with only ninety percent effort and after a gruelling 10.5 kilometre training session earlier in the day.

I was determined to do well in my first event, the 800-metre freestyle, and so was Michelle Ford. Extra motivation came when my dad made a surprise visit. He had been working in California but took time off to watch his girl in action. Bill Sweetenham organised it so Dad and Mum walked in together, hand in hand. Grampa Dave was there to point them out to me. My spirits soared. Dad sat right next to the ABC television commentators, 'Nugget' May and Forbes Carlile, with another proud father on his other side, Michelle's dad, Ian Ford.

The gun went and we dived in for the first leg of the 800 metres. When I shot to the lead, Dad was deadpan like a poker player. By contrast, Ian Ford kept up a constant stream of chatter, repeating the mantra that Michelle was a fast finisher and was about to make her move.

'Really?' asked Dad.

'Oh yes,' Ian went on. 'Everyone knows she's renowned for her strong finish. You wait and see.'

They waited, but the move never came. I led by a body length at 100 metres and by the same margin at the finish. Michelle came second and we both broke my world record, but I had broken it by 6 seconds, clocking a time of 8:24.62. It was a whopping 14 seconds faster than Petra Thümer's winning time for the same event at the Montreal Olympics.

That record was to stand for almost ten years. When I saw the time and the asterisk that meant it was a world record, I looked exultantly at Dad and 'Nugget' in the stands and punched the air in delight. They stood up cheering. I splashed around in the water, waving and somersaulting over the lane rope in ecstasy. The capacity crowd, mostly Canadians, gave me a standing ovation. Mum was so nervous she sat with her back to the pool and just peeked through her fingers a few times. She never saw the finish and only turned around when she knew I had won.

After calling the race for the ABC, 'Nugget' May turned to Dad and said, 'Congratulations.' He then turned to Ian Ford. 'Ian, have you met Tracey Wickham's father, Roger?'

Imagine Mr Ford's face at meeting Dad. That whole time he was backing Michelle, he had no idea it was Roger next to him. But Dad always knew I would hit the wall first.

Afterwards, I did an interview for ABC television with journalist Peter Meares. He asked what was going through my head during the race. I said, 'It's funny but I was singing to myself. It was that hit by the American group, Chicago, "If you leave me now". I couldn't get it out of my head!' That story was picked up by all the media and became part of the Tracey Wickham mythology. To this day, I get people saying how they remember me singing that song during the race.

During my interview with Peter, I asked him if I could pass on a special message to the folks back home. Puzzled, Peter replied that of course I could. I turned my back to the camera. Written on my t-shirt were the words: 'See you in Brisbane, 1982'. We were to host the Commonwealth Games that year, and I was pumped.

After the interview, I was told I was to give a specimen of urine for a drug test before the victory ceremony. A man ushered me into a bathroom and told me I had to produce a sample for him.

'Not with you here,' I replied.

'I'm sorry but the regulations say I must stay,' he said. 'I'll turn my back.'

I couldn't do it, so he got a young female nurse to come in and watch me. But still no luck. Eventually, a middle-aged lady entered, smiling as she turned the taps on in the bathroom. Sure enough, the running water did the trick, and we both had a good laugh as I handed over my specimen. At last, I could stand on the podium and receive my gold medal. I shed a tear as they played the new, semi-official Australian national anthem, 'Advance Australia Fair'. I'd become sick of listening to 'O Canada' time and time again.

I was having a great meet, but it wasn't over yet. My second event was the 200-metre freestyle and, while my pet distances were the 400 and 800 metres, I was pretty confident. Michelle and I handled the Canadians okay, but we didn't count on a 2-metre tall New Zealander, Rebecca Perrott, who swam a personal best of 2:00.63 to win. I was second and Michelle third.

Then, while still maintaining my heavy training schedule for the Berlin World Championships to be held one week after the closing ceremony of the Commonwealth Games, I nearly broke the world record for the 400-metre freestyle. I won it in a time of 4:08.45, which was just 0.79 outside American Kim Linehan's record, set only a couple of weeks before. My goggles fogged up during the race and cost me vital seconds. I forgot to wipe some shampoo inside them before the race. Still, no excuses and I had bigger fish to fry in Berlin.

I was training like mad, churning out the laps every day in Edmonton. It was traditional to hold back and taper down during competition times and my coach Bill had been criticised by everyone, including head coach Terry Buck, for pushing me. I had tendonitis in my shoulder and the media played it up and made out as if I was an absolute crock. But when I won two gold medals, plus two silver in the 200-metre freestyle and the medley relay (where I swam butterfly) and a bronze in the freestyle relay, they got off Bill's back.

Strolling down a corridor at the Edmonton Games Village, my mind on other things, I was nearly knocked off my feet. Bang. I collided with someone. I began apologising, then looked up to meet the eyes of a strapping young man. There he was: a shock of blond hair, a nice smile and the biggest, muscly thighs I had ever seen. I remembered meeting him before at the flag-raising ceremony a week earlier, but I couldn't remember his name. All I knew was he was gorgeous.

'Sorry, Tracey,' he said, blue eyes twinkling. 'I'm Kenrick Tucker. We met the other day.'

'Oh yeah, I remember. You're the cyclist.'

That was how it all started, and it became my first serious relationship. He was nineteen, four years older than me and 182 centimetres tall. He was to win a gold medal in the sprint at the Games and we used to meet in the cafeteria to celebrate our joint successes. It was all very innocent but the media made a big thing of it when the story broke. Whenever we went out together there seemed to be photographers and our pictures bobbed up everywhere.

After I returned from the Games, I made the front page of the Brisbane *Sunday Sun,* clutching a photo of Kenrick in one hand and my pet dog, Susie, in the other. This was a new Susie, different to the one that was hit by the car before I left for America. In fact I had three 'Susie' dogs throughout my childhood, two corgis and the poodle that was photographed with Kenrick and me.

12

Three weeks after the Edmonton Games, I went on to Berlin for the World Aquatics Championships with eleven other Australian swimmers. More than eight hundred swimmers from forty-nine countries were taking part in the meet, making it the biggest sports event held in Berlin since the 1936 Olympics.

It wasn't a luxury holiday, by any means. Seven girls shared two bedrooms and poor Rosie Brown ended up sleeping on the floor of the bathroom in order not to wake the rest of us with her nagging cough, which had already kept us awake for hours. The only bonus was the snug feather-down doonas in the bedrooms, something we had never seen before. In Australia in those days, it was all woollen blankets, and plenty of them, in winter.

We went shopping on a free morning in West Berlin and we could see the Brandenburg Gate and the infamous Wall, which had been erected in 1961. It was a symbol of the Iron Curtain and we were curious but too scared to get a closer look. In those days Berlin was a divided city, grey and depressing on the western side, but even worse in the east. It was to be another eleven years before the Wall came down.

For the Australian swim team, Berlin was a chance to prove our worth and make up for Montreal. Unfortunately, other than Max Metzker in the men's 1500-metre freestyle, Michelle and I were the only

Aussies to make a final. There I was to achieve my greatest 400-metre win ever with my time of 4:06.28, against the American and East German champions. It was the best swim of my career.

After the 400 metres, the 800 wasn't far behind. I've always viewed the 800 metres as the Melbourne Cup equivalent. It's for stayers and I was a thorough-bred stayer. I swam as well as I could and it felt easy compared with the same race in Edmonton, where I was pushed through by Michelle. Michelle and I were great together because we needed each other to gain the experience of tough competition.

During the 800 metres in Berlin, I was always in front of the Americans Kim Linehan and 'Sippy' Woodhead and was never threatened. I swam a time of 8:24.94, only a fraction, 0.32 seconds, outside my own world mark in Edmonton three weeks earlier. Were I able to see the clock I might have squeezed out a faster turn or a stronger push-off. I also mis-judged the finish, lunging with my left hand but then having to bring my right hand over to touch the wall. These are the tiny margins that make the difference between good and great. Still, I hadn't done badly. Two meets, four gold medals, plus two world records. Not bad for a skinny fifteen-year-old! The Australian media was all over me, as Dad remembers:

> After her Berlin performance where she was the only Australian medallist, one of the Sydney papers, I think the *Daily Telegraph,* wrote an edi-torial one day, which said the entire country could

learn a lesson from Tracey Wickham. Whenever she represented Australia, it was full on. No excuses. She never let her country down.

The thrust of that editorial was that Tracey triumphed when no other team member did. As a fifteen-year-old girl, she carried the Australian team, not the other way around. Does the youngest player in his first run-on game in the NRL carry his team or vice versa? All members get a psychological lift if their teammates are performing well. There is an equal and opposite effect when they all perform below expectations.

There is a world of difference between running or riding with an all-conquering team and carrying your team on your back – the so-called 'one-man team' syndrome. What other Australian swimmer has ever done this? She was a girl, a small girl, but when Australia had its back to the wall and none of its champions had stepped up to the plate, she was the one that came thundering through in lane one, screaming, 'CHAAAARGE!!'

***

I had some major wins in Berlin, but it could have been an even greater success. Bill Sweetenham always regretted not entering me in the 200-metre freestyle:

I wish I'd entered Tracey in the 200 metres at the World Championships in Berlin. If you can swim 2:02 at the back end of a 400 you can probably go 1:57 for the 200. And that's in a thick lycra swimsuit, with no anti-splash lane ropes and no wet-deck pool. She had the 'white fibres', that is, a combination of sprint and endurance fibres in her muscles, so she could handle any distance from 200 to 1500 with equal ease. These days she would have gone on swimming until her mid-twenties and she could have swum all three, as the scheduling is over a longer two-week period. We never really saw her best.

I don't want to upset anyone but I've trained some great ones, like Michelle Ford and Hayley Lewis, and I have watched Julie McDonald, Bronte Barratt and the rest. There's no doubt Tracey was the best middle-distance swimmer Australia has seen.

My dad, Roger, agrees with Bill wholeheartedly, and is as proud as punch of my world records:

Tracey Wickham set four world records in 1978: the 800metre freestyle twice, the 400 metres and the 1500 metres. The 400-metre and the 800-metre records stood for all but ten years. These were world records, not underage records. She was fifteen years of age when she set them. She had a minimum of international competition beforehand.

Today they consider girl swimmers at eighteen on their first international to be babies and they get huge amounts of international competition and no expense is spared. Who sets world records today at fifteen, let alone have them stand for ten years against the best the world can throw at them, with all the advantages of later technology and resources?

Tracey's times in 1978 were faster than those which won the gold medals at the Atlanta Olympics in 1996. Her 400metre time in 1978 was faster than the silver medal time in Sydney 2000. Her 800-metre time in 1978 would have been pipped for the bronze medal in Sydney 2000 by 0.33 seconds. In Athens 2004, her 1978 400-metre time would have missed a bronze medal by 0.05 seconds. Her 800-metre time would have earned a silver medal. These were times posted twenty-six years later.

I know of no other Australian female athlete of any age in any sport, who held one world record let alone two, for ten years. Come to think of it, I can't recall any Australian male in any sport, who held one world record let alone two, for ten years. At age forty-four, Tracey Wickham still held a Commonwealth Games event record. It lasted for twenty-nine years. I don't think she shares that feat with any other Australian.

***

I was a media darling and gave dozens of interviews on my Berlin trip. One question kept cropping up time and time again.

'What's the secret of your tremendous energy? What do you eat?'

The interviewers seemed disappointed when I said that there was no magic formula, just good, wholesome food and plenty of it. I steered clear of red meat for a few days before a race, preferring chicken or fish, and I loved raw vegetables and hard-boiled eggs.

The press brightened up when I confessed to some weaknesses: ice-cream, cream buns, lollies and meat pies. I don't know why I loved pies so much but it probably stemmed from Dad and his American business venture. I loved the smell of his delicious, crusty pies cooking in our house at Mission Viejo. Back in Brisbane, I became addicted to pies from a little shop at Stones Corner. They were so fresh, with proper meat inside and would just melt in your mouth. I had three for lunch every day for three months while training for the 1982 Commonwealth Games.

My other favourite routine was downing a Mars Bar and a chocolate milk on the way back from training. Then, in the evening, I would finish dinner with my favourite: 'Icecream and jelly and a punch in the belly.' I know it sounds bad, but remember how many calories I burnt up each day at training!

The interviewers would also ask me about my style, which was up-tempo, more like a sprinter than a distance swimmer. I had a two-beat kick, kicking once with each leg per arm stroke, and I never varied it. Some swimmers, like Ian Thorpe, use a four-beat kick and change to a six-beat kick when they swim their last lap. The thing was, I had very powerful legs and my two-beat was plenty. I rode high in the water and I knew if I was a bit flat and not having a good day because my back would sink lower, letting the water flow over my shoulders.

***

At last, after ten weeks away in Hawaii, Canada and Berlin, the team flew back into Brisbane in September 1978. The media asked me what the first things I wanted to do were, and I had no hesitation in replying, 'After being away for so long I'm looking forward to a good, home-cooked meal and seeing my friends at the pool.'

A tickertape parade in our honour was planned for the Commonwealth Games team the next day. I had no idea how huge it was going to be. It was organised by the editor of the now-defunct Brisbane *Telegraph,* Lionel Hogg Snr, whose son, now a lawyer, was a swimmer in our squad. A senior police officer estimated that the crowd lining the route exceeded fifty thousand, making it the largest crowd in Brisbane streets since the welcome to soldiers returning home from World War II.

I was blown away. The roads were jammed full of people and we were driven in open vintage cars through Queen, George and Adelaide streets to King George Square. Mum had a half-day off work and I had my sisters Kelly and Julie with me for moral support. Wearing a cowgirl hat I'd got from a swap with a Canadian swimmer, my Games blazer and my medals draped around my neck, I couldn't stop smiling.

In the lead car were Dr Jazz, Mileham Hayes, and his band. They were a hit in Edmonton and set the festive mood with some foot-tapping music. Behind me among the other medallists was my boyfriend, Kenrick Tucker, who had won cycling gold. There were signs everywhere shouting, 'Well done, Tracey.'

As I climbed out of the car, the crowd started chanting: 'Tracey is a champion.'

I knew who started it: the All Hallows girls. I spotted the familiar brown uniforms and blue-and-white streamers of my school and, although I was supposed to go up to the balcony of the City Hall, I was besieged by my schoolmates, screaming and giggling. Eventually I made it to the balcony and waved to the crowd. They would cheer and I would wave. And so it went on. I couldn't believe the commotion.

Little Tracey Wickham was now the talk of Australia. Soon I was asked to fly down to Melbourne to be a special guest on the *Don Lane Show,* a popular national variety program. While in make-up backstage, I learned that the band Sherbet would also be performing on the show that night. Like most fifteen-year-olds at the time, I was a huge fan of their music, but I thought there was no way I would get to meet Daryl Braithwaite, the lead singer, or anyone else in the band. They were huge stars and I was just some teenager, albeit a teenager who had swum at the Commonwealth Games and World Championships just two weeks previously.

But word got around Channel 9 about my crush on the band and during my live interview Don asked me whether I was a Sherbet fan. As I was telling him how much I loved them, Daryl Braithwaite came out from behind the curtain and stood beside me. I tried to stand up to greet him but, as Don pointed out, 'Your legs have gone to jelly!'

It was true: I could hardly support myself, I was so overwhelmed. In front of the live national television audience, Daryl gave me a kiss on the cheek and we had a quick chat. My face was bright red, I was so embarrassed.

Later on that night, I met the whole band in the green room. They signed autographs and gave me six backstage passes for their Lang Park, Brisbane show. The generosity didn't end there: a couple of months later it was my birthday and lo and behold, Daryl rang to give me his best wishes. That Christmas he sent me a personal card, and I started to write him back a very long letter. It was full of teenage emotion and I cried as I wrote it. I told him that I loved him very much, that I knew I was the right girl for him and that I wanted to marry him. I never had the guts to actually post it though.

At the time, I meant every word but who knows what he would have thought of it all? He would have received a tonne of letters like that in those days. Many years later, I bumped into Daryl and we had a laugh about the old times. I'm still a huge Daryl fan and love listening to my favourite track of his, 'Rise'. I'll never forget those grand days and my puppy love.

Another brush with fame was getting to meet the powerhouse rock group, Chicago. After they found out that I sang their hit 'If you leave me now' in my head as I swam my world record, they invited me to their Brisbane concert on their Australian tour. I took my sisters and some friends, and we got to go backstage to meet the band. They presented me with their whole collection of LP records in a special edition boxed set. I treasured it for twenty years, but unfortunately it was lost and probably stolen, along with other precious items, by removalists when I moved house in the 1990s.

13

The rest of 1978 was an absolute whirlwind of training and catching up on my school work. I was nervous about how much I had missed. Ironic, wasn't it: a swimming superstar one day and a struggling schoolgirl the next.

In January 1979, I was made a Member of the Most Excellent Order of the British Empire (MBE) in the New Year's honours list. At just sixteen years of age, I was the youngest Australian ever to receive the award. It was presented to me on the lawns of Government House by Queensland Governor Sir James Ramsay. This was the beginning of many awards. I was named ABC Sportsperson of the Year, Australia's Outstanding Sports Personality and the Berlei Australian Sportswoman of the Year, all for my achievements in 1978.

For the Sportswoman of the Year award, I was given a new Toyota Corolla, valued at almost seven thousand dollars, but I wasn't allowed to accept it. This was due to the bureaucratic laws which governed Australian sport in those days. It had been an ongoing International Olympic Committee rule that only 'amateur' athletes could compete, meaning you were not allowed to accept outside payments or take part in endorsement deals if you wanted to be on an Olympic team. It meant that as an athlete, you had to be from a wealthy background to be able to afford to compete. It was so unfair that, from 1972, the rule was in the stages of being phased out and was disbanded altogether by the mid-1980s.

It was therefore within the power of the 1979 Amateur Swimming Union of Australia to be flexible with the rules and allow me to keep the car prize. I needed the car to get to and from training, as my family couldn't afford one at the time. But the ASU confiscated my award and instead offered to help out with pool entry and sundry expenses. What on earth was the difference between that offer and me receiving the car? For me, the car was a necessary expense to get to and from training. The ASU's alternative was paltry in any case, as they knew the Commercial Swim Club was paying my pool entry and related fees already. Plus, in order for me to receive my 'expenses' prize, Mum had to provide receipts and extensive details and the reimbursements were a long time coming. We faked a lot of the expenses in the end because the bottom line was, I needed a car.

I was furious with the ASU's inflexible attitudes. While I didn't whinge publicly about the injustice of having to give back my prize, I said other things to the media about the poor level of support for national athletes from the governing bodies. For example, in 1978, I had to call off a world record attempt at the Valley Pool because the heating failed and I let my feelings show. I made the point in an interview that it was unfair for amateur

Olympic swimmers or national representatives to have to pay to train and now, when I was attempting to become the first woman to break the 16 minute barrier for the 1500 metres, the facilities let me down.

That got a headline. However, it also got results. The Brisbane *Telegraph* ran a hard-hitting editorial on their back page, slamming the government for not providing adequate facilities for sportspeople. It was no wonder we failed in Montreal, they said, when we can't even provide a heated pool in winter. The local council was embarrassed, and quickly fixed the facilities.

Some people, like Wayne Smith, the Queensland sports journalist, admired my determination to fight for what's right:

> Tracey wouldn't stand for what she perceived as injustice and she always spoke her mind. These days swimming in Australia is well-run and extremely professional, thanks to people like Glenn Tasker, Don Talbot and media manager Ian Hanson.

> In those days, Australian swimming was very authoritarian, with the last vestiges of the Avery Brundage era [the infamously conservative President of the International Olympic Committee]. It wasn't what you might call a swimmer-friendly era. So when Tracey vented her feelings to the media, the wrath of officialdom came down hard on her.

Another person who knew I was right to speak my mind was my Edmonton roommate, Lisa Forrest. In Lisa's own words:

I was a bit younger than Tracey, so I admired her enormou sly. When people said that we couldn't beat the drugboosted East Germans, I would reply, 'Tracey does.' She made me believe that I could beat them too.

You have to understand what it was like to be a female athlete in that era. After the Montreal Olympics, the nadir of our sporting history, Australian coaches were read the riot act. They were told that our sportsmen and women had let the country down and it was not to happen again. So the period after that saw some brutal training methods, especially for fourteen-and fifteen-year-old girls. The mantra was 'more is better' and we were the guinea pigs. The problem was that, whilst we trained our guts out, we were not treated well.

I remember our training camp in Hawaii before the Edmonton Games, when I was just fourteen. My regular 5-kilometre sessions suddenly became 8.8 kilometres and I ended up in hospital, being treated for exhaustion. It was the amateur era and swimming administration was authoritarian but not very efficient.

Being a world champion and more experienced than most of us, Tracey was outspoken in her criticism. I couldn't do it. Perhaps at times she might have been a bit too blunt but she at least got the message across. If they didn't do something about it, she went to the media. So she got little support from Australian swimming and many saw her as a whinger.

It's a funny thing about Australian sport. We love our sports heroes, but only if they behave in a certain way. Pat Rafter was the quintessential Aussie sports hero and we loved him, but he never won Wimbledon. Both Pat Cash and Lleyton Hewitt won Wimbledon, but never won over the Australian public. Tracey was in that latter category, a bit too volatile for our blood. She was highly strung and incredibly focused. She didn't suffer fools gladly. She got fed up with officials expecting her to be the best but not providing the best support.

The officials saw me as a whinger and I always seemed to manage to put my foot in it in some way. But I believed in having a strong point of view, and I knew I had a point. I wanted to help my teammates and the team members of the future. I didn't want anyone to be treated the way I was. I suppose I was just the person who 'made things happen'.

My international experience had taught me how much easier swimmers had it in other countries. Australia was the only place I knew where national representative swimmers had to pay to enter a pool for training. In Russia, East Germany, Canada and the US, swimmers were paid generous expenses for both training and competitions. For example, Canada spent six million dollars on coaching in the four years leading up to the Edmonton Games, while Australia spent a hundred thousand. The Canadian government picked up all expenses for their swimmers and also paid them about a thousand dollars a month as compensation for swimming time.

If the public want gold medals, the Australian government should have to help athletes financially. At the very least, we should have been able to receive a hundred dollars a week allowance for food, petrol, pool entry, vitamins, swimsuits, goggles and such like. Laurie Lawrence and I went a few times to beg the Minister for Sport and Recreation for financial assistance. It was always a flat, 'Sorry, can't help you', every time from the bureaucrats.

14

With money so tight, I decided to get a job. I was still only sixteen, but after the first term of school in 1979, with the 1980 Moscow Olympics looming, Mum and I decided that it was pointless continuing with my studies as I would never be able to catch up. When I went on swim trips, I took my schoolbooks with good intentions, but could never concentrate properly. School would have to take a back seat.

When Channel 7 expressed interest in having me work for them, I jumped at the chance. I would be reporting on sport and, for the most part, on their kids' show, *Wombat.* Best of all, I would actually be paid. For the first time in my life, I was able to afford to buy a treat, go to a movie or out for a meal without having to ask Mum for the money. It gave me a newfound sense of freedom.

Channel 7 were great to me and I only had to be there for about three or four hours a day. Sometimes, though, I would fall asleep at the desk because of my heavy training for the Moscow Olympics. The station paid me seventy-nine dollars a week, which was a huge amount in my young eyes. I bought a car using a personal loan of four thousand dollars and was making repayments of a hundred and thirty dollars a month. It was a second-hand Toyota Corolla Liftback and I loved it. I cleaned it every week and bought all the trimmings: lambswool seat and steering wheel covers and great speakers.

***

Kenrick and I were still going strong as boyfriend and girlfriend, even though he was based in Rock-hampton and I was six hundred kilometres away in Brisbane. He was sweet and gave me a brand new Peugeot bike, a gift from his sponsors, so I could share his love of cycling. He would make the trip down to Brisbane during the cycling season nearly every weekend to compete. I enjoyed going down to Hawthorne Park to watch him cycle and sometimes he would come over to our place for dinner. However, with his work as an apprentice motor mechanic, he always had to get back to Rockhampton.

At Hawthorne, and through Kenrick's cycling cir-cle, I became really good friends with Lee and Stephen Goodall. I first met Stephen at the Montreal Olympics, when he was a cyclist in the team sprint, then bumped into him at the Edmonton Games, where he won bronze in a team sprint. At Hawthorne I met his wife, Lee, who was pregnant. The Goodalls were five years older than me but we got along like a house on fire and have never stopped chatting since. After Lee gave birth, I would visit their house virtually every weekend. They always backed me and have been a huge support through my darkest hours.

Finally I was seeing a life outside of swimming and I began to think about alternatives. Instead of getting up at 5am and training four to five hours a day, I occasionally allowed myself to dream about the life I could have: friends, parties and dancing. And sleeping in. The ultimate luxury was Sunday morning when often Bill would let me stay in bed late and sometimes have the day off.

Don't get me wrong, there were some fun times during those days. I remember one party I organised at my place. I got a big garbage bag and filled it with lollies: snakes, Chicos, strawberries and cream and Smarties. I thought it would all be really innocent and that most of us were too young to drink alcohol. Still, the music was pretty loud and three carloads of police eventually came to check up on us. As they walked in, a whole group of young swimmers were snogging in the corner. I felt really embarrassed, but the cops were understanding. We turned the music down and got back to having a good time.

Lucky the police hadn't noticed the car parked outside, gently rocking with the windows all fogged up. Swimmers have a lot of energy to burn and they would sometimes use swimmer Stephen 'Fossil' Fry's car to do so. It was a brandnew red Celica. I'm sure there are a few people who will never forget it.

Another fun time we had was New Year's Eve, when we knew we would all have the following day off from training. We set out to chuck Bill Sweetenham in the pool. He was a cagey fellow and as strong as an ox. Even though there were half-a-dozen of us, Bill managed to wriggle away and run up into the grandstand. He cringed in the top corner of the stand and threatened all kinds of revenge involving hard training sessions. That didn't stop us. We got hold of a fire-hose and turned it on him, full bore. I still laugh when I picture Bill trying to shield himself with a little handtowel. Boy, did we pay for it at the next training session!

***

In those days, there was always another big meet looming and training was a hard slog. Bill loved playing mind games in order to motivate me and he was up to his old tricks at the March 1979 Australian Championships in Perth. I had swum brilliantly and won four titles, including the 200-metre freestyle in a time of 2:02.98, less than half a second outside the national record, but Bill had his eye on me breaking my 1500-metre world record in my final event. He tipped off all the media and said that I was going to try for the record. All I had wanted to do was qualify for the upcoming Coca-Cola trip to Europe the following month. I was furious, but Bill knew that whenever I was angry, I focused and swam well. That's why he nicknamed me 'Tiger'.

That morning of the 1500 metres, Bill nearly pushed me too far. In his own words:

> Tracey's training had been patchy and she seemed down in motivation, so I tricked her that final day. I called out slower times than she was actually swimming, hoping she would speed up her tempo that night. But you couldn't fool Tracey, she has a clock in her head!

Not only was Bill lying to me, but every 100 metres he would make a snide remark like, 'Looking flat', or, 'Can't break the record at this pace.' I just snapped. I got out of the pool and started screaming and swearing. Bill yelled back at me. It got louder and louder, with other coaches and the media all interested onlookers.

'I'm not going to do this,' I shouted. 'You can stuff your world record up your arse!'

'Get back in the pool! You don't leave until you're bloody well finished,' he screamed.

I slammed down my cap and goggles, grabbed my towel and stormed off to our motel across the road from the pool. Bill followed and tried to appease me, but I lay on my bed in my room and didn't say a word, didn't answer the phone calls or the knock on the door. That afternoon I relented and let him in. We had a good chat about how to swim the race and tactics. He apologised for losing his temper and said, 'Don't worry. You'll be fine tonight.'

Bill was a clever sports psychologist. He knew how to light a fire under me but those tactics wouldn't work every time. As I grew older and smarter I began to question his instructions and the first cracks began to appear in our partnership.

**

The pool for the 1979 Championships was in Beatty Park. In 1962 it was the location of Dawn Fraser's record-breaking 100-metre freestyle at the Commonwealth Games. It was an outdoor pool and a bit old-fashioned, but Perth people love their sport and a full house was on hand for the women's 1500-metre freestyle event. No doubt they were expecting a world record.

I was incredibly nervous. Just as the gun went for the 1500 metres, a massive storm hit. Now I had thunder, lightning and winds to compete against as well as all the pressure. It was so murky, the commentators could barely see the swimmers for the first eight laps. They knew I was winning though. I was about a lap in front at the halfway stage but when I had only four laps to go, I got a stitch. The crowd, knowing it was touch and go, roared me on. I put my head down and bum up and gutsed it out.

I won by 80 metres, breaking my own world record by more than eight seconds in a time of 16:06.63. Funnily enough, the storm stopped the moment I touched the wall to finish. The crowd gave me a standing ovation. I had broken my fifth world record in less than twelve months. I was rapt!

When I got back to Brisbane there was another nice surprise. A sports commentator, Kev Kelly, had written a poem about me and it was printed in the *Courier-Mail.* Kev was famous for his passionate rugby league calls, but this time it was swimming that had excited him. His poem was entitled 'Ode to a Champion' and ended with the lines:

It seems both right and proper that tribute should be paid, To a really great performance: our gallant super-maid.

15

Soon, it was off again to London, Bremen and Tokyo for the four-week Coca-Cola International in April 1979. It was quite a trip and I swam every freestyle event and the 100-and 200-metre butterfly. Exhausting.

I had a ball travelling. At the Crystal Palace in London, about eight swimmers got stuck in an ancient lift and couldn't get out. I had massive giggles. In Japan, my photo was constantly being taken, I was followed everywhere and showered with gifts. I thought the Japanese probably related to my small stature and admired my success over the bigger competitors. The Germans were also mobbing me after my stellar performance at the World Championships the year before, but there was one awkward moment in the Bremen pool.

I was swimming the 200-metre freestyle in Germany when I realised my togs were so tight that they had pulled in across my chest. My breasts were showing. I didn't care really because I was face down, but on the second lap I realised that there were portholes on the diving end of the pool where a television camera was filming. I stopped halfway down the lane and quickly pulled my togs back into position. I had fallen behind by 2 metres now, but I swam extra hard and won by a stroke. By the end of the meet, I walked away with five gold medals.

***

It was all too good to last. I was one of Australia's most recognisable sports stars, the envy of my friends. But those who knew me well realised that I was having problems in and out of the pool. On the surface it seemed everything was fine: I had a job and a boyfriend. I was a triple world record holder whose face was splashed across papers and magazines every week. But, at home, things were far from happy.

Dad was still in the States and, although he came home from time to time, we knew his heart was overseas. After I returned from Europe in May, Dad paid one of his fleeting visits. My parents had an argument over something trivial but it escalated. I took Mum's side, as I always did, because I felt it was unfair for her to always bear the burden of bringing up the family while my father was away. When Dad retorted angrily, I snapped. All the simmering discontent of the past few years came pouring out as I swore and threw things at him.

'You can't treat my mum like that. Just get out! Just bloody get out!'

He tried to defend himself but eventually left. We both needed some space to cool down. For some reason I always felt that I had to prove myself to my dad. Was I good enough as a daughter? I knew he'd always been proud of my achievements in the pool, but I wondered if he would have been as proud of me as plain old Tracey. Today I know better, but at the time I wasn't sure.

The next week it was school holidays and, with Julie away on school camp, Mum took me and my sister Kelly to Hervey Bay for a week. When we got home, I had a feeling that Dad had gone for good. It felt surreal. I told Mum to wait at the front door while I went into their bedroom. I opened the wardrobe: it was empty. He often left like that but I knew this time it was far more serious. He had taken all his books and his personal possessions. I went back down to the front door and told her. 'He's gone, Mum.' It was the last time I was to see my father for two years. This was the beginning of another chapter in my life. I was confused and angry.

Mum blamed herself, even though I was the one who had told him to go. She felt she was a failure and became seriously depressed. She was often crying and started taking pills. I thought she was on the verge of a nervous breakdown. One time, I wrestled the pill bottle off her. It was an awful time and I felt so sorry for her. There was so much pressure with having to raise three kids on her own, especially when one of them was a world-class athlete. As Mum recalls, life was extremely tough:

> I was Tracey's cook, chauffeur, sports psychologist, masseuse, media manager and general dogsbody. And I loved it. After rising at 5am to drive Tracey to training, preparing breakfast for Kelly and Julie and working as a secretary all day,

I would pick up Tracey from training and prepare dinner, before cleaning and washing up. Then I would collapse, exhausted, into bed at 9pm, only to do it again the next day.

I became a swimming mother by stealth. I had no idea of what I was getting into and by the time I realised, I had to go along for the ride. But what a ride! If someone asked me would I do it again, I'm not sure what I'd say. Yes and no. Yes for the good times, and Tracey really did have very good times, but no for the heartache along the way. Not to mention the stress.

When you've got a daughter with a special talent you want to nurture it for her sake. That was my philosophy. I also had two other talented girls and, with a full-time job and no partner for support, the pace was hectic and nonstop.

I never had time to stop and think why? Why all this frenetic pace? Now I know. I did what I did because I loved them and wanted them to achieve in whatever field they chose.

Despite Mum killing herself looking after us, and my pay from Channel 7, we were still not well off. Sometimes bills would go unpaid simply because we had nothing left over after buying food to put on the table. One day Mum sat there looking at the electricity and phone bills and began crying. She knew she only had one dollar to last for the next two days and the bills were already four weeks overdue. It used to make me so upset that we had to go through all this. I remember one time having to ask our neighbours for potatoes and toilet paper because we couldn't afford to buy any. It was incredibly embarrassing, and all the while I was a world record holder! If only people knew, they would have realised how hard done by we were.

***

In August 1979, news came through that American Kim Linehan had broken my 1500-metre world record. I remembered her from when she had finished third to my 400metre world record time in Berlin. But now, she had taken 2.14 seconds off my 1500 mark of 16:06.63. That was okay because Bill Sweetenham and I were certain that, given the right conditions, I could break the 16-minute barrier.

The trouble was I had too many problems to allow me to concentrate on my swimming. There were numerous commitments outside the pool in the lead-up to the Moscow Olympics: press conferences, sportsmen's nights, Olympic fundraisers, school functions, all usually requiring a speech from me. For a young swimmer with little formal education, this was always a strain. And there was no payment, of course, because of my amateur status. Furthermore, due to Mum's poor mental state and financial problems, my focus shifted and I was no longer Bill's star trainee. I missed the odd session and seemed to lack my usual boundless energy.

Things weren't all bad and there were upsides to all the Olympic hype. On one occasion I was presented with a magnificent sapphire and gold pendant, specially made for me by four admirers. Gemmologist Rod Beattie, gem carver Flynn Wallace, miner John Warner and jeweller John Doolen combined to create the pendant, which featured a blue sapphire mermaid set in a white gold map of Australia, hanging on a gold chain. They said that it was symbolic of their support for the Australian Olympic team but, because they felt they had come to know one athlete in particular, it was presented to me. I was speechless.

Then, in September, I was invited to Central Queensland for a week's holiday, with some promotional work on the side. It would be a great way to unwind, with a few days on the beach at Great Keppel Island. I was the guest of honour at the Yeppoon Pineapple Festival and Kenrick was there to meet me at Rockhampton airport. The photo of our welcome kiss made not only the local *Rockhampton Morning Bulletin,* but just about every other paper in Australia.

It was on that trip that I lost my virginity. I was nearly seventeen and had been dating Kenrick for over a year. Mum was with me and we were staying at a motel in Pialba, where Kenrick and I were guests at a sportsmen's dinner. Each night, I had been spending more and more time with Kenrick, kissing and cuddling like any teenage couple, before I returned to the room I was sharing with Mum.

Finally I decided: I wanted to spend the night with my boyfriend. I can still remember the date, 24 September 1979. I was really nervous asking Mum about it, but she was great. She didn't even look surprised. She just said, if I loved him, it was okay. She trusted me and I was only two months away from being seventeen.

Kenrick and I were very happy together but, at that age, it was all just puppy love even though I thought that I would marry him and have his kids. We wrote letters and phoned each other at least once a week but ultimately the relationship fizzled out after nearly two years. Both of us led busy lives, with training and competition precluding a social life. We drifted apart and he ended up marrying the girl next door, quite literally. She actually lived across the road. I was happy for him. We were, and still are, great friends to this day and Kenrick and his wife now have two little girls.

***

My problems with swimming came to a head in November 1979. It was Melbourne Cup day and I was supposed to organise the newsroom sweep at Channel 7. I felt ill. My head ached and my glands felt sore and swollen. I had a high temperature so I went home to bed.

The doctor diagnosed me with the mumps and a viral infection, although five months later we would discover I had actually contracted glandular fever by that point. This was bad news, with the Australian Championships just a couple of months away, and the doctor recommended at least two weeks out of the pool and probably another month before I could resume full training. I tried to soldier on but it was hopeless. Even my sister Julie could beat me in training. I managed half a session then went home.

The next week I was still out of the pool despite it being a vital time in my Olympic preparation. I was so sick that I ended up with cold sores around my mouth. I had a fever that made me feel frozen under the blankets in bed, even though it was summer and my body was hot. My teeth felt loose, like they might fall out. My face broke out in the worst acne I've ever experienced, and my whole mouth was so infected I could hardly eat.

Still, I had to get back to training and I dragged myself to the pool. I had lost 4 kilograms off my already skinny frame and my body felt flat and weak in the water. Everyone was thrashing me in training, even the twelve-and thirteen-year-olds. It was depressing and I felt so confused. They say that a week missed in training takes two weeks to make up, but I was only seven weeks away from the Olympic Trials. Nevertheless, if I could put in a good six-week training block and come at least second in a race, I would make the team.

At the trials, I won the 400 metres but came second to Michelle Ford in the 800. I just didn't have the stamina to win the longer race. At least I had guaranteed my selection into the Moscow team, although my times were miles outside my own world records which were still standing. For example, Michelle's winning time in the 800 metres was 8:43.37, 18.75 seconds behind my record, and I was a further 3 seconds out. I felt lethargic and weak.

Bill had no sympathy. Rather than try to help me, he started telling the press that a youngster in his squad, Suzi Baumer, was capable of breaking my records. I was confused and upset. After all the work I had put in, this felt like betrayal. I didn't know what to do. It would have helped if Kenrick had been around but he was in Rockhampton, training hard for the Moscow Olympics, so I scarcely saw him. I had nobody to share my problems with. Then, in December 1979, the Russians invaded Afghanistan and somebody started talking about a boycott. Everything was spinning out of control.

16

The headline in the *Courier-Mail* on Thursday, 29 May 1980, said it all: 'Tracey is OUT: the pressure got to me'.

My decision to withdraw from the Moscow Olympics caused public outrage and was the hardest decision of my life. But it was mine to make and nobody else's. I'd talked it over with Mum and rung Dad in America and they both supported me. I felt as if a huge weight had been lifted from my back. With so much going on in my life – my parents splitting, my illness, our lack of money and the political turmoil over the boycott – I knew I couldn't swim my best.

I wasn't the only one who would be missing the 1980 Olympics. The Americans had pulled out completely following the Russian invasion of Afghanistan. Our own Prime Minister, Malcolm Fraser, whilst not directly calling for a boycott, announced that the government would support any athlete who withdrew. Raelene Boyle announced she wasn't going, then boxer Phil McElwaine and pentathlete Alex Watson. Next were swimmer Mark Morgan, athlete John Higham and archer Terence Reilly. Then the hockey, yachting, volleyball, shooting and equestrian teams and, finally, our swimming head coach, Forbes Carlile.

While I wasn't alone in my decision to withdraw, it certainly felt that way when the press were crucifying me, and only me, in the media.

***

The six months prior to my withdrawal from the team were fraught with difficulty. The Australian Olympic Federation had finally decided to do something to help ease the financial pressure on athletes and released a list of names, including mine, of athletes who would receive special training grants of two thousand dollars.

Lisa Curry, Kenrick Tucker and I appeared on a telethon to raise funds for the Olympic team and were each presented with envelopes. These were supposed to contain our cheques, but when I opened mine, it was empty. I was told that, while others had received their money, my cheque had been held up due to uncertainty over my swimming future on account of my illness. I was livid. Mum rang the Australian Olympic Federation and was told that the money was to be placed into a trust account. It was ridiculous.

Then came the first of three training camps for the Olympics. It was held in Brisbane in May, where we were to spend three weeks training before repeating the experience in Sydney and then Melbourne. Between each camp, we would return to our own swim club for two weeks before meeting up again in the next state.

I managed to complete the Brisbane camp, but trained like a dog. I didn't know what was wrong with me. My arms felt like lead and everyone was passing me in the pool. I just didn't have the v-voom that

Tracey Wickham usually had in her tank. Bill Sweeten-ham refused to coach me because he wanted someone fit enough to win gold. He ended up coaching Michelle Ford, my arch-rival, which was a boon for her. Now she had a teacher with insight into my training methods and the knowledge of how to get to gold in Moscow. In return, I was trained by John Rodgers, Michelle's coach.

The final nail in the coffin at the Brisbane training camp came when team manager Peter Bowen-Pain gave me a dressing-down in front of the whole squad. He accused me of being slack and lazy and even threatened to chuck me off the team. I wish, was what I thought at the time.

That was it. After the first camp had ended, Mum and I talked over my decision, and then we drove up to the Valley Pool to tell Bill Sweetenham what I was going to do. I told him straight: 'Bill, I'm pulling out of the team. I'm not fit enough and you know I have been sick and not training well for months.'

Bill simply replied, 'Okay, if that's what you want to do.' I was confused by this reaction. I thought he would at least have tried to encourage me to stay on, and I expected him to rant and rave, but he just walked away. I left the pool feeling disillusioned and despondent.

I think, in a way, Bill was relieved. Now he could concentrate on coaching Michelle to the Olympic gold that was there for the taking. He knew she was second only to me in terms of world ranking for the 800 metres. With the Americans and Germans boycotting Moscow, Michelle would be a redhot favourite. I know Bill was desperate to be an Olympic gold medallist coach. I also later heard on the grapevine that he considered me washed-up and was keen to work with my potential successor in the squad, fourteen-year-old Suzi Baumer. Fine.

Michelle's coach, John Rodgers, hearing of my withdrawal, offered to train me for the nine-week period leading up to the Olympics. Wouldn't that have been ironic! It was a generous gesture but I couldn't accept. After informing Bill of my decision, Mum and I drove home. As we made our way down our street in Kedron, we saw a huge convoy of television trucks surrounding the house. The media had found out quickly because I had told my boss at Channel 7 just before I went to see Bill.

We drove past our house, trying to work out what to say or do, but the street was a dead end and I was forced to face the music. A posse of pressmen gathered around and questions were fired at me from all directions. I was flustered and confused. I felt like I couldn't say that I wasn't swimming well because I was ill or because of the stress over Mum and Dad splitting up. Even though it was true, it would just sound like an excuse.

I was a bewildered little seventeen-year-old girl and I had no idea what to do. Then someone in the crowd asked if my withdrawal was part of the international boycott. I wasn't a political commentator and

I wouldn't even have known where Afghanistan was at the time, but shakily I replied, 'It just seemed like the right thing to do.' The media appeared to like that and they packed up their cameras and left.

The public outcry was enormous. Some people wrote to me saying how much they admired me for taking a stand. Others sent hate mail, death threats and white feathers. I was called every name under the sun. Talkback radio seemed to discuss nothing else. My God, did I cop it! I was 'evil' and my actions were 'sour grapes'. People acted like they owned me, but what right did they have to dictate how I lived my life? What would they have done under the same pressure at the age of seventeen?

17

In July I went to Sydney to see Kenrick off to Moscow. The press flocked around us at the airport like a pack of vultures. I used to love being in the limelight and doing interviews after winning races, but this was completely different. Now I was nervous and defensive and always worrying about saying the wrong thing. I didn't have a clue about politics and I still don't care for it much. I just wanted to be alone with my boyfriend.

In Moscow, Australia won two swimming gold medals. One of them went to Michelle Ford in the 800-metre freestyle, my pet event. The media came to my house to film my reactions to the race and I felt uncomfortable. A journalist from the Brisbane afternoon tabloid, the *Telegraph,* was there and I put my foot in my mouth again. I was accustomed to reliable sports journalists like Wayne Smith and Frank O'Callaghan, to whom I was inclined to be trusting and give expansive answers. After all, they had always done the right thing by me. This *Telegraph* journalist was a guy called Mike Holliday, a young gun journo looking for a great headline. I had never met him before and he asked a lot of obvious questions which made me a bit peeved.

Firstly, he asked how I felt about Michelle winning the gold medal and not me. 'Well, she deserved to win. She swam well and it was an excellent swim. I wasn't there, so I'm glad she won for Australia.'

Then he asked whether I felt I could have won had I been there. 'Well, Michelle's winning time was 5 seconds outside my record, so yes, I think I could have. I know I would have swum my best time and set a world record if I was fit and well.'

Holliday kept fishing and asked, 'Would Michelle have won if there had been no boycott?'

'I don't know, but it's a shame they weren't there. It's not the same without the Americans and Germans because they're the best in the world at swimming.'

Holliday seized on this. 'So you mean that the medal is tarnished like a 9-carat rather than an 18-carat gold medal?'

I was confused about the carat question, not being familiar with the terminology. I didn't know what he meant. Holliday was trying to get me to say, 'I would have won if I was in Moscow and, of course, beaten Michelle.'

I just replied, 'Yeah, I think so.'

The huge headline in the paper the next day read: 'Medals only 9-carat, says Tracey'. I was also quoted as saying, 'I would not be proud of winning any medals in Moscow, knowing the best in the world weren't there.'

There was some truth to this because, in my mind, the World Championships have always been the ultimate as they were non-political and had the most countries competing. But Holliday took me out of context. I had said something along the lines that any medallist would have been disappointed that the leading nations were not there, as their win was devalued. I didn't mean to attack anyone in particular. Holliday's hatchet job failed to mention the fact that I praised Michelle for a great swim and for winning gold for Australia.

The nasty story spread like wildfire. Not only was it in the Australian press, but it was picked up by international newspapers. My dad, Roger, was extremely upset with the way I was being treated by the media and wanted to protect me. In August 1980, a month after the Olympics, he wrote a letter to the editor of the *Australian* which was published under the headline, 'A champion example':

> I recognise that stirring sewage only makes it smell worse, but I am prepared to pay that price to comment on media reports that Tracey Wickham boasted that she would have beaten Michelle Ford in the 800-metre freestyle in Moscow. I know Tracey reasonably well. To the best of my knowledge, I helped start her off in life. I then had the opportunity to watch her closely for almost all of her seventeen years. So, I feel as well-qualified as any journalist to comment on any remarks she is reported to have made.

> Boasting is not the hallmark of a champion and I have never heard Tracey make one boast

in her short life. She was taught very early in her career that swimming races are won in swimming pools, not in the cesspool of newspapers. Her achievements in that regard are a matter of record. It has also been continually impressed on her from day one that the day would certainly arrive when the same press that hailed her would turn against her. Despite that preparation she was not ready when the day arrived. Alas and alack!

Difficult to believe, isn't it, that despite her globe-trotting experiences representing her country at Olympic and Commonwealth Games and World Championships and doing nothing else but bring great glory to her country, she should remain so girlish and naïve as not to be able to deal coolly, calmly and professionally with the vultures of Australia's media. And she is almost eighteen years of age!

Time and again that poor, unsuspecting little girl has been reduced to tears as Australia's journalistic elite have distorted and twisted and edited her answers to their loaded questions, so that the only thing the truth and their reports had in common was the English language. Imagine, at seventeen years of age, not being able to see through their plausible guile. How could a girl get to her age and still be so unsophisticated and trusting of human nature? She will probably pass the same qualities on to her children. How sad!

See the pitiful spectacle we present to an unbelieving world, Australia. See how, in one fell media swoop, we diminish the glory of the thoroughly deserved victory of a new champion, who won an individual gold medal in Olympic record time. Where else in the world would a media be so pathetic as to divert attention away from Michelle Ford's proudest moment? She earned the top step on the podium and deserves nothing but our salutes and tributes. Nothing else is relevant – not even the opinion of Tracey Wickham.

I salute you, Michelle, and your family too, because I have an insight into the price they paid to allow you to express your talent into the ultimate sporting victory. And I know Tracey does too. I also know, because I know Tracey, that any competitiveness she feels toward you outside of the sporting arena is a figment of the imagination of a very sick media.

As for you, Tracey Wickham, you have been a constant source of pride to a very grateful father. For your sporting achievements certainly, but mainly because you are a wonderful, warm human being who has served her country well, been generous to a fault with your time to all sorts of organisations, oblivious to any form of compensation, a wonderful sister and daughter and an example to all those potential champions coming on.

You are a real champion, Tracey, and you do not have to justify yourself to anybody else. So don't bother.

I salute you.

Roger J. Wickham

At least there were some people on my side. Wayne Smith, who covered the whole debacle, thought I was hard done by:

Tracey just didn't get the breaks. She was ten times as good a swimmer as Lisa Curry but didn't have the glamour-girl looks and the Ironman husband.

Tracey didn't really want the glamour, she wanted recognition of her achievements. A bit like Jodie Henry really, both tortured souls. Perhaps it was because swimming doesn't prepare you for life. If anything, spending five hours a day looking at the black line on the bottom of a pool actually inhibits the development of your social skills. A seventeen-year-old girl should not be expected to comment on the rights and wrongs of politics.

Tracey had no media coaching. In fact, I was probably her media coach in a sense. In an interview she would often make a comment that gave me a mixed reaction. The journo in me would be thinking, 'Wow! Here's a big story.' But the friend in me was also thinking, 'Watch out, Trace, this will get you into hot water. Reconsider.'

She gave me heaps of headlines, but I think I can say we had mutual respect and trust. That's a wonderful thing in my game. At the end of the day, Tracey should be revered for what she did for Australian sport. Even today, if you conducted a poll around town, I think you'd find that the majority of Australians still remember her and admire her for what she achieved. She's a great Australian and I hope she enjoys the happiness she deserves. It's long overdue.

Bill Sweetenham, despite not putting up a fight to get me to the Olympics, missed having me at Moscow and brought me back a surprise present. In his own words:

A mate of mine in Moscow, Hans Fassnacht, was the manager of Arena swimwear, the brand Shane Gould used to wear. Hans asked if I could get him some Australian gear for a charity back home in the States. I knew there was not much available, as we had gone to Moscow against the wishes of the government, on a really tight budget. So I went to Peter Bowen-Pain, our sectional manager, and he gave me a couple of tracksuits. Not many people knew, but Peter had paid for our team tracksuits out of his own pocket. I managed to scrounge a couple of swimsuits and towels plus some kangaroo pins and a stuffed koala. It wasn't much but Hans was delighted.

When we left at the end of the Olympics, Hans called and said there was a bag waiting for me in reception at our hotel. Sure enough, he had given me a huge Arena bag, with about fifty swimsuits, both race and beachwear, inside.

When I got back to Brisbane I felt sorry for Tracey, missing out on the Olympics. So I said, 'Take a few swimsuits and give the rest to your mates.'

I found out from one of the girls that Tracey had given them out to the youngest kids in the squad, to make them feel special, and only kept a few for herself.

She had a good heart, but it was a shame that she decided not to go to Moscow. I knew she had issues, with her parents' split, her glandular fever and poor training but I still thought she would have won the 800. Michelle Ford trained with us for a while before the meet and her form was even worse than Tracey's. Anyway, Tracey didn't go, which I think was the worst mistake she made in her whole career, but she had her personal reasons.

The media and the public continued to attack me merci lessly. Being so young and in the spotlight is extremely difficult. I remember feeling so much em- pathy for Queensland swimmer Hayley Lewis, who won five gold medals at the 1990 Auckland Common- wealth Games as a fifteen-year-old. She was seen by the media as painfully shy and inarticulate and they were happy to criticise her weight and appearance, but people forgot that she was just a teenager with no media training who was suddenly an overnight superstar. At least nowadays Hayley's a confident and poised celebrity host of the *Biggest Loser* television show. She looks fantastic.

As for my public backlash experiences, the absolute worst was at a greyhound meeting at Wentworth Park in Sydney shortly after the Olympics, where I was asked to present a trophy. As I walked onto the track, someone in the crowd started booing. Then another person threw a can of beer at me and finally I was hit by a half-eaten hotdog. The officials had to form a ring to protect me and help me off the track.

I was humiliated, furious, upset and hurt. If that's what you get for swimming for your country, then I'm out. They can stick it, as far as I'm concerned.

Fuck swimming! I've had it! Australia can pick on someone else!

And so I retired.

PART 3

STARTING AGAIN

18

The sun beat down, making me drowsy, as the roar of the surf mingled with the cries of a flock of seagulls overhead. I drifted in and out of consciousness, revelling in the luxury of being able to relax, without feeling guilty, for the first time in memory. I was on the beach at Coffs Harbour, working on my suntan while my new boyfriend, Glenn, enjoyed himself by riding the perfect waves coming around the point. The peaceful spring morning reflected my mood, an equanimity that I hadn't felt in years.

I first met Glenn, who was three years older than me, at the Valley Pool, where he interviewed me in his role as a sports reporter for Channel 7. Later, I worked alongside him in the sports department and we started dating. His happy-go-lucky nature was the ideal antidote for my depression following the events of the past few months. He had a great sense of humour and we laughed a lot.

Unfortunately, following my retirement, the Channel 7 bosses let me go. They had the broadcasting rights to the Moscow Olympics and had wanted 'Channel 7's Tracey Wickham' to win gold for Australia.

They made it plain that they disapproved of my stand and I didn't bother explaining the circumstances. I just cleaned out my desk and left.

It was a shame, really, as I'd enjoyed the job, especially reporting for *Wombat* and working with people like producer Dina Browne and hosts Fiona McDonald and Eric Summons. I also enjoyed working for *Sportscene* with David Fordham and Pat Welsh. Not to mention the fact that the money came in handy. Channel 7 looked after me, giving me taxi fares to get to and from training and had shown me the skills needed to work in television.

I had loved sharing a workplace with Glenn. He lived in a flat at Bardon, just down from Mount Coot-tha where the Channel 7 station was located. We would often pop down the hill for lunch. We got on well and I enjoyed driving with him in his old blue Charger, surfboards strapped on top, as we made our way down to Coffs to visit his parents. They were kind and made me feel at home.

I soon forgot about the pressure of training, the glare of the media spotlight and my own parents' problems. I ate what I liked, enjoyed the odd beer and revelled in doing what others regarded as normal things, like going to movies, parties and restaurants. I had never been able to indulge in these things so, for about nine months, I had a ball. But all good things come to an end, as they say. I had virtually moved in with Glenn, but Mum disapproved. Her attempts to talk me out of the move had fallen on deaf ears and I 'ran away' to Glenn's place. So she rang Uncle Graham.

I have three uncles and they are all terrific blokes: Graham, Terry and Jon. Uncle Terry is an accountant who has always done my tax over the years and Uncle Jon was blinded in a car accident in 1967 but manages to live a normal life. It made me angry that, after surviving Vietnam, six months later his mate fell asleep at the wheel and Jon went straight through the windscreen, glass shattering his eyes. The mate got away with a few scratches. I love taking Uncle Jon shopping and reading his mail to him, and we chat about the good old days.

Uncle Graham was a property developer and has always offered me excellent advice over the years. He also used to give me free boxes of chocolates when I was a kid, which I loved. He has a great sense of humour but a serious side too, so when he talks, I listen. After Mum rang him up, he came down and spoke to me. He said simply, 'Trace, what are you doing?'

He gave me that old-fashioned look of disapproval and I got the message. I had just turned eighteen and was pretty rebellious but I knew right from wrong. I packed my things and went home. My rebellion had lasted just three days. What *was* I thinking?

Around that time, December 1980, I had a call from Don Talbot, Director of Coaching at the newly formed Australian Institute of Sport in Canberra. He asked me to consider a comeback for the Australian

Championships in Adelaide the following month. It sounded fantastic. I would be the first swimmer accepted into the AIS and I would actually be paid to swim. The fact that it was only a measly twenty-five dollars a week for petrol was immaterial. They offered me free room and board, as well as top-line coaching.

I had unfinished business with swimming. I wanted to go out on top and I was still a teenager. So, while I had reservations about living away from home, and was especially hesitant about Canberra, I said yes. Glenn didn't like the idea of me going back into the water full-time. He tried to talk me out of it, reminding me that he would be in Brisbane and I would miss him. It was true but, once I set my mind to something, I do it. We broke up, but there were no recriminations and no hard feelings. We're still friends.

***

Training in Canberra was not how I imagined it would be. Have you ever tried to train for a sport on your own? It's hard, even at a social level. I was unfit and had been out of the water for nine months. Top American coach Dennis Pursley was supposed to be head coach but had been delayed in the United States. Bill Sweetenham had come to fill in for Pursley temporarily, but he didn't coach me. Don gave me a basic program however, busy with his duties setting up the Institute, he left me to my own devices. There was nobody there to push me and hardly anyone to talk to.

I could never understand why they located the AIS in Canberra. Freezing in winter and blazing hot in summer, I would have thought it to be the worst place to base an institute for sport, especially swimming. I had to chip the ice off my car windscreen to drive to training at 5am, and this was in March, not even the dead of winter. At least everything was done indoors, which made the training bearable, but I missed the sun on my back at the Valley in Brisbane.

The AIS food was pretty good, but the accommodation was lousy: tiny monastic cells with bare brick walls. And I was still dirt-poor. Out of necessity, I got a job working at Myer's Miss Shop for four hours each weekday. As my Mum, Elaine, puts it:

> Swimmers these days don't know how easy they've got it. Can you imagine Stephanie Rice working as a checkout chick whilst she was at the Australian Institute of Sport? Tracey did.

In my experience, the AIS was hardly the sportsperson's dream it was made out to be.

19

At this point, the Amateur Swimming Union of Australia showed its typically ugly and self-interested side yet again. In the short period of time I had retired, Mum and I took part in a television advertisement campaign to make ends meet. In Mum's words:

Tracey and I did some commercials for a new brand of margarine called 'Queensland Gold'. It was a clever link in with Tracey's chance at winning gold medals at the Brisbane Commonwealth Games, and they took out a fullpage newspaper advertisement declaring, 'The Queensland gold rush is on!' Still, I was the main focus in the television commercials, preparing healthy sandwiches for my children and so on. Tracey and I were paid six thousand dollars for our work.

However, when Tracey came out of her retirement, the ASU decided that the payment might jeopardise Tracey's amateur status. They made us pay all the money back, directly to the ASU, who confiscated it and kept it in their own coffers for evermore.

Thank heavens for the advertising company, George Patterson's, who generously paid Tracey the six thousand dollars again, handing over the cheque on the *Don Lane Show* after she seriously retired. That meant they paid twice in the end, six thousand to the ASU and six thousand to Tracey.

Having only been in training for a few weeks at the AIS after nine months out of the pool, I decided to enter just two events, for fun, at the Australian Championships: the 100metre butterfly and 200-metre freestyle. I was pleased to come second by a whisker to Suzi Baumer in the 200 freestyle, but then was ecstatic to win the 'fly, Lisa Curry's pet event. She was shocked, considering my lack of training. Up until that point, we had always been friends but somehow that day everything changed.

Following the championships, other swimmers began arriving at the AIS but I had already been there for a month. It was difficult to get close to the swimmers because I had befriended a group of gymnasts who were the first athletes to arrive and was used to hanging out with them.

I found one consolation, a sweet young diver from Tasmania called Andrew Quick. He was in Canberra for the Australian Diving Championships, which I went to watch out of boredom. We hit it off and spent a lot of time together away from the pool. Andrew invited me to take the Easter break in Tasmania with him and I accepted. I asked Don Talbot if that would be okay and he said, 'It's fine with me, as long as it's all right with Bill.'

Bill said pretty much the same thing, so I went out and bought a return ticket to Hobart. I even sold my bike to meet the cost of the fare, but I didn't mind, I was just really looking forward to the break.

Then it all went pear-shaped. There was a major airline strike over Easter and Bill Sweetenham called us all together. He told us, 'All leave is cancelled. You might be able to get out of Canberra, but there's doubt over return flights, so you all have to remain here.'

I was stunned. I had my ticket and my guy was waiting for me. I had to go. Then I found out that Neil Brooks had been allowed to leave for Perth because he was homesick. Neil was a star freestyler who had won gold at Moscow and was part of a group nicknamed the 'Mean Machine'. His leaving gave me confidence. I would go.

I quietly approached Bill afterwards and sternly told him that I was going to Tasmania and that neither he nor anybody else was going to stop me. Bill warned me that there would be ramifications, but I was desperate for a break and I was going, hell or high water.

The gymnasts and I formulated a plan to drive me to the airport at 5am so I would be first on the list for a seat, since all bookings were up in the air following the strike. They dropped me off and helped me in with my bags, then stayed until they knew I could get on board. I made it onto a flight and was off to Tassie. Yes! While this was all behind Bill's back, I still felt it was okay considering I had been given consent earlier, before the group meeting.

Andrew and I had a terrific Easter, camping in the beautiful Cradle Mountain area, but I knew I was in for it later. I didn't have to wait long. On my first day back, I was sent to Don's office where he and Bill were waiting for me. I was ready for a showdown. They both said that I was told not to go anywhere and I blurted out my reasons. I was furious and swore at them both. They told me I was to be suspended for two weeks, which meant I could stay and pay for my accommodation and meals myself or fly back to Brisbane at my own expense.

After my Tasmanian holiday I was broke and barely had enough money for a bus to Brisbane, let alone enough to pay for the AIS out of my own pocket. The decision was made for me, but it didn't matter. I just wanted to get out. I didn't like it there anyway and, if they were going to treat me like a criminal, I didn't want to stay. I left and never went back. They can stick the AIS where it fits.

Bill Sweetenham has his own version of the events that led to the tumultuous break-up:

> When Tracey was asked to join the Australian Institute of Sport, I had misgivings. Some people were suited to institutional life, but not Tracey. I passed on my feelings to Director of Coaching Don Talbot. I had taken Forbes Carlile's place as head coach of the Australian swimming team for Moscow when he withdrew and then I was asked to fill the job at the AIS temporarily. So I was in the chair when Tracey arrived. She had trouble

settling down and the Easter incident was the final straw.

I didn't want anyone to leave because, given the airline strike, Don and I were worried that our young athletes might go home for the holiday, live it up, and then try to drive back when they were tired. We didn't want a road fatality. Tracey was not happy, but you can't allow one swimmer to go when the others had to stay.

When she came back from that holiday, Don and I agreed to suspend her, not realising she would just walk away for good. But, ultimately, it was probably the best thing that could have happened. The one thing I always say about Tracey is, she was very easy to train but extremely hard to coach. Coaching is all about life skills and this is where Tracey and I clashed.

She was stubborn and fiercely independent. It was like the old 'Don't Walk on the Grass' sign. People like Tracey go out of their way to walk on the grass if there's a sign telling them not to. We had similar personalities, strong-willed and fiery, so there were always going to be some fireworks.

∗∗∗

I caught the bus, feeling smug about sticking it to my bastard of a coach. Then I realised: I had no money for food. I raided my coin jar but there was only around seven dollars left. It was a long trip to

Brisbane and I was famished so a girl on the bus offered to lend me ten dollars, which I accepted gratefully. I promised I would pay her back, but I lost her name and address. To this day, I'm ashamed of what she must have thought of me.

Nevertheless, I made it back home to Brisbane where the sun was shining and the water was warm. I heard about a new complex at Chandler, on the south side of town, which would be the venue for swimming and diving for the 1982 Commonwealth Games. I thought that attending the Games in my home town would be a fitting swansong to my career, so I rang up Laurie Lawrence and joined his squad as soon as I could.

The deal was simple. There was no need for a written contract, we just settled on a handshake. Laurie's only comment was, 'You're looking for a world-class coach and I'm looking for a world-class swimmer. How can we fail? You give a hundred percent and I'll give a hundred percent. We'll make a great team.'

Laurie is one of a kind. Effervescent, energetic and kindhearted, he grew up in Townsville, where his father 'Stumpy' Lawrence ran the Tobruk Pool, the famous training centre for Olympic swimming champions in the 1950s such as the Konrads, Dawn Fraser, John Devitt and Murray Rose. Laurie later played rugby union for Australia as a halfback. He only had one lung, but that didn't deter him. As a swimming coach, he managed to imbue his charges with the same enthusiasm and determination he had. He trained Stephen Holland to break thirteen world records and later led two relatively unknown Brisbane swimmers, Jon Sieben and Duncan Armstrong, to gold medals at the Los Angeles Olympics.

At that time in my life, Laurie was a godsend for me and, best of all, he was training my old swim mates from Bill's squad. The decision was easy.

20

After all the criticism and heartache I'd suffered after pulling out of Moscow, I was beginning to feel unsure of myself as a great swimmer. But Laurie, with plenty of psychological tricks up his sleeve, used his skill. When I arrived for training at the brand-new Chandler Aquatic Centre in 1981, Laurie would call out, 'Here comes the world record holder. Who wants to carry her bag?'

Then half-a-dozen young kids from the Lawrence Swim Club used to race down to the pool entrance and fight over whose turn it was to help me with my gear. It made me feel important and special and I had no idea at the time that Laurie was working on my psyche.

He'd get the kids to walk up and down the side of the pool and watch my stroke. I was training hard and was always red in the face from doing sets of 20x100-metre freestyle with five seconds rest. Laurie would shout out, 'That's how a world champion trains. See that!'

That's right, I thought, I'm still the world record holder over the 400 metres, 800 metres and the 1500 metres, twice over, and I've still got what it takes.

The kids in Laurie's squad would also argue over whose turn it was to do their land exercises next to me before training. Each day we'd do 10x100 sit-ups (half-sits, harder than full ones) and 10x100 leg raises, plus rubber stretch bands for 2000 repetitions, 1000 in the morning and again in the afternoon. Laurie got the kids to count out all my exercise reps, which made me feel important. I was so fit, I could chat right through it all. Then I had to swim 8–10 kilometres twice a day, hurting the whole time. After a couple of months, my confidence began to return.

Financially, I was helped out by a generous Brisbane businessman, Ron McConnell, who sponsored me for a year. He was the money-man behind Queensland's acquisition of the cricket stars Greg Chappell and Allan Border, and he also assisted me financially by donating fifty dollars a week to help with petrol and entry fees. To this day, I can't thank him enough.

Furthermore, despite all his hard work, Laurie refused to take any money from me for coaching. 'A world champion doesn't pay coaching fees,' he would say. But this didn't stop the Chandler Pool charging me fifty cents twice a day to train there, even though I had no job (so I could concentrate on swimming) and didn't qualify for the dole. I would get so worked up about the fact the Brisbane City Council wouldn't help me out and waive the fees. It stank.

Laurie's offer of free coaching was particularly generous when you consider that there was no money in elite swim coaching in those days. I admire Laurie so much for giving his heart and soul to the squad just for the love of the sport. Like all of us, he was on a tough regime and ran a learn-to-swim school as well. No wonder that when Federal Sports Minister Graham Richardson wanted to share in the glory of Duncan Armstrong's epic 200-metre freestyle Olympic gold medal in Seoul 1988 by posing for a photo with swimmer and coach, Laurie refused.

'Where were you when we did the hard yards?' spat Laurie vehemently. 'If you want gold medals, why don't you help out the coaches? Why don't you give grants to swim coaches like you do for swimmers?'

While certainly outspoken, Laurie was also a genius in his field. As a struggling young physical education teacher, he quit his job and went to the United States to learn how to coach swimming. He spent three months with Don Gambril, at the famous Phillips 66 Club in Long Beach, picking up lane ropes and coaching tips. Gambril's stable included world record holders Gary Hall Snr, Hans Fassnacht, Gunnar Larson and Bruce Furniss.

Then Laurie went to Sacramento to work with Chem Chavoor, mentor of Mark Spitz, Debbie Meyer and Mike Burton, all legends in the sport. He earned no money but gained a wealth of knowledge about swimming. When Laurie returned to Australia, he went down to Sydney where he studied the methods of Forbes Carlile at the famous Ryde Club. I was so grateful to have him.

***

My first competitive test during my comeback was the Australian Winter Titles in Adelaide, August 1981. It went like a dream and I won three races: the 400 metres, 800 metres and 100-metre butterfly. It was a heartening effort after nine months out of the pool. Dad has his own story to tell involving that particular meet:

I was working in western Victoria in the mallee country around that time. I happened to be at a farm one day where the farmer's wife asked me, as people often did, if I was related to Tracey. I said I was and that, in fact, I was en route to Adelaide to watch her swim.

The woman took me to her ten-year-old daughter's bedroom and there on the wall was a king-size poster of Tracey. Her mother said Tracey was her hero and everything was 'Tracey this' and 'Tracey that'. She then wondered if I might be able to get Tracey's autograph for the little girl. I told her I would use my considerable influence with my daughter to see if we couldn't just make that happen.

Tracey won the 100-metre butterfly in Adelaide and I spoke with her immediately after the medal presentation. I told her about the little girl in Victoria and asked if she had a photograph she could autograph for me to take back. Unfortunately, Tracey had exhausted the supply the *Courier-*

Mail gave her, so couldn't help with the autograph until she got back to Brisbane. Then she said, 'Give her this instead.' She took her medal from around her neck and gave it to me. This was neither the first nor the last medal Tracey gave to children. I doubt she has any left and she had boxes of them.

I called in to the farm on my way back to Brisbane and the little girl and her parents were waiting. The tears flowed when I sadly announced that Tracey was out of photos. 'She did send this though!'

I pulled out a program which Tracey had auto-graphed for the girl. She lit up like a Christmas tree and gave me a big hug and a kiss. I then pulled a brown paper bag out of my jacket and said, 'Tracey thought you might also like this.' When she opened the bag and pulled out the gold medal, the child just burst into tears. So did her mother and her tough farmer father.

Some months later, the mother called me and said the girl had still refused to remove the medal from around her neck. People often tell me I must be proud of Tracey. They don't know the half of it. She is a great and generous human being.

***

After Adelaide came a short trip to Tokyo for the Eight-Nations meet, my first international competition in two years. Despite some negative press back home about my defection from the AIS, I shut them up with wins in the 400 and 800 metres.

By September, I had broken the Australian short course record (short courses are competed in 25-metre pools as opposed to an Olympic 50 metres) for the 1500 metres and just missed my own 800-metre mark en route. I cut 7 seconds off the old record by swimming a time of 16:20.54. Laurie was delighted, saying the effort exceeded his wildest expectations.

Before I could swim to triumph in the qualifiers for the Commonwealth Games, Laurie entered me in all the freestyle events at the January 1982 Queensland Championships. When we got closer to the races, Laurie decided that it wasn't worth tapering back my Games training in order to be fresh enough to compete, so each night of the state titles he would send me up to scratch or withdraw from my event. The media covering the competition made a big stir about my behaviour, as Dad remembers:

> The Brisbane *Telegraph* complained that many of the public had gone out to the championships every night in good faith and paid their money to see the world champion perform, and each night Tracey scratched from the event. It went on to say that Tracey had now boxed herself into a corner, because the only remaining event was the 100metre

freestyle and it featured a 'hot' field which included four of Australia's best female sprinters.

They were right. I was boxed into a corner. The eight-day meet was nearly over and as the Executive Chairman of the Queensland Amateur Swimming Association, Greg Lalor, pointed out to Laurie, I had to swim in order to get selected for the national titles. Furthermore, I would have to place in the top three to prove I was fit or else there was no Queensland team spot and no paid ticket to Sydney for the championships. And I had to achieve this in the 100 metres, a sprinter's race.

'Laurie, I can't swim the 100. I'm a distance swimmer,' I wailed. 'Why do I have to qualify when they know I can swim? Why do I have to keep proving myself? I'm the world record holder!'

The main problem with the sprint was that for months I had been logging 24 kilometres a day in distance training, in accordance with our grand plan of focusing on the nationals. It was the most mileage I had ever done in a session, so how could I win a flat-out sprint against other swimmers who had tapered their training to be fresh for the event? It's like asking Steve Moneghetti to win a 100-metre sprint race the day after marathon training. Impossible!

Laurie 'generously' dropped my sessions by 5 kilometres the day before the 100 metres. Well, how kind, I thought sarcastically. I was angry with the whole business, but there was no choice. I tried to think positive. After all, how often did I get to swim the 100-metre freestyle? It could be fun.

It certainly didn't start out that way. The day of the race, I sat in the stands at the Chandler Pool for three hours waiting for the heats to begin. I walked up to the marshalling area to get my name ticked off, feeling lethargic with a t-shirt over my togs and my thongs, cap and goggles in hand. As I got there, a group of girls I knew started to give me a slow clap.

'So we've decided to swim at last, have we?' taunted Lisa Curry, one of my oldest 'friends' and rivals. Normally I wouldn't have minded but there was no hint of a smile on her face. Right, I thought, I'm going to show the whole lot of them.

'Thanks, girls,' I sniped. 'Is all that applause for me?'

The only seat left while we waited for the heat was the one next to Lisa and I sat down, confused. I didn't know how to react to the animosity. Should I leave in a huff or stick it out? I didn't want to be a chicken. Up until this point, I had treated the 100 metres as a chance to just swim and prove my fitness, but now I was furious. I was going to win no matter what.

I was in the same heat as Lisa, but I was focusing on the final and let her win, with me coming in second and qualifying fifth fastest. The 100-metre freestyle was Lisa's best event and she had tapered for the championships, picking up plenty of golds.

After the heat, I stormed my way back to Laurie. When I told him what had happened he tried to calm me down. 'Trace, you're getting carried away. They didn't mean any harm, surely.'

'Well, I don't care. I'm going to teach them a lesson tonight. I'm going home to sharpen my claws. Why are you smiling?'

Laurie replied, 'Because when you're angry, you always win.' He was delighted. It was his job to motivate me and the girls had done it for him.

I went home to eat and sleep, which was my usual prerace preparation. Trouble was, I couldn't do either. I was so het-up.

***

It was time for the 100-metre final. I knew that in order to win, I would have to stay with the other freestyle sprint specialists over the first lap and my back-end stamina would see me home at the finish. As I walked out to the starting blocks, the crowd gave me a standing ovation. Word had spread that this would be a showdown and they were backing me as the underdog.

I got a terrific start and swam the first 50 metres as fast as any lap in my life. With each two-beat kick, I repeated a mantra over and over in my head: 'Take that! You bitches!'

I was just under a body length behind Lisa Curry as we approached the wall and she was pushing it. I didn't slow down at all and flipped, pushed off and rebounded like a coiled spring. It was the best turn I'd ever made. I came up fractionally ahead, put my head down and headed for home. Dad recalls the rest:

> When the field reached the 75-metre mark of the second and final lap, nothing separated the swimmers. They were headed for a blanket finish, as is common in sprint events. Ten metres from home, Tracey simply changed gears and pushed the pedal to the metal. No one remembers the minor placings and those who witnessed the demonstration had no idea of the significance of what they had just seen. These girls were all sprinters and were tapered for this particular race. Their places in the Queensland team rested on their performance.

I had done it. A distance world champion achieved the impossible and upset the sprint champions! It was my personal best time, 58 seconds, not bad after swimming 160 kilometres in the previous seven days training and now I was the Queensland Women's 100-metre Freestyle Champion. How sweet is revenge! But I wasn't going to gloat. I stayed cool, took my cap off and politely acknowledged the others by saying, 'Nice swim, girls.' Then I ducked under the water and, in a mass of bubbles, screamed, 'Yeehaa!'

I swam to the other side of the pool, hopped out and sauntered off as if it was just another day at the office. Dad remembers one other little detail:

When Tracey climbed out of the pool, she said (and not in a modest whisper) to the badly-beaten hot favourite, 'That was just to let you know, that the only time you will *ever* win a race, is if I'm not in it!' State of mind is eighty percent of victory.

I rate this race as one of the best performances of my career, almost equal to the 1978 World Championships 400 metres and the Edmonton Commonwealth Games 800 metres. I thank those girls for that slow clap and their 'kind' words in the marshalling area because it proved a point to me. Mind over matter can win!

21

The 1982 Commonwealth Games in September continued to be my main focus. However, two months before the qualifiers were due to begin, my doubts and fears returned. Did I have it in me to win? Second place was not an option. If I was going to make a successful comeback, I wanted to prove that I still had some fuel in the tank. I started sleeping in and lagging a bit in my training. The hard slog was getting to me, but Laurie pushed me through and for a few months would personally come and pick me up for training each morning, ensuring I never skipped a session.

Laurie was a hard taskmaster with a simple philosophy: if you weren't winning, you just had to train harder. He used to flog us until we protested that we were tired and sore, and then he would say, 'Have you considered why the Americans are swimming faster times than us? It's because, when you're too tired to swim another lap, they're doing two more.'

He knew how to get me fired up. My shoulders would ache, but Laurie knew when to back off. Like the Melbourne Cup champion trainer, Bart Cummings, Laurie had the gift of bringing his charges to a peak at the right time. After six months of preparation, I made up my mind. I was going to have a crack at making the team. I ground out three hundred and sixty laps a day over eleven sessions a week. I was back in the winner's circle again thanks to the master motivator.

Speaking of motivation, there's a funny story that Laurie likes to tell. One morning during the months leading up to the 1982 Games, at 5am, in the dead of winter, Laurie came by my unit at Stones Corner and knocked on my door. It was in a block of six, one of several similar buildings in the street which all looked the same in the dark.

'Come on, Trace. Get out of bed. Time to hit the water.'

Knock, knock.

'Come on. I know you're in there. I haven't got all day. Let's get cracking.'

No response, so Laurie kept knocking and yelling. Eventually the door opened and standing there was a little old lady clad in a dressing-gown.

'I think you must have the wrong unit. Have you tried the one next door?'

Red-faced, Laurie apologised profusely and retreated. He tried the next building and there I was, twiddling my thumbs, waiting for him.

When we got to the pool and were just about to start the session, in walks the little old lady, in swimsuit and pink cap, still wrapped in her dressing-gown. She walks up to Laurie and says, 'All right, Mr Lawrence. Here I am. Which lane do you want me to go in?'

Now, I wouldn't say this story is exactly true, but there's no doubt in my mind that Laurie could motivate an eighty-year-old if he tried. What a champ.

***

By May 1982, I was fit and confident going into the Australian Championships and Commonwealth Games Trials at Sydney's Warringah Pool. However, I felt ancient compared to most of my rivals and teammates. There was even an article about it in the paper under the headline: 'Grandmother of Australian swimming – at nineteen!' That was why, six years into my international career, I made up my mind that the Brisbane Games would be my farewell to swimming. I had to move on and let others take up my reign.

While taking part in the nationals, I stayed in a separate location to the other competitors, at the Bellevue Hotel in Kings Cross where I paid for my own accommodation and expenses. I just wanted to be able to concentrate on my races with no distractions. A journalist, Richard Sleeman from the *Australian,* gave me a lift to the pool one morning and offered to lend me his car for a couple of days. He said he wouldn't need it and it would be cheaper for me than paying for a taxi.

I gratefully accepted and, after qualifying for that night's 200-metre freestyle race, drove off in the direction of the Cross. Somehow, I got lost. There were one-way streets, no signs and the traffic was so fast. Growing more and more frustrated, I drove round and round for over three hours, totally disorientated. Eventually, almost in tears, I pulled over and asked two businessmen for directions.

'Tracey!' one exclaimed. 'What are you doing in Richard's car?' It just so happened they were his workmates from the *Australian.*

'He lent it to me, but I'm lost and I've been driving around for hours. Where's the Bellevue Hotel ... please.'

I was in a panic, with tears streaming down my face.

'All you have to do is drive down this street. Turn left at the roundabout and follow it all the way along. You can't miss it.'

God, I hope they don't write a story about this, I thought.

At last, I found my hotel. I felt hugely embarrassed but relieved. I barely had time to shower and change before I had to get ready to go back to Warringah. My pre-race routine went out the window. No sleep, no shaving the legs. I bolted down a sandwich and caught a cab to the pool. I was unbelievably stressed but, would you believe it, I won the 200metre final in a personal best time of 2:02.69. There's nothing like swimming under pressure! To this day, I've never driven through the Sydney CBD again.

I breezed through the rest of the nationals, setting myself up nicely for the Commonwealth Games. One

of the most satisfying events I competed in at Warringah Pool was the 800 metres, where I was up
against my 'heir apparent', fifteen-year-old Suzi
Baumer. The press had promoted her as one of their
favourites and I had been portrayed as the bad guy
out to get her, even though Suzi and I were friends
from way back when we'd trained together under Bill
Sweetenham at the Valley Pool.

As we were introduced for the 800 metres, the
applause for her was louder than mine, but it didn't
deter me. I was more determined than ever to win.
I took the lead from the start and never lost it, winning by 12 metres over Suzi, in a creditable 8:39.39.
That was the third time I beat her at that meet, the
other times being the 400 metres and the 200 metres.

I wasn't so lucky in the 100-metre butterfly,
where I came third and my old rival, Lisa Curry, won
with a fast 62.09. At the press conference, Lisa
seemed to prefer to talk about beating me rather
than the fact that her time was a new Australian
record.

> It's only the third time I've ever beaten
> Tracey. The first time was when I was ten and
> the next when I was twelve. You can understand
> why I'm excited!

Bear in mind, it was her pet event. For me, it was
a novelty and I wasn't fresh, having won the 400-
metres freestyle an hour before. Despite my third
placing, I was deemed ineligible to swim the butterfly

at the Games. This was because in those days, once you made the team, the coaches could decide who was going to swim what. There's politics everywhere, even in swim teams, and despite my better time, another girl was chosen to compete in my race because one coach wanted to 'give her a go at more medals'. I earned my spot and I was upset I couldn't swim it. Nowadays, denying a place-getter their position just cannot happen.

***

Training with Laurie Lawrence became even tougher in the lead-up to the Games. At least, as he used to say, I had the perfect build for a swimmer, which helped me somewhat.

'No tits, slim hips and no bum.'

At 164 centimetres tall, with a snub nose, a dusting of freckles and auburn hair bleached by sun and chlorine, I seemed like a typical Aussie girl. But there was one quality that separated me from the pack and enabled me to withstand the relentless grind of training, the pain of injuries and the single-minded sacrifice of my teenage years: a ferocious will to win.

Laurie also thought I had a perfect 'boat' for swimming. Technically, I was ideal: good acceleration, well-balanced and streamlined, with hyper-extension in the knees and flexible ankles. For a woman I was abnormally strong in the shoulders and my rhythmical, two-beat kick lifted my hips with a dolphin action that made me ride high in the water. If I could handle a compressed, heavy workload and stay healthy, there was no way I could lose.

Some people, like Michael Bohl who was also on Laurie's squad, thought I was overtraining:

> When she was with Bill Sweetenham, she used to run to training every day, but Laurie had to yell out under her window to wake her up. You can't keep logging those huge distances all the time, something's got to give.

He was right in a way. As I got older, training became more and more of an effort. I was just more hungry and eager when I was in Bill's squad. Nevertheless, I was convinced that hard work was still the way to go. I endured the mind-numbing ordeal of swimming 80–100 kilometres a week. It was gutbusting but Laurie somehow made it enjoyable. After all, who would be willing to stick their head in a bucket of water for five hours a day if it wasn't fun?

In many ways the secret to logging those hours lay not so much in Laurie himself but in the squad, especially the boys. There were fantastic blokes like Michael, Adam Sambrook, Justin Lemberg, Stephen Fry and Gary Watson. We went through the same kind of torture together and we always laughed about it.

I was even going out with squad mate Mark Stockwell at the time. Mark started competitive swimming later than the rest of us and just missed the team for Brisbane 1982. He was really disappointed but more than atoned two years later with a silver medal in the 100-metre freestyle at the 1984 Olympics. While we were dating, I knitted him a woollen sweater. It took me months but I didn't mind, because it filled in the time between sessions. My life was pretty boring, just 'knit, sleep, swim and eat'. In the end, Mark went on to marry another Tracey, the American swimming champion Tracy Caulkins. But I'll bet he's still got that sweater somewhere. I know he wore it for at least fifteen years. He loved it.

Another squad mate I remember warmly is Jonno Sieben. He was only fifteen in 1982 and it was his first selection for a senior Australian team. Later, he would win the 200-metre butterfly gold at the 1984 Los Angeles Olympics, setting a 4 second personal best and executing one of the greatest swims I have ever seen. These days, he's a swim coach in Townsville and, reflecting on his past, says my gruelling work ethic was hugely inspirational to him:

> Tracey was the toughest competitor I've ever seen. She was as tough as anyone, male or female, when it came to hard training. There was no challenge she wouldn't accept and there were no short cuts. Fair dinkum, she should have had balls.

Those boys on the squad meant a lot to me, and I'm so glad that nowadays they are all happy and successful in business, due in no small way to Laurie. He was a father-figure to his swimmers, tough but fair, and he was especially kind to me.

***

One Sunday morning in June 1982, when I would usually have time off, I decided to get in some extra kilometres and planned to meet Laurie and a couple of other training mates at the pool at 8am.

Problem was, I was living in Kedron at the time, which was a good fifty-five minute drive away. I was running late and had half an hour to make it in time. The main street where I lived was called Rode Road (pronounced Ro-dee) and it was dead on Sundays. I started going around 89kph, up and down hills, when a policeman waved me down. Damn, a radar. Hell, I knew I was going way over in a 60kph zone, what excuse could I give them?

'I'm late for training and Laurie's going to get upset,' I said.

The cop was a big fan and a nice guy, and he started asking me a heap of questions like, 'Not long to go now, hey?', 'Do you think you will win gold for Australia?' and 'What's Laurie really like?'

Soon the other cops who had been monitoring the radar came crowding round and we had a good chat. The sergeant radioed in to ask what was going on, and when he was told I was late for training, he replied, 'Okay, just tell her to slow down and leave earlier for training in the future. And let her know that we wish her all the best for the Games in September.'

I couldn't believe it, I was let off! Thank God, because otherwise I would have had a two-hundred-dollar fine and three demerit points. When I finally arrived at training, I told Laurie the story. He had a good laugh. I got in the pool, counting my blessings that I didn't have an accident and was very, very careful from then on. I learnt my lesson: 'Speed in the pool, not on the road.'

That incident wasn't the first run-in I'd had with the traffic police. Another time, about six months after getting my licence, I was driving with Mum when I noticed a radar on the south end of the Story Bridge in Brisbane. I thought I'd be nice and let the oncoming traffic know that the cops were there.

I started flashing my lights on-and-off for ages. Lo and behold, an unmarked cop car pulled me over, just on the other side of the bridge. Yikes. The cop asked why I was flashing my lights and I tried to say, 'Well, I'm getting confused with the indicator and lights and I keep flashing instead of indicating.' But it was yeah, yeah, they've heard that before.

Anyway, I couldn't get out of that one and landed a seventy-five-dollar fine and one demerit point. The lesson there was, if you see a radar, don't warn the oncoming traffic. If they're speeding, tough!

Apart from these incidents, I've never had a problem on the roads. I know I am a very careful driver, a bit of a leadfoot, but I know how to handle the roads very well. It's the other drivers one has to be careful of. My family has always said I'm a safe and reasonably fast driver. I manage to get myself through the traffic with the greatest of ease!

***

It was such a great feeling to know that I would be representing my country in my own home town for the Common wealth Games. Adding to my excitement was the launch of the official Games swimsuits which I was asked to model at Chandler Pool. I was thrilled to be chosen to wear the new, Speedodesigned green lycra one-piece. It had a white and gold sash, bearing just one word: 'Australia'.

That great experience was in total contrast to the nightmare that was to come when we attended a team training camp in Sydney. Our forty-three-strong swimming team was scheduled to stay at the Migrant Endeavour Hostel in Maroubra for a month, before moving to the Games Village at Griffith University in Brisbane. The Amateur Swimming Union of Australia had apparently been short of funds and gone for the migrant hostel as the cheapest accommodation available, basing their decision on the location, which was near the heated indoor pool and gym at the University of New South Wales.

I couldn't believe my eyes when our Commonwealth Games team bus pulled up outside the Endeavour. It was completely shabby, with poky little units that barely fitted any of us. The beds were also hilariously small. We took a photo of the 2-metre tall Neil Brooks lying down on one of them, and his legs from the knee down were over the end of the bed!

In fact, the building was still operating as a migrant hostel and we would share our paltry meals consisting mainly of rice with the Vietnamese refugees in the cafeteria. It was completely shameful that this was the best that Australia could offer its national representatives in its own country. Can you imagine today's champions putting up with those conditions?

I was sharing a unit with Kiwi-born Rickie Binning, a lovely girl and a lot of fun. We needed a sense of humour with this kind of accommodation. The unit had one tiny bedroom with a single bed which Rickie got to sleep in. I was left with the lounge room and a vinyl divan that converted into a bed. It was as hard as a rock and I kept falling into the crack down the middle. I was supposed to sleep like that for a month.

The first night was horrendous. I tried to doze off for three hours, tossing and turning. I was incensed. At 11pm, I tucked my pillow under my arm and went to Bill Sweetenham's room to bang on his door. He was sharing with the team's head coach, Terry Buck, and when they answered I let them have it.

'How the hell am I supposed to get a good night's sleep on a rock-hard divan? Are we going to put up with this for a month? I have so much pressure on me, swimming for Australia, but we're being treated like we're from a Third World country. What's more, the food's crap. We need steak and vegetables, pasta and fruit. Healthy food, not mushy rice at every meal.'

Bill and Terry were useless and I went back to bed. Bleary-eyed the next morning, I rang Mum and burst into tears. I was so disappointed with what was happening, considering the fact that the team was about to carry the hopes of the nation on our shoulders. I know Michelle Ford rang her father to ask if he could send a mattress, so she could get a decent night's sleep.

Mum rang Wayne Smith from the Brisbane *Telegraph* and the paper ran a front-page story on our Spartan living conditions. It was picked up by the other papers and went national. I still can't believe we had to put up with what we did. It might have been understandable if we were in a foreign country with a different culture. But we were the host for the Games, we were in our home nation and our swim team was the one with the best medal prospects. No expense should have been spared to ensure we did our best.

Fortunately, the exposure of the controversy led to some much needed changes. We all received hired television sets and ten cases of fresh fruit were delivered to the team every few days. Our structured meals improved and they switched our main meal from the evening to midday, so we felt more comfortable going into the 6pm training session. Furthermore, the media coverage attracted sponsorship for our team. This included the Sealy mattress company, which got some national publicity in exchange for several truckloads of first-class, king-single mattresses. At least now we were better prepared for the Commonwealth Games.

22

On September 30, with my heart pumping, I announced:

> We declare that we will take part in the Commonwealth Games of 1982 in the spirit of true sportsmanship, recognising the rules which govern them and desirous of part icipating in them for the honour of our Commonwealth and for the glory of sport.

Three thousand pigeons were released. Guns fired a salute. And I breathed a big sigh of relief. I had delivered the Athletes Oath at the Opening Ceremony in front of a capacity crowd of sixty thousand and a worldwide television audience. We were at the appropriately named Queen Elizabeth II Jubilee Stadium in Brisbane, standing in front of the Queen herself and the Duke of Edinburgh.

It was a great honour to be chosen as spokeswoman but it hadn't been easy. Apart from my nerves, there was the wind: a rare stiff, chilly westerly, which sent papers and dust swirling through the stadium and threatened to blow my Aussie slouch hat off my head. Worse still, it whipped right through my thin team uniform and made me shiver. Despite being as fit as I had ever been, I knew I was coming down with something.

It's a funny thing about athletes. The more you train and the fitter you get, the more bugs you seem to catch. I suppose having such a low body fat percentage and working to exhaustion just shoots your immune system. You walk a fine line being an elite sportsperson.

The next morning, I had a sore throat and a runny nose. I visited the Australian team doctor, Tony Millar, and he prescribed nasal drops and garlic tablets. Anything stronger was regarded as a banned substance and strictly forbidden, so I just had to sniff and suffer in silence.

***

My first event on the opening night of the six-day swimming meet at the Commonwealth Games was the 800-metre freestyle heat. I cruised through as second fastest qualifier in 8:41, just behind my main rival, England's Jackie Willmott. The press had been expressing doubts about my form after my long break from international competition, whereas Willmott had won the 800-metre silver medal at the recent World Championships in August. I pulled out of the Worlds because I wanted to train solely for the Commonwealth Games.

I was still feeling strangely lethargic and had a sore throat in the lead-up to the final. Nevertheless, I knew how much hard training I had done and, of course, I was the world record holder and defending champion. This was my event and no Pom was going to take it off me.

I revelled in the hometown conditions with the local crowd, including all my family and friends, and the state-of-the-art pool at Chandler. It had an innovative 'wet-deck' design and anti-turbulence lane ropes to keep backwash to a minimum. There were also two empty outside lanes so, once you got your nose in front, it was as still as a millpond. An added advantage was that I had trained there for the previous eighteen months and knew every tile on the bottom of the pool. I loved it.

In the final of the 800 metres, Willmott went out fast and led at the end of the first 100 metres. I was in the next lane, content to ride along in her wake and settle into my usual rhythm. I took the lead in the third lap and, with each succeeding lap, further increased it. I got the gold, Michelle Ford snatched the silver and Willmott got the bronze.

The problem was, when I touched the wall at the finish, roared on by the huge crowd, I looked at the time and cursed. 8:29.05! Less than 5 seconds outside my world record. I was hardly even trying and still had plenty in reserve.

Believe it or not but, right throughout my career, I never felt as though I really gave a hundred percent in a race. My hesitation to give my all was a hangover from the butterfly race I swam as a twelve-year-old when I hit the wall in the second-last lap and almost drowned as I floundered home. That memory continued to haunt me throughout my career. I didn't want to make a fool of myself and so my strategy, once I got in front in a race, was just to stay there comfortably. For some strange reason, when I was way out in front of the other competitors, my body tended to hurt more than when someone was right beside me.

As I recovered my breath after the 800-metre final, I reflected on why I didn't go harder. If only someone had been pushing me. Oh well, I had a gold medal, which wasn't a bad start, and there were two races still to come. I made the most of the moment, waving to Mum, Dad and my sisters in the stands and acknowledging the standing ovation I received from the crowd.

'Congratulations, Tracey, you've done Australia proud.' Those words came from Malcolm Fraser, the Prime Minister of Australia, as he hung the gold medal around my neck while I stood on the podium. I felt so relaxed and happy that I forgot protocol and gave him a kiss on the cheek.

When we marched down the side of the pool afterwards, I took off my Aussie slouch hat and threw it to the crowd, but people kept throwing it back. I broke out of the line and ran over to the Prime Minister and placed it on his head. He didn't mind at all, waving to the crowd and joining the three placegetters for photographs. He was a great sport, and while I have absolutely no interest in politics, I once had morning tea with Malcolm and Tamie Fraser during the Moscow fiasco and liked them both.

Then I spotted Grampa Dave in the grandstand. I had promised him that the first gold medal I won at the Games would be his. I raced up and hung my medal around his neck. He was so proud, and tears rolled down his cheeks. Heaps of people were patting me on the back and asking me for autographs. They all started chatting to Grampa as well and he was so proud to be Tracey Wickham's grandfather.

***

The next morning, I competed in the heats for the 200 metres and my cold had worsened. I really didn't feel like swimming. June Croft of England, a classic sprinter, was a hot favourite with a personal best of 2:00.08. In her heat she clocked 2:00.87 and made it look easy, whereas I struggled home in 2:03.95. At least I was the fastest Australian into the final.

By the next night's final, I was feeling lousy and knew I'd be lucky to break 2:10. Laurie tried to pep me up but I felt exhausted and lethargic as we filed into the packed Chandler Pool. I was coughing and sniffling because I didn't want to blow my nose in front of everyone and show them I wasn't well.

As we stood on the starting blocks, I was aware of June Croft next to me. She was a strapping girl, at least 7 centimetres taller than me and very broad-shouldered. I felt beaten before we started. I convinced myself that it wasn't my pet event and that it didn't matter if I didn't win. It was stupid of me, as an elite swimmer, to think so negatively. The truth was, I had the ability, sick or not.

To my surprise, my fellow Aussie, Rosemary Brown, was first to turn, just ahead of Croft and another Aussie, Suzi Baumer. Brown's lap time of 28.83 was fast. Too fast for me.

Brown and Croft were level at the 100 metres and I moved into third place ahead of Suzi. I started to feel better and by 150 metres I was a clear second. As we came down the pool for the last time, I suddenly felt I could win. I was actually gaining on Croft in the last 25 metres. One length became half a length as the crowd's roar lifted my spirits and my tempo.

'I can win this!' I thought. I changed gears in the last 15 metres and sprinted. Too late. I finished second. I looked up at the scoreboard and couldn't believe my eyes. My time was 2:00.60, more than 2 seconds inside my personal best. June Croft had made history, winning in a Commonwealth and Olympic Games record time of 1:59.74, the first Englishwoman and only the sixth in the world to break the magic 2-minute barrier. I realised as I touched the wall that I could have won. I just kept thinking, 'Can we start the race again, please? I went out too slow the first time.'

***

I had two days now to rest for the 400 metres and, as sick as I felt, that 200-metre time was the best medicine I could have had. There was only one race left in my career and there was no way I was going to bow out with anything else but a gold medal.

But I got sicker. My cold had gone to my chest and I kept coughing all the time while my nose was blocked and ran continually. I was so scared of failure and to make matters worse, everyone was acting like my win was a foregone conclusion. Mike Wenden, a dual freestyle gold medallist at the 1968 Olympics, forecast that I was 'the only certainty of the Games' in the 400 metres. Norman May, the ABC's veteran swimming commentator, predicted that I would go close to my world record time from Berlin four years earlier. Nobody considered the possibility of me losing. Except me.

I swam like a log in the heat, clocking a slow 4:19 compared to Willmott's 4:15 and Croft's 4:17. Even though I was the world, Commonwealth and Olympic Games record holder and again a defending champion, I couldn't stop the feelings of pessimism. I was sick. I didn't want to embarrass myself in front of all my family and friends and Australia. Not in my home town. It would be easier to just withdraw. No shame in that, was there?

Once again, I couldn't sleep. My old bugbear of noisy distractions had returned to haunt me on the eve of the most important race of my career. I tried resting after the 400-metre heats but tossed and turned. As other athletes finished their competition, it was party time and there was a lot of shouting around the dorms.

I had one night to get some sleep before the 400-metre final, and there was no way I was getting it in the Village. My mind was made up. I'd call Mum and get her to pick me up. Bugger the officials, if they wanted me to win gold for Australia, they'd have to put up with me going home for a night. My house was only ten minutes away anyhow.

I called Laurie and told him what I wanted to do. He backed me: 'Don't worry. I'll take the flak. Just do what you have to do.'

Laurie sneakily told team management that he wanted me to have an extra training session then drove me to the front gate where Mum picked me up. I had a good, homecooked meal with roast chicken and vegetables followed by my favourite ice-cream and jelly and went straight to my own comfy bed.

***

By morning, I felt a bit better but my mindset was still negative. I decided I was going to pull out of the 400 metres and to hell with the officials, the press and the public. It was my decision, nobody else's. I had won a gold and a silver medal for my country, what more did they want?

Mum drove me back to the Village at Griffith University and told me that whatever I did, it was fine with her. As soon as I walked in to our accommodation, Dick Orbell, a fellow swimmer, warned, 'You better watch out, Tracey. They're looking for you.'

The team management had twigged to my going AWOL the night before and wanted an explanation. I was summoned with Laurie to appear before them in the auditorium immediately.

Sure enough, the management tore strips off me and Laurie, who could hardly get a word in. How dare I leave the Village without telling anyone! Who did I think I was? This kind of selfish behaviour was undermining team morale and I deserved to be suspended, they said. I was infuriated that they were trying to tell me what to do when it was the last race of my career. All I had wanted was a good night's sleep.

Anger welled up in me. Memories of missing out on Moscow, the AIS debacle, the ASU taking the car I won and the six grand I had to give back for doing the margarine TV commercials kept flashing through my mind. After all I had done for Australian swimming, what made them think they could treat me this way?

I exploded. 'What right do you lot have to talk to me like this? At least I earned my Australian blazer. What did you do to earn yours? Just try and suspend me when the whole of Australia is crying out for this gold medal I'm expected to win tonight.'

I was swearing a fair bit and poor Laurie just sank into his seat in embarrassment. He whispered to me to calm down, but secretly he must have been glad I was worked up because it improved my swimming.

I knew there would be outrage from Australia if the officials banned me from the 400-metre freestyle, particularly with the Queen presenting the medals for that event. She only presented at two events, the other being the 400-metre athletics which Raelene Boyle had won for Australia. I turned and walked out of there, struggling to open the big double doors of the auditorium. I fired a parting shot: 'Anyway you're all just a mob of fucking bastards.'

I slammed the doors behind me. I was fuming, shaking, steam coming out of my ears. That would show them. But what had I just said? I had insisted I was going to swim when I meant to say I was pulling out!

For the record, after that little blow-up my card was subsequently marked NTA: 'Never to tour again'. It didn't matter to me because I was never going to swim again. In fact, I had a bit of a chuckle when I saw my negative team report. As if I cared anymore.

By lunchtime I had cooled down but felt scared. Even though my best time was 8.72 seconds faster than Jackie Willmott swam in the heats, I wasn't sure that I could beat her. I was feeling worse than ever and decided again that I would pull out of the race. I had to tell Laurie.

I searched the Village, looking everywhere, but couldn't find him. I rang and left messages but there was no sign and I got angry. How dare he desert me at this crucial stage of my career! After three hours of searching, there was nothing to do but to trudge back to my room. Well, wouldn't you know it, just as I had given up there was Laurie, making his way towards me.

'Where the hell have you been, Laurie?'

He had his arm behind his back, but brought it forward to reveal a dozen beautiful red roses.

'What are these for?' I asked.

'For when you win tonight and get your gold medal from the Queen.'

'Laurie, I'm sick. I can't swim and I can't win.'

'Oh, Tracey, you could win with one arm tied behind your back and doing backstroke. Come on, off to your room. Get ready and meet me in the car park in twenty minutes. The team bus has already left but we'll go together.'

'But ... but—'

'Go get ready.'

I'd lost the argument. Suddenly, I knew I had to get organised and focus, focus, focus. My whole mindset had changed. I thought, 'Who's in the race? What lane am I in? How am I going to do my race tactics? Oh shit, I've got fifteen minutes. I gotta pack and go swim the race of my life!'

I raced up to my room, had a quick shower, packed my bags and was out the door. I sprinted to the car park looking for a Commonwealth Games car but couldn't find Laurie.

'Where the hell is he?'

I heard a *beep! beep!* and there he sat in a beat-up old council bus that he'd bought for a grand. It had the 'Laurie Lawrence Swim Club' written on the side and graffiti from all the swimmers covering it inside and out.

'I'm not going to go to the pool in that thing. We'll never make it!'

But it was no arguments and away we went. I knew we were up for a good half-hour drive in that bus. I sat in the front left side seat in my Australian tracksuit with Laurie driving and cranking the old stick shift every time he changed gears. It was so embarrassing.

Laurie was singing 'Advance Australia Fair' and every other Aussie song he could think of, trying to psych me up. I was quiet of course, not in a real good mood. Every red light he would honk the horn and yell out to the people, 'I've got Tracey Wickham in here and she's going to win a gold medal tonight given to her by the Queen!'

People went crazy, jumping out of their cars and coming on board to shake my hand. He did this at about eight sets of red lights. At this rate, the race will be over before we get to the pool, I thought. He even stopped on the side of the road where three kids were playing and told them I was in the bus. They shook my hand and wished me luck and said they were going to watch me on TV that night to see me win the gold medal.

I began to focus on my race plan. I have to win this, I thought. For my family, my friends and for the rest of Australia. I can't let any of them down now.

After ten years of swimming competitions and thousands and thousands of laps at training, it all came down to this, my last race. There was no turning back now.

23

When Laurie and I walked into the foyer at the Chandler Pool, we were met by Mum and her partner Ashley, both with worried looks, and my best friends, Lee and Stephen Goodall. Everyone was worried about my health problems and, as Steve gave me a hug for good luck, I saw Lee look towards Laurie and mouth the words, 'Is she swimming?'

'Of course she's swimming,' thundered Laurie. 'Now let us through, we've got to warm up.'

I half smiled and went straight through to the changerooms. Running through my mind was the simple knowledge: 'This is it.'

As I slipped into the warm-up pool, I knew that I couldn't let the people close to me down, especially Mum. She was my rock and always has been. I felt like I was in a dream. As I swam slowly up and down, I stared down at the black lines and recalled how many times I had counted the tiles as I trained over the past eighteen months. It had been a wild ride and tonight it was about to end.

Suddenly it hit me. My normal preparation had gone out the window and I didn't even know who was in the lanes next to me or what times they had done in the heats. Mental preparation is equally important as physical preparation and now I felt out of my comfort zone and rattled.

But, as I walked out to the starting blocks, my spirits lifted. My whole family was there. Even Dad had flown in from the United States, and he was my good luck talisman, having seen me through in Edmonton and Montreal. Sitting next to Mum was my grandad, Dave Colborne, old and frail after several severe strokes but happy and excited. He had originally been seated right up the back of the stands until the ushers, realising his poor health and failing eyesight, moved him right down to the centre of the front row. Even Mim was there, my sisters, my cousins, my aunt Denise and my old coach Bill Sweetenham, willing me to victory alongside my team. A further boost came when I saw Kenrick, my ex, who had just won a gold medal that afternoon at the velodrome next door. He smiled and gave me the thumbs-up.

By the time I stood on the blocks between the two English girls, June Croft and Jackie Willmott, I felt supremely confident. As I was introduced to the crowd I thought to myself, 'This is my pool. This is my crowd. These Poms are not going to beat me.'

I relished the deafening roar which greeted the announcement of my name and raised my arms high above my head. I wanted to let the Poms know they were in for a hell of a fight. As always, I cracked my knuckles and said my usual little prayer, 'God give me strength.'

As soon as the gun went, I was in front, determined to finish my career in style. I had never been overhauled after leading in a major race and wasn't about to start now. Forgetting my cold, I went through the 200 metres in 2:03, under world record pace, but in the last lap something strange happened. I felt as though I didn't want to finish. I wanted it to keep going. I was lapping up every moment and never wanted it to end.

I wanted to savour every stroke and so I actually slowed down. As I went to touch the wall, I came up short and had to take another full stroke. That never happened to me before and I can't explain why it did this time. It probably cost me a Games record. My time was 4:08.82, just outside my 4:08.45 in Edmonton. If I'd stretched out and glided I needn't have taken that extra stroke. Anyway, who cared? I finished nearly 5 seconds in front of Willmott and Croft, who came third.

As I looked up at the clock, I burst into tears. Perhaps it was the release of all the pent-up emotion of the past few days: the drama of my cold, the run-ins with the ASU officials and team management and the ending of a career that had been my whole life up until this point.

The crowd were on their feet, cheering and stamping, so I swam slowly down the pool, waving to everyone and soaking it in. When I came back to the start, I was blubbing like a baby and Suzi Baumer, who finished fourth, put her arms around me and comforted me. I didn't want to get out of the pool. It was surreal. Time stood still.

As I walked back up the deck of the pool for the presentation, I saw Mum sitting next to Dawn Fraser near the Royal Box. She was trying to hold back tears, but Dawn advised her to let it all out. When I saw Mum crying, I started again myself. Someone threw me a koala mascot with the Games symbol on it, so I clutched it to my chest as I walked to the dais. To this day, that koala sits on my dressing-table, next to my daughter Hannah's teddy.

With England having the two fastest qualifiers going into the race, the Queen probably thought she would be presenting the gold medal to one of her own swimmers. But, if she was disappointed, it didn't show. She placed the medal around my neck and said, 'Well done. Very good swim. Congratulations.'

I clutched her hand in both of mine and replied, 'Thank you so much, ma'am.'

The Australian anthem piped up and tears were rolling down my cheeks again. When it finished and I walked down the pool deck, I saw Grampa Dave. He was standing, leaning on his stick, and crying as he wore the 800-metre freestyle gold medal I'd given him around his neck. I knew he was gravely ill and that he'd held on just to see my swansong. When I saw him, he was just howling with emotion. I'd seen him shed a few tears before, but never like this. I started to cry again.

Then I saw Laurie and we hugged each other without a word. We both knew what we had been through that day and we were overcome with relief and joy. I owed him so much. Thank God he'd conned me into swimming that night. The master motivator had done it again and without all his hard work and dedication, I would never have swum, nor won for that matter. Next to Laurie, ironically, was my former coach, Bill. We had our differences in the past, but he smiled when he saw me and put his arm around me. He said simply, 'Well done, mate.'

As I gave my last post-race press conference, Grant Kenny burst into the room and announced that Lisa Forrest had come first in the 200-metre back-stroke final. I really wanted her to win because she was such a great mate of mine and my roomie. The announcement just added to the euphoria in the room. Grant and I had been friends for a long time, so I was pleased when he gave me a big hug of congratulations and said, 'Come outside. There's a present for you.'

I walked out and saw a red Mazda RX-7 with a massive pink ribbon wrapped around it. I had always had my heart set on that model and this was the icing on my cake. So Grant and I took off and painted the town the same colour as the car. My cold seemed to evaporate as we danced the night away, without a care in the world. Later, I found out that I had to return the car as it was just a loan and part of a publicity deal with Mazda that my so-called manager had arranged. That company certainly got their money's worth, as a photo of me in the car made the front page of the *Courier-Mail* the next day. I had only been retired for two hours and already I was being exploited.

***

The huge high of my final swim was followed by tragedy the next day. Grampa Dave was rushed to hospital after another mild stroke. I visited him in intensive care and spent as much time as I could in between my PR commitments. Grampa was in and out of hospital over the next month, declining rapidly.

Five weeks after the Commonwealth Games, I was in Weipa, in the far north of Australia, staying with a local family while I opened the new town swimming pool. One night I was having dinner when a peculiar sensation overcame me. I didn't feel ill – I simply had no appetite, even for my favourite dessert, ice-cream and jelly. I felt sad and wanted to be alone. I tossed and turned all night, with no idea of why I couldn't sleep, and sat up on the edge of my bed a few times, knowing something wasn't right.

The next morning, I got a phone call from Laurie who told me Grampa had passed away that previous night, 17 November 1982, around dinner time. Mum couldn't bring herself to call me. I just screamed, everything was a blur and I felt sick. I hung up on poor Laurie and raced to my room, where I bawled my eyes out. That lovely family in Weipa kindly organised to fly me home immediately and I never did get to open the new pool. I promised I would return one day, and I will. They were so kind.

At the funeral parlour, I again had the chance to place my 800-metre gold medal around Grampa's neck. I told him how much I loved him and said my goodbyes. To this day, I wear his medal for Best All-Round Athlete at Nudgee College 1924 – made of real 9-carat gold – around my own neck.

It was around this traumatic time that the press revealed to the public that I had received six thousand dollars from the Fraser Government in compensation for not going to Moscow. About three months after the Olympic Games, a cheque had arrived in the mail with a letter saying that it was equal to the amount it would have cost to send me to Russia had I gone. There was also a green-and-gold striped Australian team blazer.

Sure enough, once it became known and I had come out of retirement to swim with Laurie Lawrence, certain factions within the ASU yet again tried to strip me of my amateur status even though others, like Raelene Boyle, received the same amount. Some members of the union even said that it was a bribe and, because I was hard up, I took the money instead of competing in Moscow. That doesn't even make sense. The ASU made a veiled threat to seize my medals and the press had a field day over the contro-versy. I had a good line for them though.

'They'll have to dig up Grampa first.'

***

At last, at the age of nineteen, my life such as I knew it was over. Not a bad career I suppose, with five world records, two world titles, four Commonwealth Games gold medals, three silver and a bronze, and twenty-three national championships. I had broken three hundred and sixty-five Queens land records, two hundred and seventy-five Australian records and twelve Commonwealth records and won numerous other international gold medals.

There was still that little annoyance: my lack of Olympic medals. It was a matter of bad timing. I was too young at Montreal in 1976 and Moscow 1980 was a blowout for health and family reasons. I should have won, given that I held every freestyle title from 200 to 1500 metres at the 1979 Australian Championships and won the 100-metre butterfly in 1981 and the 100-metre freestyle at the Queensland Championships in 1982. Plus I still held my world records for the 400 and 800 metres. But it wasn't to be.

In 1984 when the Los Angeles Olympics came around, I was two years into retirement, forced out of the sport by a lack of money. Ironically, universal professionalism and sponsorship came to swimming that same year, 1984. Too late for me.

For a decade, my life had been confined to the pool with my eyes constantly glued to the black line as I churned out lap after gruelling lap. Now I had another life to live.

PART 4

DOWNWARDS SPIRAL

24

Even though I was no longer swimming, there was still a whirlwind of publicity and television appearances to get through post-Commonwealth Games. As well as appearances on *It's a Knockout, Blankety Blanks* and various other shows, I was a return guest on the *Don Lane Show.* After the Games in 1982, they gave me the biggest surprise of my life. I was interviewed by Don, but asked to stick around and help out with the rest of the show. As usual, the program ended with the Lucky Wheel, where a contestant would pick something on the wheel and, if it came up, they got to keep it. After the contestant had finished their turn, Bert Newton told me to give it a go. I always wanted a car, so I went for it and sure enough, the wheel stopped spinning on the car prize. I won!

I later found out that the odds were certainly in my favour, as there had been three extra panels with the car prize than usual and Bert had surreptitiously slowed the wheel to ensure it stopped there. The show's producers purposely rewarded me for my swimming career on express instructions from the station owner, businessman Kerry Packer. He found out about the car I wasn't allowed to accept in 1979 at the Australian Sportswoman of the Year Awards, and wanted to make up for it. I went to see him in person the next day, as he didn't want any publicity, and I gave him a huge thanks.

When it came to collecting my prize, I was given a choice of a Holden Gemini, a Toyota Corolla or a Mazda 323. Barely able to control my joy, I chose the latter as it had always been a favourite of mine. The following week, back in Brisbane, I picked up my shiny new steel-grey car. At last, after all those years of borrowing and bludging lifts, I had wheels of my own, thanks to Kerry Packer.

My own celebrity meant I got to meet a heap of other celebrities. As well as the bands Sherbet and Chicago, I rubbed shoulders with Suzi Quatro, Kiss and Dr Hook. I felt like a groupie!

I also flew a lot in those days, travelling to functions around the country on Qantas and Ansett. I almost always got upgraded from economy to business class and often there was a complimentary bottle of wine for me to take home. All I had to do was be polite (as I always was), smile and sign a few autographs. I loved it. You don't earn money from swimming, but the perks almost make up for it.

Another fringe benefit came through my friendship with Kenrick. When I accompanied him to a Great Keppel Island sports function in 1979, the manager at the resort told me to come back anytime, at his expense. After I retired, I rang him and asked if the offer was still good. He said he was more than happy to have me as he was about to open a new pool and I could be the guest of honour at the gala opening. Flo Bjelke-Petersen, the wife of the Queensland Premier, performed all the formalities, so all I had to do was socialise and mingle with the guests. No problem.

I went back to Great Keppel as a guest three more times over the years. In return for doing a bit of promotional work, I could sit at the Captain's Table for dinner each night and enjoy the facilities of the beautiful resort. On my first trip they had a 'Lovely Legs' competition among the guests. We all had to parade in high heels and a short skirt behind a screen which hid the upper half of our bodies, then spin around and walk back again. My pins were pretty good and shapely after churning up and down the pool so many times and, you guessed it, I came up a winner.

On those three occasions, I was also allowed to bring a girlfriend with me. We just swam, sunbaked and swanned around like a couple of movie stars. What a life!

***

There were downsides to the fame as well, as I soon found out in the wake of the 1982 Games. Walking down Queen Street Mall, I felt that everyone was staring at me. As people passed me I could hear a constant stream of them saying, 'That's her, that's

Tracey Wickham' and 'Isn't she tiny! How did she swim so fast?'

Others were just pointing and staring and some were even making snide remarks. It was like I was a two-headed monkey at the zoo. Why couldn't they just leave me alone? I knew people meant well and I suppose it was a shock for them to see me doing everyday things like shopping, but I suddenly couldn't take it any more. I turned into the nearest shop, which happened to be Sportsgirl, and hid behind a clothes rack, holding my head in my hands.

'Oh God, can't I walk down the street without being gawked at or whispered about?'

I burst into tears.

Another downside to celebrity is that other people want to exploit you and leech off your fame. On the last night of competition at the 1982 Games, I was approached by a fellow called Geoff Ramsey. His company made swimming pools and he was looking for a famous swimmer to be his figurehead. He offered fifty dollars for every pool sold if I would lend my name to his project and he reckoned he'd sell thousands. The 'Tracey Wickham Pools' company was born and my photo duly began featuring in ads in the *Courier-Mail.* Soon enough, cheques for amounts between two hundred and four hundred dollars began appearing in my mailbox at a rate of about once a month.

Doing the maths, that equated to around eight pools being sold every four weeks, which was ridiculous. I truly believe the company would have sold twenty times that number through all the franchises. I knew I was being robbed. Ramsey refused to send me the company financial records and when finally he did, the documents showed that plenty had been sold and I wasn't receiving even close to the percentage I had been promised.

After about two years of our partnership, the cheques abruptly stopped. My name was still being associated with the pools, however, and all attempts to contact the company came to nothing. We ended up in court twice and my solicitor calculated that I was owed about thirty thousand dollars. Ramsey even tried to argue in court that he owned the trademark 'Tracey Wickham'. How ridiculous and how dare he try to steal my name.

I won my case, but Ramsey declared the pool operation bankrupt. He had milked the company dry so all that was left in the account was one dollar. I got nothing and had the added expense of the legal fees. I lost a bundle.

My 'manager' also turned out to be a disappointment. Aside from the Mazda loan fiasco, although that might have been more the car company's fault than his, there remained precious little emanating from his 'deals'. He became more of a hindrance than a help when it came to real opportunities.

SPC, the canned fruit company, had approached me directly and offered sixty thousand dollars to do a series of television commercials. Doing the right thing, so I thought, I passed the matter on to my manager. I thought the offer was great and was ready to sign, but he was strangely quiet. I kept asking him what was happening and he kept saying it was still in the works. Little did I know, he had been holding out for a hundred grand without consulting me. More money would have meant more for him in his twenty percent cut. SPC had declined that ridiculous offer, and me altogether, and my manager just didn't have the guts to tell me. That ended our relationship quick smart.

I had another manager after that who was equally as hopeless. He organised for me to do a television commercial with a drink company, who paid me twenty thousand dollars for a six-month contract. Later on, they wanted to extend the broadcasting of the advertisement to the southern states, so I was offered another eight thousand and accepted. That money went directly into my manager's bank account, and I never saw it again. He was going bankrupt, which I never knew. He knew though! I was so angry.

That was the last straw and I finally decided to manage my own affairs. I had a simple formula, just a flat fee for speaking at a function. It was time to cash in.

***

In early 1983, I was approached to write a book called *Swimming to Win.* I sat down and tried to pass on everything I'd ever learned about the sport. The book was short, about eighty-nine pages, but I was proud of the result. It was mainly about stroke techniques, like a swimming bible for beginners. Sometimes people would stop me in the street and say how much they had learned from the book, which was gratifying.

I was becoming more comfortable with my fame. I have a policy to always be nice to fans who are friendly and polite to me. Dad gave me some sage advice at a very early age: 'Never refuse an autograph. That may be the only time this person ever meets you, so they'll form a lasting impression from that one meeting.'

Whether there were a handful or a hundred people waiting for an autograph, I'd sign with a smile, no matter how tired I was or how bad my day had been. I also tried to reply to every letter I received, in longhand, and always wrote to thank the organisers of any function I'd attended. Dad always said it's the little things that count: 'It costs a stamp and five minutes of your time but it's worth a million dollars to them.'

I still do that to this day, longhand letters. I wish other people would too, it's a shame it's not done.

By now I was getting plenty of offers for promotional work and was asked to speak at functions. I had been pretty nervous about public speaking back when I was fifteen, and used to write out every word of my speech. I had a set selection of five topics and it must have been pretty boring for my audience. But now I was older and more confident, I began to adlib and tell stories. I found I really enjoyed it, especially if the audience reacted to what I was saying. I began running the whole gamut from state school morning teas to major corporate launches. Some people would even tell me that I was like a female version of Laurie Lawrence up on the stage, which was a huge compliment.

I made some memorable blunders though. One came about when I was asked to emcee a prestigious corporate function, something rare for me as I was normally a guest speaker. I always wore a smart suit on these occasions and, as my legs were one of my best assets, a short skirt above the knee. I stuck to the rundown and the presentation went smoothly. However, as was my habit, I called the organiser the next morning to thank him and to check if everything was okay. He seemed strangely hesitant.

'What did I do wrong?' I finally asked.

'Well...' he said, sounding embarrassed. 'What you said was fine but every time you sat down we could all see your knickers.'

Oops! I have crossed my legs on stage ever since.

25

'Tracey Wickham, coach'.

That was the caption under the front-page photo in the local paper, the *Suburban Express,* the day I started work in October 1983. It was my first real job and I was coaching the Everton Park State School Swimming Club. I was a bit nervous about my qualifications. I still held two world records and I was probably the most famous swimmer in the country, but could I pass those skills on? I had three categories of classes – learn-to-swim, semi-advanced and advanced – and they were all full. That meant a hundred and fifty children were depending on me for advice and perhaps even to save their lives. I had to get it right.

I was at the Houston Pool from 6am each day and would take two groups for a ninety-minute session until 7.30am. Then in the afternoon, I would take three more sessions from 3.30pm to 6pm. The pool was named after Tom Houston, the former Everton Park school principal, who had fought long and hard to get it built. It was worth the struggle, because it was a beautiful little pool and I was excited to have this opportunity to use my skills in a profitable way. But it was difficult, hot work coming into summer and I felt drained after dealing with kids all day.

As for me, I had no desire to swim at all. After all those years, I didn't want to go anywhere near the water, except to coach. Even when I went to the coast, I spent most of my time just lying on the beach. Secretly, I was afraid of sharks and even though there were nets and lifesavers, I didn't want to take the risk. Although Dad had been Australian Surf Belt champion and surfing was in the Wickham blood, it wasn't in mine.

I had to give up the coaching after one season. The problem was, to be a good coach you need to be with your squad day in, day out. Unfortunately, I had too many speaking and travel commitments and so coaching had to take a back seat.

***

In November 1983, I turned twenty-one. I was living in my own unit in Indooroopilly and loving my independence. I threw a big birthday bash and hoped Dad might be home for my party. Unfortunately he was in Cairo on business but at least he called to wish me well. I was having a terrific time catching up with my friends and doing things they had always taken for granted. I had a memorable birthday but it would have been better if Dad was there.

At this time, I was travelling around the country to raise money for the future Commonwealth Games Australian teams. I was brought into it by Benny Pike, an affable boxer from the Sunshine Coast. We had met at the 1976 Montreal Olympics, became mates at the 1978 Commonwealth Games and had gone on a few fundraising trips together at the time. After retiring from the boxing ring in 1981, Benny had started work in promotions for Carlton & United Breweries, major sponsors of the Games teams. Soon enough, he called me in.

Little did I realise my breezy acceptance would lead to twenty-odd years of trips to numerous country towns and countless fundraising functions. 'Nugget' May was nearly always involved too. We would bowl into town, head for a pub and have a drink with the locals. Benny and I would take a plastic bucket around, shamelessly asking for donations and plugging the sportsmen's night that evening. At the function, Benny would interview me, then 'Nugget' would do his famous 'Gold, gold, gold' call and an auctioneer would sell sporting memorabilia.

I recall one such evening in 1986, raising money for the Commonwealth Games in Edinburgh. The town was Redlynch, just a dot on the map near Cairns in North Queensland and the function was at the only sizeable place in town, the pub. As the official party arrived, a brawl broke out on the footpath.

'My God, I'm not going in there,' I said, stunned.

'Don't worry, I'll look after you,' comforted Benny.

To my surprise, the place was packed and we got a standing ovation as we walked in. When the bidding started in the sports memorabilia auction, people went crazy for my old pairs of togs and even signed t-shirts fetched hundreds of dollars. When I made a passionate plea for support, the sports-mad locals, fuelled by

214

plenty of beer, donated thousands to the team. They threw money, even shirts and thongs, in a riotous display of patriotism, Redlynch-style. Even an old war veteran with only one leg ended up throwing in a cheque for a thousand dollars, all on the quiet. He didn't want to cause a scene. We were so grateful.

I also went on fundraising trips for the Olympic team. These were organised by Ian Guiver, the boss of the Queensland Olympic Council. I would often be joined by former stars like weight-lifter Dean Lukin, swimmers Stephen Holland, Jon Sieben and Justin Lemberg and the athlete Raelene Boyle. We mainly used to tour country areas but several times we made appearances at State of Origin rugby league games at Lang Park.

I was so busy throughout the early 1980s that my family and friends kept telling me to slow down and take it easy. After all, I'd earned it. But I'm the sort of person who has to be running around and doing things in a hurry. I just want to devour life.

Unfortunately, that proved to be my undoing on a skiing holiday in 1984, when my ambition to conquer the slopes exceeded my ability. The result was a badly injured knee: torn ligaments which required a reconstruction. My knee would affect me for the rest of my life and I continue to suffer to this day. It certainly slowed me down for a while.

***

In August 1984, I watched the Los Angeles Olympics with interest. Jon Sieben's incredible win in the 200-metre butterfly was an absolute highlight, but I was keeping a special eye on the 400-and 800-metre women's freestyle, where my records still stood. American Tiffany Cohen won the 400 in a new Olympic record time of 4:07.10, but missed my world mark of 4:06.28. She also went close to my 800-metre time but missed out by 0.33 seconds, clocking 8:24.95, another Olympic record. Six years of my records holding and counting!

My star still hadn't dimmed by the 1986 World Aquatics Championships in Madrid. As far as *Age* swimming journalist Ron Carter was concerned, I was sorely missed and he wrote an open letter to me in his sports column. He said that Australia had taken me for granted for too long and 'only now is the sporting world appreciating your greatness ... Tracey, you are still the best. Wish you were here.'

Another touching tribute I received around this time was from the Gosford rose showman and breeder Eric Welch. He created a new type of miniature rose and named it the 'Tracey Wickham'. A 'fragrant, hardy, vigorous grower', it won numerous awards at the Sydney Royal Easter Show and the Australian and State Rose Society shows. What a thrill!

26

I was leaning over the bar in a nightclub in 1985 when a familiar figure bumped into me, accidentally on purpose. It was Rob: tall, dark and handsome, in a bearded, Italian sort of way. He had a cheeky look and certainly wasn't shy.

I remembered him well. We first met when my girlfriend and I were on the town a day or two after the 1982 Brisbane Commonwealth Games finished. My swimming commitments were over and I was as free as a bird. As we walked into a popular nightclub, the Underground, where a lot of Games athletes hung out, three guys sitting in the lounge turned and looked at us. The bearded one said, with a smirk, 'I've got a gold medal too.'

'Oh yeah,' I replied. 'What for?'

The answer came in Italian and his mates hooted with laughter. Even though I didn't speak the language, I got his drift. Cheeky bastard! But he had a nice smile. We chatted for a while about the Commonwealth Games and what it was like meeting the Queen. My girlfriend and I moved on through the club, mingled with some other swimmers and forgot the cocky Italians.

A year later, I was driving back from Toowoomba, where I had been speaking at a sports function. I stopped at a roadside fruit barn. A dark-haired fellow with a beard had just made a sale to the barn and was stacking packets of nuts onto the shelves. There was something familiar about his face. He looked up and saw me.

'Hi, Tracey, remember me?'

I just looked blank, so he gave me a clue.

'We met at the Underground after the Games last year.'

The penny dropped and we had a brief chat. Rob was so charming I even gave him my number. As I kept driving back to Brisbane I mused about him. Funny really, as I had always gone for blond, sporty guys like Kenrick Tucker, Mark Stockwell and, more recently, rugby player Michael Broad. Robert Ciobo was about as different as you could get, but there was just something about him.

The phone call never came but there we were, two years later, standing at the bar. His cheeky grin was still there, so I decided to get on the front foot and quipped, 'Is that a gun in your pocket or are you just pleased to see me?'

His eyes lit up. 'Just excited. What about a drink?'

Rob told me that he worked for his family's peanutprocessing and distribution business that had started up about two years before, Meriram Nuts. The name, he explained, came from the Christian names of the Ciobo family: Mehmet, Rita, Robert, Antonetta and Max. It sounded like a close family of hard workers. No problem with that.

We arranged to meet up again at Ekka, the Brisbane Exhibition, the next day. I remember two things about our first date, apart from the fact that I had a ball. One was that, being August 16, it was the eighth anniversary of the death of Elvis. The second thing was that Rob was petrified to go on any ride faster than a merry-go-round! But we got on like a house on fire.

The following day, I went to a Tupperware party and saw some old friends and parents from swimming. After a couple of drinks I confided to a girl-friend, 'I've just met the guy I'm going to marry.'

'What's his name?'

'Robin Something...' I couldn't even remember what his first name was.

'You don't know his name and you're going to marry him?'

'Yep!'

It was an old-fashioned courtship. Rob took me to a lovely little restaurant, Olivetto's in Red Hill, the next night and we talked about our hopes and dreams. One thing we had in common was a desire for marriage and children. At twenty-eight, Rob was ready to settle down and, at twenty-three, I was thrilled to be realising my childhood dream. Ever since I could remember I wanted to get married and have kids ... four, five, six ... the more the merrier.

Soon, Rob invited me to dinner with his parents at their home in Keperra and we had a lovely Italian meal. It seemed that I passed scrutiny, even though I wasn't Italian. As long as Rob was happy, they were too. They were pleased that Rob had met a nice girl who was down-to-earth.

*****

In January 1986, five months after we first started dating, I had my wisdom teeth out. Rob visited me in Brisbane Private Hospital and brought me flowers ... and a ring. Rob knew his jewellery as he was previously a gem cutter with his own shop in Melbourne. What he gave me did not disappoint, it was a gorgeous gold ring with a three-quarter carat solitaire diamond. Although my face was all swollen and I could barely talk, he proposed. I accepted. I was genuinely head over heels in love.

I wanted a big, traditional wedding and the Ciobo family was more than happy to comply. My dad, Roger, was back in the US, but he gave his blessing when I rang with the news. I remember him saying, 'Don't worry, I'll fix it for you. You can have a big wedding and invite whoever you want.' Unfortunately, the financial situation never worked out. I ended up having to pay for it myself. Dad promised he would pay me back one day when he could. Anyhow, family is more important and that's all in the past now.

Although I rarely saw my father, I still loved him and forgave his absences. He and Mum finally divorced and Mum remarried in 1983. It was an unusual match in that Mum was eighteen years older than her new husband, Ashley, and they had been introduced through my sister, Kelly. But the age difference never proved a problem. He's a real gentleman and was working as an accountant at that time. He's smart and kind and loves Mum to bits, which is what she deserves after all the time and effort and love she gave to her children. They are still married, twenty-seven years later.

Mum gave her blessing to my wedding and helped out with the preparations. It took nearly eleven months to organise and was going to cost a fortune. Happily, the bridal-wear company Gardam's offered to provide the dress and *New Idea* paid two thousand dollars for the engagement story and another two grand for exclusive rights to cover the wedding. That was huge money in those days.

Our big day was 1 November 1986, at St Stephen's Cathedral in Brisbane. The reception was at one of the city's top hotels, the Mayfair Crest. We had two hundred and seventy guests and no expense was spared. The matron-of-honour was my best friend, Lee Goodall and my sisters, Kelly and Julie, were among the five bridesmaids. My idea had been to have a 'rainbow wedding' with each bridesmaid in a different colour: mauve, apricot, pink, lemon and blue, with our little flower girl, my six-year-old cousin Natalie Gilday, in white. Lee and Stephen Goodall's little five-year-old, Matthew, was the pageboy. The men were in soft-grey suits with tails and cummerbunds and bow ties that matched their partner's dress.

The giant, eighteen-tiered wedding cake was lit with fairy lights and rotated. It took Ipswich baker Ted Salmond a month to make and weighed over 20 kilograms. My wedding dress was a masterpiece. It had crystal beading over the entire bodice and was made of double-layered pearl organza with a tulle and satin underlay. The train was nearly 5 metres long. It cost three and a half grand and took over a hundred hours to make. I felt like a queen.

Everything went perfectly, just as I had planned. The best thing was that Dad walked me down the aisle. His return from the States was the greatest wedding present I could have had. There were plenty of exciting moments during my swimming career, but I've never been happier than I was that day. It ended up costing me eight thousand dollars, but I didn't care, it was well worth it.

***

Rob and I were blissfully happy for a while. We honeymooned in Italy for three months and visited members of his family in Calabria. We travelled the whole length and breadth of the country and I even picked up a few basic phrases of Italian.

The Ciobo family lived in an old house at Keperra on two and a half acres. They bought the property next door to move into, but it had to be gutted and renovated. I had major input into the design for the new place, to help Rita, Rob's mum, make it her dream home. Rob and I then moved into his parents' old house, where we lived for four years before we built our own dream home on the land behind. Rob liked to call the area Ciobo Hill.

Rob was busy working in the family nut business while I wasn't doing much, just the odd promotional work for Meriram. I revelled in my freedom and the fact that, for the first time in my life, I didn't have to do what someone else told me to do.

I slept in occasionally, ate whatever I liked and took up smoking. It was a bit of rebellion on my part, I suppose. At last, I could do what I liked and no one could tell me otherwise. I had the odd drink but never really took a fancy to alcohol. Perhaps a session with the toilet bowl after my win at sixteen years old at the ABC Sportsperson of the Year function in 1979 had something to do with my distaste for champagne. I really like a Scotch in cold weather or a beer on a hot day, but I'm not much of a drinker.

***

I was overjoyed when I found out that I had fallen pregnant on our honeymoon, but it was quite a shock that I could conceive so easily. I just thought I would have a little break from the pill with no real intention of getting pregnant. Soon after the good news, however, I started spotting and Rob rang the gynaecologist, who told me to lie down. I ended up going to hospital where we lost the baby and the doctor gave me a curette. It had been just ten weeks.

I conceived again two months later but once again lost the baby, miscarrying at home, in agony. Mum was there with me and I was crippled over in pain. It was then that I began to fear I would never be able to carry a baby to term.

In July 1987 it felt like I had lost yet another part of me: my 800-metre world record was broken by the tiny American, Janet Evans. Funnily enough, she looked just like I did when I set the record, a skinny fifteen-year-old. Janet clocked 8:22.44, taking over 2 seconds off my mark which had been set in Edmonton in 1978, nine years earlier. A month later in Germany, Anke Möhring lowered the record further, to 8:19.53.

There was one huge consolation, however. By October 1987 I was again pregnant and this time I would keep the baby. Rob was delighted and I as good as wrapped myself in cotton wool until I was sure the baby was safe. I had major morning sickness, if you can call it that, since I always had it in the afternoons. Thankfully, both the sickness and my fears of miscarriage had gone by the twelve-week mark.

Another historic moment came in December 1987. I had been out Christmas shopping and came home to find a note pinned to my door by my sister-in-law.

'Janet Evans just broke your 400-metre record.'

Well, I collapsed in tears. I wasn't expecting it to go then because it was the American winter, but Janet did it. My 400-metre world record had been the longest-standing record of all time. Janet clocked 4:05.45 and so, after nine years and four months, my name was erased from the world record books. That record was my 'baby' and I'd wanted it to last at least a decade. Both my records had survived two Olympics and three World Championships, but now it was over. Oh well, at least I was pregnant.

***

On Wednesday morning, 13 July 1988, Hannah Lee Ciobo arrived. She was born at the Royal Brisbane Hospital, weighing in at eight pounds and two ounces (3.86 kilograms). It was a six-hour labour with no complications, and I had been given an epidural after an hour because I was scared of the unknown. With a healthy head of curly dark hair which later turned blonde-brown and clear crystal blue eyes, Hannah was a gorgeous, lively child. She looked very Italian!

After the labour, I was wheeled back into my room and was starving. I had a craving for a massive hamburger: not McDonald's-style, but a traditional one with 'the lot'. Rob combed the streets at 7pm and was gone for ages. Finally, he came back with the biggest burger you've ever seen and took a photo of me tucking into it in my hospital gown. I certainly deserved it.

Hannah was the first grandchild in both Rob's and my family and everyone came to visit the new baby, with the exception of Mim's side, much to my disappointment. But Pop Wickham snuck out behind Mim's back and caught the bus to see his great-granddaughter. I was so rapt. Pop was a true gentleman, the kind who opened car doors and raised his hat for women. Kind and gentle with a distinctive husky voice, he always wore a hat and tie. They certainly broke the mould after they made him.

Once I had Hannah, I couldn't believe how life could change so quickly. I just couldn't get into the swing of things, which on reflection was probably connected with undiagnosed post-natal depression. I was constantly tired and slept most of the time. Luckily, Mum took time off work and stayed with me for a month. When Hannah cried for a feed, Mum would wake me up and bring Hannah into my room. I would breastfeed her, then Mum would take her back to her cot and nurse her or change her nappy.

Being a mother was a shock to my system. I was like a zombie, walking around in my pyjamas in the middle of the afternoon. I felt like I was constantly running to catch my own tail, but never got things done. All I seemed to do was eat, feed Hannah and sleep. Without the help of my own mother and Rob's mother next door, I could not have got through it. After about five months, I began to settle down.

However, Hannah was a poor sleeper and didn't sleep through the night until she was two and a half. I was always sleep-deprived. Eventually I checked in to a Sleep Centre on St Paul's Terrace in the city. It was a hospice where mums with troublesome babies could stay to get help weaning them off the breast and regulating their sleep patterns. The nurses were great and we were there for four days while I got Hannah into a routine.

On the very day she turned six months old, Hannah began to crawl and by ten months, she was walking. I loved to dress her up in cute dresses to go out and she was a very placid child. Everyone doted on her. When she was eleven months old, I took her up to the hospital where she had been born to see Pop, who was being treated for a minor heart attack. He was delighted to see us and chatted away happily. He said, 'Trace, you should make a comeback. You can beat all those other girls, even now. I reckon you should do butterfly, you can break the world record.'

He always believed that. I loved 'fly and, at my peak, probably could have broken the record. It was such a shame it didn't fit into meet schedules alongside my other middledistance freestyle events. Nowadays it would be possible, as meets are stretched out over seven days instead of the four I had to contend with.

Pop passed away a few days later in his sleep. I was so pleased that he got to see his great-granddaughter one last time.

After Hannah's birth, my weight blew out by 24 kilograms. I'd always been a skinny athlete so this was a weird experience for me. I looked in the mirror one morning and saw Porky Pig staring back at me. I weighed 84 kilos at the time I gave birth and I couldn't even get my wedding rings on for nearly two years afterwards. I remember someone coming up to us at Brookside Shopping Centre, six months after Hannah was born. They asked, 'So when are you due again?' Talk about embarrassing!

I was really upset and was wary of anyone seeing my stomach. I felt like a blimp and I simply had to do something about it. So, for the first time in my life, I watched what I ate, and began some gentle exercise. Luckily, thanks to my fast metabolism, this was the only time I ever put on a significant amount of weight. I'm definitely thankful for that, but I've been careful with my diet ever since. I love my fruit: I eat about six to eight pieces a day and only really have about three main meals a week, generally at lunchtime.

I do have my weaknesses, of course. I love Italian food, the authentic cuisine having been introduced to me by Rob's family, and Japanese teppanyaki. I also can't go past a great T-bone with potato and pumpkin mashed together, corn, beans and homemade gravy. Then there's my big love, icecream. These days, I am hooked on Baskin-Robbins and go to the shop in Ashgrove every two days. I'm one of their best customers and I only ever order one flavour: 'World Class Chocolate', naturally.

27

It was the summer of 1990 and the stands wer. full. A hush descended over the excited crowd as I dived into the pool. There was no starting gun and no opponents, but over three hundred and fifty kids and their parents were watching as I swam slowly up and down the lanes. This was the first Tracey Wickham Swim Clinic, in the northern New South Wales town of Cessnock. Thanks to Rob's uncle who worked there, AMP had agreed to sponsor ten clinics throughout country centres in New South Wales, Victoria and Queensland.

At this first one, good old Laurie Lawrence agreed to help me out by commentating while I demonstrated swimming techniques. A born enthusiast, Laurie was a master at getting the kids involved and we got a great response. I was overwhelmed by the turnout, so it was wonderful to have Laurie there helping. All I had to do was swim a few lazy laps, answer his questions and sign autographs. But they were tiring days. We went from 9am to 5pm on Saturday and Sunday, then flew to the next town the next weekend and did the same thing again.

I did this the whole summer. I toured rural Victoria, towns like Bendigo, Sale, Ballarat and other northern New South Wales towns, and I got better all the time. Rob and I organised the whole thing ourselves, from the sponsorship through to the negotiations with the schools and the transport in between. Rob would attend the clinics with me and a few times we were able to bring Hannah along too.

***

In December of 1989, just prior to beginning the clinics, Brisbane was undergoing a heatwave so I walked to a local pool in Ferny Hills for a cooling dip. I hadn't seriously swum for years and the feel of the water was wonderful. I started doing a few easy laps and it all came back to me.

I returned the next day and the day after. As I got fitter, the intensity increased. After ten weeks, I was doing 8 kilometres a day and had lost 10 kilograms. I began going to the gym and then running home. I got a new hairdo and some new clothes. Before long I was feeling like my old self again and ready for a challenge.

I rang Laurie Lawrence and told him about the hours I'd been logging in the pool. What should I do with all this fitness? He thought about it for a few days and then rang me back.

'How about marathon swimming?'

I was shocked. Yuck, I thought. I'm always scared of the unknown in water, particularly when there's no black line to guide me. But Laurie gave me a goal. He told me that two women would be chosen for the Australian team contesting the World Aquatics Championships in Perth in early 1991. I went away and thought about it. The idea began to appeal to me. All right, Laurie, let's do this.

I started training again, eight years after retiring from competition. Would I still have it? How would I be able to swim 25 kilometres, more than double my longest training swim? That distance takes about five and a half hours, an eternity for me. And then, what would it be like swimming in open water in Perth's Swan River?

For our first challenge, Laurie and I decided to attempt the annual Magnetic Island swim, 7.6 kilometres across Cleveland Bay, from the island to Townsville. It was May 1990, and the field would include Susie Maroney, one of Australia's outstanding open water swimmers. She was just fresh from winning the Round Manhattan Island Race and swimming the English Channel.

I was really nervous, not because of the distance, but because of sharks and sea snakes. I'd always had a morbid fear of them, which was why I didn't like swimming in the surf. And I hated seaweed. I had to swim the distance with a cage around me for my protection and I felt really constricted. My fingers kept hitting the front of the cage and barking my knuckles because the water was choppy and the boat was nearly stalling and going backwards. The bottom of the cage was open and I kept looking for dark shapes under the water, thinking a shark was going to come and attack me from underneath, having smelt the blood dripping from my knuckles.

But Laurie knew me well. He would write signs on a whiteboard, words of encouragement and smiley faces, which made me angry sometimes. I'd scream out to him because I wasn't real happy in there. As the gun went on Magnetic Island, we were last to get going and, with all the bickering, several hundred metres behind Susie Maroney and the other leaders.

Once I settled down, however, I caught up and was out in front. My rhythm was good and I felt like I could keep going for eternity. How good was it to be back! Eventually, there we were, 400 metres off the sandy beach. Laurie said, 'Okay, now you can swim up over the cage and go the rest of the way to the beach.'

'Hang on, Laurie,' I protested. 'There's still a fair way left and there are sharks in this water. Can't we go a bit closer?'

'No, we can't. The boat will run aground. Hurry up, get out and swim. Maroney's almost level with you.'

I was panicking, but took a deep breath and did what he said. I swam as fast as I could to the safety of the beach. Not even Thorpey in his prime would have caught me, I was so eager to get safe and sound. I had done it. I had won my first marathon race and now all I had to do was swim a distance three times as far just six months later.

***

Lake Tresamino is a freshwater lake in Italy, between Rome and Florence in Tuscany. In July 1990 the water was warm and as flat as a pane of glass. It was the venue for the 20-kilometre Gran Fondo race, my first big international marathon.

Thanks to sponsorship from AMP, I had been able to afford the trip and paid for Rob and Laurie and his wife Jocelyn's airfares and accommodation. I was missing Hannah, who stayed behind with Mum and Rita, Rob's mother, but I had a good support team and my sister Julie, who had been staying in Austria with her boyfriend, came to lend moral support.

I had put in months of hard training and felt confident that I could go the distance, but I was venturing into the unknown against a field of seasoned competitors. Silvia Dalotto of Argentina, Anita Sood of India and Gisela Slavicek of Yugoslavia had all won open water swims before. I was an absolute novice.

This time we were better prepared than at Magnetic Island and got away well. Unfortunately, the exhaust fumes from the boat made me sick and I felt like I wanted to throw up in the first half of the race. At the halfway mark I was 5 minutes behind the leader, another Australian, Jacqui Robinson.

Laurie worked out the problem and instructed me to swim on the far side of the boat. I immediately felt better and began passing other swimmers. I was gaining on Robinson and had my old rhythm.

It was two days after Hannah's second birthday, so I used her as motivation and promised myself that I would buy her a lovely present with the prize money. I didn't feel tired at all and stormed home to victory.

My time was 4 hours, 20 minutes and 47 seconds, 6 minutes better than the race record and a time that would have won the men's competition the previous year. As it was, I beat fourteen of the twenty-one male swimmers in the race, which was won by another Aussie, Peter Galvin from Perth.

When I tried to get out of the water my arms felt like lead and my legs were like jelly. I was simply exhausted, but I knew I had it in me now for the World Championships. First, though, I would have to finish in the top two at the October trials back home.

My prize for coming first at Gran Fondo was fifteen hundred dollars. It was the first money I ever won in swimming and I gave Laurie five hundred to thank him, then spent the rest the next day at the Florence markets. That soon helped me forget all about my aches and pains.

The following day, Laurie, Jocelyn, Rob and I all went to Pompeii to see the ruins. It was blazing hot and I was in shorts, t-shirt and joggers. With my flat chest and small bum, I suppose I looked like a boy, because when I went into the ladies toilets, one of the attendants stopped me and pointed to the men's. Rob had to explain to him in Italian that, although I had boyish muscles, I was a girl. In fact, I was his wife! Eventually I was allowed to go in, thank God, because I was busting by that stage.

Laurie was brilliant at coaching, as always. He eased away my doubts and kept reassuring me as my training regime increased. Two months after Italy, staying at a unit near Laurie on the Gold Coast, I was doing two workouts a day, six days a week. I would do a hundred and sixty laps in a session, often finishing in the dark. In the morning, I sometimes ran up Heartbreak Hill, a steep set of a hundred and thirty-eight concrete stairs leading to a lookout on Currumbin Hill. I would run up, jog down and run back to my unit.

Rob and Hannah would visit midweek and Hannah would stay for a few days with Rob's mum or my mum, and I went home to Brisbane on weekends. The rest of the time, it was just a hard slog. Eventually, I was logging 15–20 kilometres a day and felt as fit as ever. I was ready for stage two.

***

Come October, I was primed for a big performance in Perth for the qualifiers for the Inaugural Open Water 25-kilometre World Championship. I was still a novice and would be up against the likes of Susie Maroney and Shelley Taylor-Smith, the unofficial world champion and winner of the Naples – Capri race in July, who knew every ripple of the Swan River. But Laurie was convinced that I had improved enough to win a place on the team for the World Championships in January. I would have to place in the top two to qualify.

I had absolute faith in Laurie and, while he sometimes pushed me too hard, the results made it all worthwhile. So when he suggested a radical solution to the cold water, I went along with it. The Swan River felt like it was freezing with a temperature of 16 degrees, very cold by Australian standards. Laurie's idea was to use wool fat, which is basically lanolin, as an effective combatant against hypothermia. In our hotel by the riverbank, he and Rob smeared the greasy mixture all over me and my swimming costume. I felt like I weighed a tonne and I looked like the Creature from the Black Lagoon.

When I went down to the start in the Swan River, I was wrapped up in a long terry-towelling robe from the hotel. In the tent set up for officials and competitors, I saw all the champions of the open water events and felt intimidated. They had so much more experience than me. I had never swum a 25-kilometre race before, and never in saltwater. My only previous experience was the 20-kilometre swim in freshwater in Italy. I felt I shouldn't have been there, but one thing cheered me up: at least I would be warm.

I looked across at swimmers getting their rub-downs. I didn't partake because I was so heavily caked with grease, so I just tried to loosen up my shoulders and legs. I noticed the other girls had a bit of Vaseline under their armpits and on the tog lines, but I had my lanolin slopped on everywhere: over my chest, bum, stomach and even my feet. I felt conscious of other swimmers glancing sideways at me, the 'glug swimmer'.

Finally, we gathered at the water's edge, ready for the race. The men started twenty minutes earlier and then it was our turn. Our boats (each swimmer had a support boat with a driver and coach) were about one kilometre away, ready to join us after the start.

The gun went. I did two strokes and sank! Water was coming into the top of my costume and became trapped around my chest and hips because the lycra fabric was clogged with fat. I felt like I was dragging a bucket of water on my chest and another on my bottom. The others were all swimming along normally while I floundered around like a duck in its death throes. I was panicking.

I could see Laurie peering at me from the support boat, unable to help. The other girls reached their boats within 10 minutes, but it took me at least another 7 to reach Laurie.

'What's wrong?' shouted Laurie.

'Laurie, you bastard!' I yelled in anguish. 'What have you done? I can't swim a stroke because of this bloody grease.'

My togs were just about falling off because of the weight of the wool fat. My bum was already exposed and the media boat was circling, a television camera trained on me. According to the rules, you're not allowed to touch the boat, so I trod water and peeled the swimsuit off. I had a spare suit, cap, goggles and towel in my bag on the boat. Thank God, it was a habit I always had for competition.

There I was, starkers, wiping off the wool fat with a towel Laurie threw to me. I told the media boat to bugger off. I was fuming. Eventually I managed to pull on the new suit, cursed like a sailor, then set off after the others who, by now, were dots on the horizon. The wool fat was still clogging my togs and I felt the 'bucket of water' dragging all the way, but it was not as bad.

I had given the field a head start and this was a whole lot tougher than the Magnetic Island race. There was a headwind and a choppy, one-metre swell which made it hard to swim smoothly. As the race progressed, my left shoulder began to ache. The constant buffeting had exposed my old weakness: tendonitis. Swimming 25 kilometres involves about 105,000 strokes, which is a test for the fittest of swimmers. When you have an injury, you simply can't go on.

Laurie could see what was happening and told me to pull out. At the 20-kilometre mark, I reluctantly withdrew. For a novice at this kind of marathon swimming, I thought I'd done pretty well. As it turned out, that was the end of my open water swimming career. I missed the team but still had an involvement with the 1991 World Aquatics Championships as a commentator with ABC Radio.

Rob was sympathetic and urged me to keep trying. 'All that fitness shouldn't go to waste.'

I agreed and for a while my comeback was a reality. But deep down, I wanted something else.

28

When I found out that I was pregnant again in the first half of 1991, I thought Rob would be as pleased as me. But when I raced next door after the test to tell his mother the news, there were no congratulations. On the contrary, her face clouded over and she said, 'Oh dear, what will Rob say? He's not going to be happy.'

I was bewildered. Rob and I had always talked about having a big family so I assumed he would be delighted with the news. Then I remembered that at one point, after we had Hannah with her difficult sleep patterns, Rob said he wanted only one child and no more. He found it all a bit exhausting. And then there was the fact that he was trying to get me to have a crack at making the team for the Barcelona Olympics. My getting pregnant would interfere with the grand plan.

Nevertheless, I hadn't wanted an only child and my biological clock was ticking. Hannah was two and a half years old and I didn't want too big a gap between our children. I knew the time was right, so I washed my contraceptive pill down the sink for a couple of months. At least *I* was overjoyed when I fell pregnant, and I took things very carefully given my previous record of miscarriages. My mum was absolutely thrilled. She knew that I had always wanted lots of kids.

When Rob and I went for my eighteen-week scan and could actually see the gorgeous little creature growing inside me, even he had to admit how beautiful it looked. We were dying to know the sex of the baby, hoping against hope that a boy would be possible this second time round.

'Well,' the doctor replied, 'I wouldn't paint your nursery blue yet, but I'm ninety percent sure it's a boy.'

Sure enough, our son Daniel was born at Royal Brisbane Hospital on 15 January 1992. I was induced into labour and immediately began contractions, supported by the lovely midwife who had delivered Hannah. She had been helping with another labour just down the hall in the hospital and was honoured to assist at my second birth.

During a scan the week before, I had been warned that I was going to have a nine-pound baby and I had psyched myself up. Wow, I thought, Hannah was huge and that was at eight pounds and two ounces. This is going to be a doozey!

After an hour, I was having major contractions and asked for an epidural. Two hours later, the anaesthetist was still nowhere to be seen and I had to make do on the 'happy gas'.

'Where is he?' I yelled in pain.

'He'll be here shortly,' my midwife replied.

I was only 5 centimetres dilated and knew I was in for a long labour. Another hour passed and by this time I was anxious and in absolute agony. Finally, after a grand total of three and a half hours, the doctor turned up to administer the epidural. I rolled over between contractions and he began to slowly prepare the dose. Just as he was injecting the medication, I felt a massive urge to push. The nurse tried to stop me because I had not reached the 10-centimetre dilation necessary to begin final delivery.

'No, I have to push.' I had an unspeakable urge, but the medical staff simply continued to administer the epidural.

'No, no, I really have to push.' They rolled me over to have a look.

'Oh shit!' I heard a nurse say.

The head was visible, I had dilated from 5 centimetres to 10 centimetres in minutes. I was ready to give birth. In two pushes, Daniel was out so fast he was still in shock and blue in the face. He had to be placed on oxygen straightaway. And what a huge baby he was: nine pounds and twelve-and-a-half ounces, nearly ten pounds (4.5 kilograms)! How the hell did I manage to deliver such a huge baby from such a tiny girlish frame? Daniel had a full head of black hair, just like Hannah. But while Hannah was quiet and serious by nature, Daniel was a typical boy: boisterous, noisy and full of cheeky fun. I was rapt and just adored the children.

***

Rob and I had a great relationship from the moment we met but, over time, I realised that even though I cared for him and his family, we were drifting apart. Rob was a very funny guy and we had a lot of laughs but I don't really think I was 'in love' with him. I think we were more just 'great mates', though we never admitted it to each other.

Both times I was pregnant I thought things would get better, but when a baby arrives on the scene, stressful situations escalate and things change. I ignored the warning signs from Rob. He was increasingly moody and spent less and less time at home, always citing the demands of the business.

The kids filled up my days and I loved organising birthday parties and sleepovers with their friends but it wasn't all smooth sailing. Like Hannah, Daniel was a poor sleeper and was always hungry. Up until he was three and a half, he woke during the night wanting his milk bottle, or his 'latte' as he called it, and often had two bottles in one night.

We knew we were making a rod for our own backs by giving the bottles to him – even Daniel wouldn't let us tell the daycare teacher about them because he was a 'big boy' now – but we needed our sanity. His routine when coming home from kindy was to have a 'latte' straightaway and watch his *Dumbo* movie. It was heart-warming to see him, lying on the sofa, sucking his bottle and rolling his eyes in ecstasy.

But Rob and I continued to drift apart. We both led busy lives: Rob with the family business and me looking after the kids. Our sex life deteriorated and he often came home late at night, saying that he had been 'entertaining clients' or having coffee with his cousins. It didn't help that I had stacked on the weight again after Daniel's birth and felt unattractive, tired and frustrated.

Living right next door to his parents, in keeping with Italian tradition, was no comfort. They always defended their son no matter what: he was a Ciobo and blood was thicker than water. In many ways, their constant presence in our lives made it hard for us to form our own family unit. Rob never understood why I would get upset and ask about living somewhere on our own, just our little family. Even though we had talked about living elsewhere before we were married, now he didn't want to hear it. We were staying next door and that was that, end of story.

On the plus side, Rob's mother, Rita, was great for babysitting and loved doing it. One night, however, I was washing up after dinner at their place and heard Rita screaming in the lounge room. She ran past me and out the front door, yelling, 'I can't watch. Daniel's choking!'

'On what?' I asked.

'An apple, an apple.'

I raced into the lounge room. Daniel was lying on the floor, red and purple in the face and a relative was trying to get the apple out. I immediately picked my son up by the feet and hung him upside down, then slapped him between the shoulderblades. A big piece of apple popped out and he began crying. Thank God! I cuddled him and he settled down. It was lucky I knew first-aid or he could have died.

***

I was still suffering badly from the after-effects of the poorly executed knee reconstruction I had in 1984 after my skiing accident. Five months after Daniel was born, while I was still breastfeeding, the whole thing collapsed and had to be reset. I was in a splint and couldn't walk. I had to get a lady to come and help for a few weeks. She drove Hannah to kindy and did some shopping and cleaning.

The pain was unbearable. My GP prescribed heavy-duty painkillers, which seemed to do the job at first. However I gradually began taking more and found that, while killing pain, they also gave me a euphoric 'high'. I became attached to them, like a friend. They dulled the emotional pain as my marriage started falling apart.

Nevertheless, Rob and I had our good times. One Saturday night in the early 1990s, I organised a barbecue at our place. Rob was sitting in the backyard with our family and friends while I was in the kitchen, preparing food and watching the Lotto results. Rob had played Gold Lotto every Saturday since 1975 and always picked the exact same numbers. I knew his system, which was to choose numbers in the corner of the play sheets in a triangle sequence. So when Rob called out to me to read him the results, I formulated a sneaky plan.

As the Lotto balls dropped from the basket on the television, I yelled out to Rob. After four 'correct' numbers came out, he started to get excited. When the fifth number came out he yelled with joy, just one number to go! I called out the sixth and he bolted into the house, falling over the kids' toys and racing into the kitchen yelling, 'I've got it! I've got it! I've won Lotto! Yippee!'

Only Rob's cousin Flora was in on the joke with me and I had to bite my inner cheeks so as not to burst out laughing. After about five minutes, I couldn't do it to him anymore and I told him that the numbers were a hoax. He didn't believe me at first, but eventually realised the joke.

I asked, 'So, what's it really like to know that you've won Lotto?'

'It's an awesome feeling to know you've won the big one,' he replied, sulkily.

He didn't play much after that, only every now and then and still to this day hasn't let me forget what I did. But I thought I'd played the biggest prank ever! It was fun!

I just love jokes, and love hearing them, even the dirty ones. There were times, though, when the joke was on me. In 1992, the Queensland Olympic Council organised for a special train to travel up the east coast from Brisbane to Cairns as a promotion for the forthcoming Barcelona Olympics. I flew to Rocky to board the train for two days and nights, one of a dozen sportspeople invited to come on the trip. One whole carriage was full of memorabilia, things like Dunc Gray's bike and Dawn Fraser's swimming costume.

We pulled into the port of Gladstone late one steamy afternoon and everyone agreed that a cool drink would go down well. I had been chatting to two former boxers, Fred Casey and Wally Taylor, and they escorted me into the nearest pub. There were three pubs in the main street across the road from the railway station and we visited each one in turn.

Now, I'm normally not a drinker, but on this occasion I was led astray by a couple of charming rascals. Someone suggested I have one of these green concoctions called 'Slippery Nipples', which were passed around free. I was nervous about the taste, so I summoned up my courage and skolled mine straight down. It tasted surprisingly good and I felt okay, so I had another and so on. They went down very nicely and apparently contained crème de menthe, among other potent ingredients. We had a lovely meal, sang songs and generally had a wonderful time, all the while I kept downing the drinks. I must have had four or five in an hour.

Suddenly it hit me. I was plastered. Fred and Wally realised my plight and, being thorough gentlemen, helped me back to the train. I could barely walk. When they left, I undressed and passed out on the bed, stark naked.

When Fred and Wally came back from the pub later on, they thought they would check to see if I was okay. They knocked on my door and it opened, revealing me in all my glory, lying on my back, arms flung wide, snoring.

'Oh my God!' said Wally, backing away hastily and averting his eyes.

Word somehow got around the train and I was the butt of many a joke. Since that night just the mention of a 'Slippery Nipple' sends me running the other way!

29

While married to Rob, I had been earning plenty of money but didn't have my own bank account. Everything I earned went into the Ciobo family nut business, including thirty thousand dollars I made doing television commercials for a women's iron tablet while I was training for the marathon swims in 1990. I didn't mind putting my cash in their trust.

However, when I needed to withdraw money for expenses such as school clothes, Daniel's soccer fees or the kids' birthday parties, swim lessons or ballet lessons, I had to get either Rob or his parents to sign the cheques at their business. I was made to feel like a puppy begging for a treat and Rob just didn't understand because he never had to live away from his family. I was miserable and things had to change. I felt I had totally lost my independence.

Our first serious argument came after Hannah's fifth birthday in mid-1993. I went to a lot of trouble organising a special party with cake, balloons, face-painting and, best of all, Shetland pony rides. The last item cost one hundred and twenty dollars, but seeing the delighted faces of the kids made it worth the expense. Hannah had a ball.

A few days later I had a call from Rob and, to my amazement, he was furious: 'What's going on? You want a cheque for this and a cheque for that. And now you go and spend a hundred and twenty bucks on pony rides. Who do you think we are, the bloody Bank of Queensland?'

I tried to reason with him, saying that the children deserved special treats once in a while, but he kept up a tirade of abuse. It was so loud my aunt, Denise, could hear his voice over the telephone from across the room. She took me aside.

'Tracey, you've got to sort this out, this isn't right. You can't live like this.'

I tried to get Rob to give me direct access to my money, but he maintained that it was tied up in the family business and that only our living costs could be covered. I angrily demanded that the money I made from my swimming clinics should be freely available, at least for expenses involving the kids and other incidental things. But it was to no avail.

The financial situation was incredibly stressful for me and I could barely get to sleep at night. I was emotionally drained. By September 1994 I made up my mind that I wanted to leave my husband. I confided in a friend at the time who told me that I was making the right decision. Over the next few months I began secretly packing my things and taking them to Mum's place, preparing for the day when it would all become too much. Little did I know my 'nice' friend was telling Rob everything.

Around October 1994, when the kids were playing at their grandparents' next door, Rob and I had a bitter argument. I said to him that very, very close female sources told me that Rob was making advances towards them. Rob ran to his family, protesting his innocence. Sure enough, one of his relatives came storming into my living room, yelling, 'Rob would never have affairs! How dare you accuse him of doing that!'

I yelled back, and told him that it wasn't me making the accusations and that he wouldn't know the half of the story. He screamed back, swearing in Italian and I picked up the jelly and ice-cream I had been eating and threw it. I just wanted him out of the house. It missed and smashed all over the back patio tiles. It was a huge mess.

Rob's relative walked back to the Ciobo family house and shouted out to me, 'You some world champion. You are the champion of my balls!'

I was extremely hurt. How charming, I thought. After all I had done for the family: promoting the business, renovating their house, sinking my money into their ventures, driving Rob's mother to the shops. I felt used and worthless.

***

On New Year's Eve 1994, it all came to a head. Rob and I and the kids – Hannah aged six and Daniel almost three – had been down the coast staying at the family's new unit and were due to return to Brisbane for a New Year's Eve barbecue at Rob's sister Donnie's place. It was a blazing hot day and I had to clean the unit and pack the clothes and toys into the car while Rob minded the kids. Rob and I scarcely said a word to each other on the way back. Somehow I knew it would be our last family holiday together.

When we got home I felt exhausted. Rob was raring to go, but I felt like resting for a while. So I said, 'You go ahead. I've got to do my hair and make-up and I'll be a while yet. I'll come over later.'

He packed the kids into the car and left. I just wanted to chill out. An hour later at around 7.30pm, Rob came bursting through the front door to find me relaxing on the couch with a cigarette and glass of rosé. The kids were going to swim in Donnie's pool and Rob had come back to fetch their togs.

He asked me why I wasn't getting ready. I told him that I wasn't up to going and had some loads of washing to do, plus I wanted to pop in and visit Mum who I hadn't seen for weeks. After all, it was just the usual Ciobo family barbecue. Rob started to get angry and mouth off about me never wanting to go to family get-togethers. I was always at them! Not to mention the fact he rarely came to my family gatherings, which always upset me.

We exchanged heated words and moved into the kitchen. Rob pulled out a frying pan and told me I should hit him with it if I was so angry. I just looked at him in disgust and shook my head in disbelief. Then Rob brought up the ten thousand dollars which Sizzler had paid me to do a commercial for them a few months before. Tired of being broke, I deposited the ten grand into a new personal account rather than into Meriram. Rob started to rave on about how I was a miser. Everything I ever had was tied up in the Ciobo family business, and he was calling me cheap? It was the last straw. I was livid and began to hit his shoulder with the back of my left hand.

'Go on, hit me harder! Hit me harder!' he said, gritting his teeth.

I hit him about five or six times. Then he rang the police. It was about 8pm at night.

'My name is Robert Ciobo, I'm Tracey Wickham's husband. I'm ringing regarding domestic violence by my wife.'

As soon as he said, 'I'm Tracey Wickham's husband', I knew right then and there that I would leave him that night. I just shook my head. I slumped onto the bottom step of our stairs, visibly shaken and shocked at what had just taken place. I waited for the police to arrive.

Two young cops turned up about half an hour later and Rob walked outside to greet them with an icepack on his shoulder. While he made his report to the policemen, I didn't say a word. I felt like it was all a bad dream. I had hit him several times, but I wasn't that strong. He was nearly 50 kilograms heavier than me and under all the stress of the marriage my weight had plummeted. I was incredibly fragile. The cops came to talk to me and suggested I stay somewhere else that night.

'You two are the first to know that my marriage is over,' I told them.

After making his verbal complaint, Rob decided he didn't want to take any further action. Realising it was all a storm in a teacup, the police gave us both a lecture and left. I could hear them laughing about it on their way to the car, laughing about the size difference between me and Rob.

There was nothing to be said between us. I it was over. I just couldn't stand any more. I rang Mum.

'Mum, this is it. I'm leaving. Please ask Ashley if he can bring the trailer around. I don't want to spend another night in this house, ever.'

I packed what I could and left Rob. Due to the circumstances, I also had to leave the kids who were still at the Ciobo New Year's Eve party. I could hardly turn up and take them in front of all of Rob's family. In hindsight, I should have gone to pick them up, but I knew they were having a good time with their cousins. A new chapter in my life was beginning.

30

I stayed at Mum's for a couple of months and then found a small townhouse to rent at Wooloowin. I had been there three weeks when I was served with a summons to appear in court over the custody of our children. Surely they couldn't take them away from me? Those kids were the most precious things in my life. If they wanted a fight, they would get one.

I prepared myself for the courtroom battle, gathering files and information and hiring what I hoped would be a brilliant lawyer. One day I was walking down Adelaide Street in the city and it struck me how stupid this was. Who had looked after the children since they were born? Me! I felt sick in the stomach with the fear that they could take my babies away from me. I knew how close Rob's family was and I felt that I was all alone against them. I was, but at least I had Mum's support.

Gradually it emerged that they were basing their case on the supposition that I was an unfit mother and didn't look after the kids. Well, who did then? I was always home, picking them up from school, taking them to doctors' appointments, lessons, sport, parties and so on. The only time I was away was when I did the weekend clinics with Rob and sometimes we would even take Hannah with us.

The family maintained that I never cooked meals and was always off gallivanting around the country while Rob stayed at home minding the children. This was ridiculous, as Rob had come with me to every single one of the ten weekend swim clinics and I hadn't even travelled after Daniel was born. The only element of truth was that Rob's parents helped with looking after the kids and often the kids would eat at their place, because everyone loved Rob's mother's Italian cooking. For them to say that I didn't love my children and was an unfit mother ... that was just ridiculous!

Rob was a great dad and adored the kids but I was really, really upset and confused by what he and his family were saying about me during those custody battles. They called me a 'terrible mother', but I know they didn't believe it, none of them. I never wanted to go to court, for the kids' sake mainly. After all, Hannah was six and a half and Daniel just three years old.

In the interim before the final hearing, the court decided that it was better for the kids to stay with Rob and his family because of the community environment. I was upset, but things were about to get worse.

Six weeks prior to the final hearing, my lawyer called me into his office. Mum came with me and we were both led into a huge boardroom. My lawyer and his right-hand man then began to threaten us that if we didn't come up with ninety thousand dollars in the next week, they would cease to represent me. There was nothing I could do to talk them round:

they wanted their money right then and there. I was furious, to say the least. They knew I had nothing and that their payment would come once a settlement was reached. I went into a rage and began yelling and screaming. I just lost it.

Poor Mum shrank into her seat and tried to calm me down. I ripped off my diamond ring, which was worth about twenty thousand dollars, and threw it to the back wall of the boardroom where it ricocheted off the blinds. I yelled a few more expletives and ran down to the city streets. I couldn't believe this was happening at such a crucial time. How on earth was I going to get another lawyer to work on my case in just a few short weeks? There was no way I was going to wait another two years for a final hearing.

Back in the boardroom, Mum picked up my ring and met me outside the building. I was shaking and a complete mess. To me, this was just proof that when it comes to the law, it's the people with the most money who win. I lost all my faith in the family court system.

Thankfully, my dad was able to organise a friend, Malcolm Marshall, to take over the case. He was fantastic and we ended up with an out-of-court settlement a few months down the track. I wanted equal time with the kids, but it was decreed that I would have them for five days (four nights) each fortnight. The whole situation was very distressing but there was nothing I could do.

I never did pay the ninety thousand dollars to the lawyer who buggered up my court case. His firm knew it would have been front-page news if they tried to harass me. I would have made sure of that.

While I was waiting for the divorce settlement I was so broke I applied for the single parent pension. Hiding behind huge sunglasses, I was recognised by the Social Security clerk, who asked for my autograph. I was so embarrassed I just ran out of the building. I had the feeling that my whole life had been wasted. At thirty-two, I had nothing to show for all my efforts. Fame brought me nothing and I was severely unlucky with the timing of my career. As Shane Gould reflects:

> Tracey was unfortunate to live in an era when swimming was going through a big change, from the honour and glory of representing your country to sports entertainment. I think Kieren Perkins changed all that in Australia. He became a national hero and TV networks wanted more and more.

> Nowadays swimming is a top-rating spectacle on live television but, in those days, they didn't realise its moneymaking potential. Tracey was in that no-man's-land between the two and she was very young. Unlike me, she had nobody to advise her how to take advantage of her fame. My dad was in marketing and Mum was a social worker, so they mentored me and helped me make a career out of my swimming achievements.

It's funny how people assume that if you are a well-known person you must be wealthy. If only they really knew. Standing in the line at Centrelink for the first time was the lowest feeling I've ever had. For me it was intensely embarrassing. There I was, with my high profile, having to line up to apply for a pension.

Another emotionally distressing event following the split involved a Mazda 626 that Rob and I had bought during our marriage. I took it with me after our split as it was my only way of getting around. One day, I lent it to Dad when I went on a short business trip. On my return, Dad rang to tell me that Mim, who he had been staying with, had heard a commotion at 2am in the morning out the front of the house where the Mazda was parked. They awoke to find all four tyres slashed. I was so afraid.

When Rob and I finally sorted out our settlement, I fixed up my debts and had enough left over to put a deposit on a house at Bridgeman Downs, on the northern outskirts of Brisbane. I worked hard and paid it off in two years. For a much deserved treat, the kids and I went on some terrific holidays. We went to the Capricornia Resort at Yeppoon, which also gave us a generous deal. I was thrilled to see how the kids enjoyed themselves. Nothing pleased me more than knowing how much fun they had, usually with a friend each. God, I miss those days!

***

Breaking up with Rob had bruised my self-esteem badly. Ten weeks after we separated, I made the decision to go to a plastic surgeon on the Gold Coast in March 1995. I had always been flat-chested, which was great for swimming but not so good for my ego. I finally decided to do something about it and had breast implants inserted.

About six weeks earlier I had been staying at Mum's and found an old Berlei sports bra. I tried it on and, to my dismay, found that I didn't even come close to filling it out. With all the stress of the break-up, I had lost a lot of weight. It looked like I had the bra on back to front! I was 49 kilograms when I left Robert and looked like a twelve-year-old boy.

At that moment, Mum walked into my bedroom and I asked her to look. She was just as surprised as me to see how poorly the bra fitted. I knew what had to happen.

'That's it! I'm getting a boob job. I can't live like this anymore.'

For years I never wore a shoestring top. I always wore a shirt or something loose-fitting. Even my wedding dress had a big piece of material with crystals hanging off the shoulder over my chest. I wanted to feel a little bit more feminine. My body shape was boyish, with no curves. I didn't want to look like Pamela Anderson. I just wanted reasonable-sized boobs.

When I saw the doctor at Pindarra Hospital, I told him that I just wanted to be in proportion to my height and weight. He showed me the various saline implants but I left the decision up to him.

'Just stop filling the implants when you think they look the right size.'

Sure enough, I ended up a 36C, which was perfect. After fifteen years, I've never had a problem with them. I regard them as one of the best investments I've ever made. Friends who already had normal-sized breasts asked, 'Why did you want to spend all that money on boobs?'

I'd reply, 'For five grand it was either going to be a leather lounge or boobs and I know which will last longer.'

I knew that if they themselves didn't have boobs, they wouldn't be questioning my surgery. They didn't know what it was like to have 'nothing up top'. It was a personal decision. I did it for no one except myself and I have no regrets.

It did the world for my morale, which had been really low after the divorce. What's more, I had lost all the weight I stacked on after having the children and I was exercising regularly. Not swimming marathons, but just enough to stay healthy. I was getting back on track.

***

Having the operation improved my outlook on life, but I was still heartbroken to be separated from my own children for the majority of the week. I remember one time in the summer of 1996 when I visited a girlfriend who was also divorced with two children. While I was there, her kids came home from their father's. There was not a kiss exchanged, she just started shouting at them, 'Where are your lunchboxes? Your school clothes are still dirty. Where are your other clothes?' and so on.

I sat there dumbfounded and thought to myself, 'At least you have your kids ten nights out of fourteen, I only have mine four nights. You should be happy to see them, and give them a hug and kiss and tell them you love them and not be irate as soon as they walk in the door.'

After about five minutes, I decided that I had to leave as I was so upset at what I was seeing. It was just on dusk and drizzling rain. I switched the engine on and drove off. Suddenly, I burst into tears and a primal groan from the pit of my stomach came out. Tears were pouring down my face and I could hardly see the road. I started banging my head on the steering wheel very hard and couldn't stop. I was in a fit of rage and emotion. I missed my children so much. How dare that woman treat her kids like that! It was not fair or right.

I grabbed my mobile phone and rang Mum. She didn't even understand who was calling as I was incoherent, screaming down the phone.

She yelled, 'Is that you, Tracey? Where are you? Are you driving?'

'Yes,' I said.

'Stop the car!' Mum yelled.

I told her where I was and both she and Ashley drove to pick me up. As I waited the fifteen minutes for them, I sat on the side of the busy Stafford Road in a daze. I knew I'd lost it. I couldn't handle the fact that I wasn't allowed to be a mother to my kids as much as I wanted to be. My children were my number one priority. Always.

Mum drove my car and Ashley drove his and we all went to my Aunty Denise's and Uncle Graham's to have a chat and a coffee. Uncle Graham and I talked about doing more swim clinics and motivational talks in country areas. He helped me put a plan together and I acted on it. I had a new direction in life.

31

I expanded on the clinics I had begun back in 1990 and started travelling, mainly through country towns in Queensland. I would be away about four to five days a week when the kids were with Rob. I extended my schedule to include motivational talks, so my days were really full. I would ring a school and ask for the sports master, explaining what I had to offer. The usual reply would be tentative.

'That sounds fine but how much will it cost?'

'Nothing. It's free. It's all paid for by sponsors.'

'Well, that's great. When can you come?'

I would start early, fly to a major country town and then drive for up to four hours to the outlying areas. I would often give ninety-minute motivational talks to three schools a day, then give a swim clinic in the late afternoon for the whole town. I would always be on my own, driving a hired car and staying at small country motels. In Queensland the distances were greater and with towns like Atherton and Charleville so far apart, I had to drive further and cover fewer schools.

One memorable visit I made to Queensland was to Charters Towers. Mum came with me to do research on our family tree, and it was great to look at the town and go to the mines and graveyards to see the old records of how our relatives died.

All in all, it was a gruelling schedule, with up to forty schools covered each summer, but the kids loved it and so did I. I never wanted to be a coach but I have always enjoyed teaching kids how to swim. I talked to them about goalsetting and discipline and spiced it up with tales from my swimming career. The kids asked lots of questions and their parents seemed thrilled to have me there.

It was great to be able to earn a living doing what I loved. Over seven years, I had various wonderful sponsors, firstly AMP, then KFC and finally Optus and Chandlers by the early 2000s. The sponsorship grew to a nice five-figure sum for a ten-week season. What's more, it was gratifying to see the response from the kids. Not only did they learn to swim, but they hung on every word when I told my stories.

Little did I know then that in 2005 I would be awarded a Medal of the Order of Australia (OAM) for Services to the Community, in recognition of my regional swimming clinics and school tours. Wayne Smith rang to tell me that I'd been nominated and that he had given me a heartfelt testimonial. I never found out who put my name forward, but I felt thrilled and very humble. Quentin Bryce, then the Governor of Queensland and a great supporter of women's sport, made the presentation on the lawns of Government House. It was such an honour.

Life was turning a bright new corner. In July 1998, when I was thirty-five, I was invited to do a guest speaking job for the Heinz company in Sydney. It was a strange invitation, and after the speaker's agency gave me the details, I rang the CEO of Heinz to check if everything was okay. He sounded a bit vague about the whole thing and I wondered if it would fall through. But, soon enough, the airline ticket arrived along with details of the accommodation and so on.

I flew down and checked into my hotel the morning before my speech. I had a call from Nicole Livingstone, the swimming commentator from Channel 9, asking if they could do an interview with me about the forthcoming Commonwealth Games in Kuala Lumpur. I said that I had a speaking engagement later on that night, but it would be fine. Nicole said they would pick me up in a limo at 6pm at my hotel and drop me at the other venue in time for the dinner.

Everything went according to plan and we started the interview in one of the Channel 9 studios. I was mid-sentence when, suddenly, the lights went out. The floor manager said there was a problem, so could we go to the next studio? I was panicking. It was getting late and I had to be at a blacktie dinner at 7.30pm. Nicole led the way along a dimly lit corridor and into the next studio.

All in a flash, the lights came on and there was Mike Munro standing with a red book in his hand and a big grin on his face. I nearly ran off the stage because I thought we had stumbled onto another show that was being recorded. I shrank back but Nicole dragged me along. At last I realised: they were all there for me.

Mike said, 'Tracey Wickham, this is your life.'

Wow! What a surprise! I was speechless. I mumbled something like, 'Well, it would be lovely but I can't tape the show now. I've got a dinner and I'm the guest speaker. I really have to go, Mike.'

'No, you don't,' laughed Mike. 'That was all part of our plan to get you down here for the show. Everyone's waiting to see you, but first Nicole will take you to a dressing-room where you can change and we'll meet you back here shortly.'

I was in a dream as I changed into the evening dress I brought for the 'Heinz Dinner' and gulped down a Scotch as I was made up. Apparently Channel 9 had been planning the show for months, liaising with Rob to get the kids and the rest of the family down to Sydney and even flying Michelle Ford in from overseas.

When I was ushered back into the studio, there were my nearest and dearest, all delighted for me. Mum and Dad, together for the first time in years, Hannah and Daniel and my sisters, Kelly and Julie, each nursing a baby. Kelly had given birth to hers just five days earlier.

There was Michelle Ford, my old friend and rival, now married and living in Switzerland. I hadn't seen her for sixteen years. Lisa Forrest and Julie MacDonald, two more friends and teammates came next, Julie with a swimming ribbon I'd given her when she was a kid on the way up. My training partner and good friend Michael Bohl recorded a message, as did Laurie Lawrence, Bill Sweetenham and my hero, Shane Gould. Even the band Chicago had sent a message via satellite, wishing me well and saying they still remembered me singing their song as I swam. It was a wonderful surprise!

Last but not least, there was my first coach, Peter Diamond, who had a photo of me standing on the podium when I won my first state age record at the age of ten. He had kept it all those years.

It was a night full of emotion and happiness. I felt so honoured and flattered. Why did I deserve this? It was so good to know that people remembered and cared. We all had a great time except for Daniel, who came down with a fever and was grumpy. I had to put him to bed early in the hotel room. It's funny, being a mum never escapes you, even at euphoric times like this. I lay there next to him while he went to sleep, thinking about that fabulous night. All for little old me!

Not long after *This Is Your Life,* the ABC's *Australian Story* chose me as the subject for one of their shows. They did a lovely interview with Mum, in which she told them how hard up we were the whole time I was representing my country. Mum was incredible during my swimming career and I owe her everything. Having met Ashley and remarried, she kept working but I insisted that she retire at sixty, have some fun and enjoy her ten grandkids.

Ashley was a godsend for Mum. He's such a kind-hearted person and would do anything for the family. He's an accountant by trade and a computer programmer, so helps us all out with our problems. Good with his hands, he can do just about anything around the house, including concreting and tiling and he even made a great chook pen for my sister. Ashley's been an excellent stepfather, even though he's only four years older than me. I'm very happy for them both and a little envious.

***

The kids and I had some terrific holidays around this time, thanks to the generosity of former Olympic runner and current Gold Coast Mayor, Ron Clarke. He used to have us stay at Couran Cove, a luxury eco-resort on South Stradbroke Island, just off the Gold Coast. Ron often put us up in his own beautiful house, free of charge, for a week or so. I would let the kids bring a friend or two and they would run free, as there were no cars on the island and transport was on bikes or on foot. We would take our own food and stock up the fridge, without a care in the world.

They were great days, but it still tore me apart to watch my children growing up in front of my eyes, separated from me for most of the time. One day when Hannah was eleven, she was strangely subdued. She came home straight from school and plonked herself on my bed. I asked her what was wrong. She was shy and didn't say much at that age. Finally, she spoke up.

'I got my period.'

I was amazed. She was too young! I didn't get mine until I was fourteen and I wasn't expecting her to start till her teens as she was such a slight build. I asked if she had any tampons and she said no. She said she had started about five days ago but was too embarrassed to tell her father. I asked, 'What did you use?'

'Toilet paper.'

She said she was too scared to talk about such things with her dad, so I sat her down and gave her a long talk about what she should do and what to use. That's when I, as her mum, really wanted to be there for her. I still felt I'd let her down in her time of need.

It was awful being without my kids. I pined for them. I began to feel more and more depressed. Some days I felt so drained I couldn't go out, I just stayed at home by myself. I had a hard time getting out of bed in the morning. It was so lonely I couldn't go to sleep at night. I'd just lie there and end up crying myself to sleep. Sometimes I would pop a pill or two to ease the pain of being separated from my babies.

When Rob and I first broke up, I felt like a load had been lifted off my shoulders and I started to get better and kick the pills I had been taking to ease my sciatic nerve pain after having Daniel. I was independent and making a fresh start. I didn't need an emotional crutch. But then I was served with a summons for the custody battle and I needed support. I went back on the painkillers.

By 1999 I knew I was in trouble, but I was too embarrassed and depressed to tell a single soul. My shameful secret had become a terrible burden. Eventually, I went to a doctor who helped me wean myself off them. It worked well for a while but then I fell apart again.

It was a vicious cycle: if I took the pills, I felt in control. But then I would get tired. I was so up and down I didn't want to see anyone. My personality changed. I was a recluse and I hated life. I felt unable to work or even go out and socialise. But if I didn't take them, I suffered withdrawal symptoms. I didn't even consciously realise it was withdrawal, but all the tell tale signs were there: clammy skin, depression, diarrhoea and cramps. I felt weak and unable to think properly.

Finally, in late 1999, I told Mum everything. She took it well and nodded. 'I knew something was wrong. You have not been the Tracey I knew for a long time.'

That year, I went to see a psychiatrist who specialised in this problem and he suggested I check myself into a hospital where they could monitor my intake and gradually lessen the dosage. It worked, at least for a while.

32

With the exposure I got from the television programs, I was in demand again. Requests came pouring in to make appearances on television and radio, to speak at functions or to give swim clinics. I was a guest on *Good News Week* and *The Panel* and various other shows. I was also asked to be a torchbearer in the relay leading up to the 2000 Sydney Olympic Games. I ran with the torch as it made its way through Queensland and then Mum, Ashley, the kids and I flew down to Sydney and dressed up in our greens and yellows to watch our nation compete. I commentated the swimming for BBC London Radio. It was an honour.

My morale, which had taken such a battering over the past few years, soared. I felt everything was turning around. I was free and independent, my kids were happy and healthy and, at thirty-seven, I thought I looked pretty good when I got dressed up. In fact I looked better than I had when I was swimming, because I finally had boobs.

I started dating again. One Friday night in November 2000, I went to a popular sports bar, Adrenalin, with a girlfriend. The bar had a regular theme on Fridays called 'The Star Behind the Bar', when a former sports personality would act as a barman and sign autographs. In return we got a meal and free drinks.

After my spell at the bar I began chatting to a group of guys. One of them was called Rick [not real name]. He was pleasant, chatty and very good-looking. With his sparkling blue eyes and blond hair, he looked like every Australian girl's dream. He said he was an engineer but, as I later discovered, he was actually a labourer. We swapped telephone numbers and the next day he asked me out for coffee. From that moment, we saw each other every day and went camping and fishing with the kids in the school holidays. Soon enough, he moved in with me at Bridgeman Downs. It all happened so quickly.

I thought this was it. Finally, I'd found my perfect match. For the first two months together, everything was wonderful. Even when I got a phone call from one of his ex-girlfriends, warning me that he had a violent temper and had bashed her, I just ignored the alarm signals.

The first time he lost his temper and yelled at me I couldn't believe it. This was supposed to be my perfect match? As time went by, he became more and more abusive, sometimes even hitting me. I told him to move out, but he ignored me. I got quite frightened. He was a big, strapping bloke and I thought he might 'get me' later if I rang the police.

I discovered his true colours on a camping trip at Christmas time. The kids – Hannah, Daniel and Rick's son – slept in one tent and we were in the other. Rick wanted sex every night and liked it rough, even at home. I hated the fact he got off on it and we often argued about it. That night in the tent I was conscious of the children so close, but he just ignored my pleas. Daniel must have heard us because he confronted Rick the next morning when I was momentarily away from the campsite.

'You can't do that to my mother. I hate you and I want to go home.'

'You little bastard,' he said, slapping Daniel across the face. 'You'll go home when I'm ready and not before.'

Poor Daniel was only eight years old. Rick had been verbally and sometimes physically abusive to him when I wasn't around. He was so two-faced and Daniel was too frightened to let me know what was going on. Finally, Daniel had had enough and ran to me with tears streaming down his face. He told me what had happened. I was shocked and angry. Nobody treats my children that way. I demanded that we pack up and go home immediately. Not a word was spoken on the return trip.

The thing with Rick was his mood swings. He could be charming and funny one minute, then nasty and aggressive the next. He had a way of winning me over after an argument, so that I always forgave him.

One night just before Easter 2001, he went too far and belted me in a drunken rage. His son was staying over at my place and was in the shower, which was at the back of the house. I was sitting in the family room with Rick, who had been drinking heavily. He started ranting and raving, abusing me and I retaliated by saying, 'Just get out of my house, you bastard.'

As I leant over him, sitting on the sofa, Rick elbowed me, flush on the jaw. I was thrown to the ground and hit my head on the tiled floor. I was stunned, seeing stars. His son heard the commotion and came running out of the shower, entering the room with a towel wrapped around his waist.

'What's going on?'

'Your father has just punched me in the jaw,' I said groggily, still lying on the floor.

'Not again. You do this to all your women, you fool.' Rick's son was furious.

I wanted to get out of there and go to my girl-friend Yani's place, but when I tried to drive the car out of the garage, Rick kept pulling the plug on the control for the roll-a-door. My lip was cut and bleeding, my whole face bruised and I was terrified. I couldn't get away. I felt so distressed and was hyperventilating. What could I do?

I rang Yani and she spoke to Rick over the phone, calming him down. She persuaded him to let me go, so I drove to her place. She was horrified at the state of my face and took me to Royal Brisbane Hospital, where I was treated and interviewed by a social worker and a policeman. We were at the hospital until 4.30am.

The police came to my place the next day and asked questions about the incident, so I told them what had happened. They interviewed Rick but he lied about everything and got his son to say that I had been throwing punches at his father, then slipped and hit my head on the floor. Rick was exonerated. Later, his son would apologise to me for lying. At least one good thing came out of the incident: Rick left. Good riddance, I thought.

The next night, Yani came over and we celebrated with a drink. To our surprise Rick suddenly burst into the room and started swearing at me, accusing us of being drunk. We were just having a laugh! I am a very moderate drinker and I'd probably have no more than a dozen drinks in a year. This was just one beer that we shared by way of celebration.

Yani protested and attempted to explain that we were just trying to relax. I'd had enough. I looked Rick in the eye and threatened to call the police unless he got out of my house immediately. He began to argue and then pleaded with me, but I was determined. That was it. Eventually Rick relented, packed up his clothes and left. I felt shattered. From my ideal man, Rick had become a nightmare, but now it was over. Or so I thought.

During Easter, five days after he had left, there was a knock at the door and there was Rick again. He looked dreadful, had lost 4 or 5 kilos and was apparently very sorry for his behaviour. He apologised and said that it would never happen again. Could I take him back? Stupid soft-hearted Tracey agreed to give him another chance. He moved his clothes back in and everything seemed to be okay.

Soon after, Rick and I went up to the Gold Coast for a sports function at Southport Sharks and we sat at a table with the former AFL star Warwick Capper and his wife. Capper was dressed outlandishly in tight leopard-skin pants and, fuelled by plenty of drinks, was swearing profusely. Rick was in a similar mood, cursing, knocking back plenty of booze and getting on well with the sports star. As they got more inebriated, the tone of their conversation dropped lower and lower. Eventually they were discussing their sex lives and, while Capper was evidently satisfied with his, Rick was complaining about ours. He told Capper he had to beg for it and I was boring because I didn't enjoy it as much as him.

I was so embarrassed at this intimate aspect of our relationship being freely discussed in front of others, including my good friends, Lee and Stephen Goodall. They were shocked, to say the least. When Lee and I went to the toilet she expressed her dislike for Rick and his behaviour. I hadn't told her about our problems and I needed some support, so I admitted to her that he had hit me.

'God, no,' she exclaimed. 'Just get out of it. Kick him out, Trace. He's not your type. You can do better.'

I was on the verge of getting rid of him anyway and told her I agreed. I would do it. I hadn't been drinking since I was driving, but Rick took a few more beers with him for the one-hour trip back to Brisbane.

When we got to the Riverside Expressway at about 1am, his mean mood exploded into a fit of violence.

He threw his empty beer bottle out of the car window, smashing it against the freeway railing. He was shouting at me, swearing abusively. I wanted to get away from the expressway, so I turned towards the Herschel Street exit, near the police station. As I veered right, Rick must have thought I was headed for the cops.

'What the fuck do you think you're doing?' he yelled, grabbing the steering wheel and yanking it.

The car tyres screeched as we slewed left, turning 180 degrees, running over the cement island and denting the whole underside of the car. We ended up facing directly back towards the way we had come. Thank goodness there was no traffic at that time of night. I managed to get back onto the right side of the road and took the Hale Street exit, which took us up to Kelvin Grove Road. Finally I found a place where we could pull over.

'Get out of my car,' I snarled.

I was trembling with rage. He got out and I was about to restart the engine when he reached through the window and snatched the keys from the ignition. He did it so violently that the ignition key bent, making it impossible to start the car again. I wound up the window, locked the doors and rang Yani. I told her what had happened and pleaded with her to come and get me. It was 2am in the morning. She told me to calm down and that she was on her way. I remembered that I had a spare key in my purse, but I waited for Yani and told her to take Rick back to our place. I refused to have him in my car again.

When we got home, I thanked Yani and assured her that I would get rid of Rick in the morning. When she left, he flew into a rage again, pushing me backwards toward my bed. The kids and his son, a young adult we had asked to babysit, were woken up by the commotion. I was flung through the air and landed flat on my back, but my hair flicked the edge of the blanket box at the foot of my bed. I had missed serious injury by millimetres.

His son saw what had happened and attacked, flailing his fists into Rick, yelling, 'Don't do that. That's what you did to Mum. Don't you dare hit Tracey again.'

I slept in Daniel's bed that night and the next day Rick got his marching orders. He was also placed under a Domestic Violence Protection Order by the police and ordered to stay away. That was it, for good.

***

Rick moved his things out one day when I wasn't home. When I returned I noticed he had left photos of us all over the house, including in the kids' rooms, the cutlery drawer and even my undies drawer. On top of the photos, I noticed that things were missing. I was about to fly to Papua New Guinea for a sports function in a few weeks and needed my passport. It was gone. My grandfather's ivory-handled knife, a favourite of mine, was also gone. A fax machine was missing from a cupboard.

Worst of all, my most important medals were missing. These were my proudest possessions: the gold medal presented to me by the Queen after the final race of my career at the 1982 Commonwealth Games and the two golds from my world record swims, the 800 metres at Edmonton and the 400 metres at the World Championships in Berlin a few weeks later.

I know this sounds funny but, yes, I did keep them in my undies drawer. The reason I didn't want them in a frame was that I liked to show them to kids at swimming clinics and I'm not one to 'show off' in my own home. I asked Hannah and Daniel if they had seen them and the answer was no. After a frantic search of the house there was no sign. Obviously, a thief had crept into the house and stolen them. He had a key and knew where everything was kept.

The police came and took my statement and promised they would do their best to recover my belongings. Several radio stations broadcast a plea for their return, but to no avail.

Could my life get any worse?

33

I moved out of Bridgeman Downs to a house in Taigum and stayed there for around nine months. As I was doing a big clean-up, I found the ivory-handled knife. It was hidden under the mat in a cutlery tray.

Sitting on the floor of the garage of the new house, I was throwing out junk that had accumulated over the years. I threw a fruit box full of old letters into the bin but then decided to double-check it. Under a pile of newspaper was a small plastic bag. I tugged and it felt really heavy. I pulled harder and there they were: my medals!

I called out to Hannah to come to the garage. When I held up the plastic bag with my missing things in it she squealed with delight. She grabbed the box and looked further down. There was some antique jewellery Mum had given Hannah for a birthday present.

I tipped all the contents out and there was my passport, as well as a photo of Rick and me together in happier times. He would have been hoping I would have thrown the box out myself since it was full of old birthday cards and newspaper clippings. People sometimes ask me these days if I ever found my medals and I tell them the story. But I never told it publicly because I didn't want him to have the pleasure of knowing I had discovered what he'd done.

That bastard Rick! I never want to see him again but if I do, I'll punch him where it hurts.

***

You would think I'd have learnt not to trust men so easily after that relationship, but I didn't. In October 2002, when I was thirty-nine, I advertised a sofa in the *Trading Post* and several people came around to look at it. One of them was a big, broad-shouldered bloke called Tim [not real name]. He was interested in the sofa, but it turned out he was more interested in me. We had a good chat when I first met him, thinking what a charmer he was.

Next day, he rang to ask me on a date and I accepted. He told me that he had just broken up with a girlfriend the day before. We hit it off really well and soon he was spending nights at my place. I had moved again to a lovely house in Kinnaird Street in the western suburbs and my life seemed to have taken a turn for the better.

Unfortunately, like Rick, Tim had some skeletons in the closet. Almost every day he would borrow my mobile phone to call his ex-girlfriend. Not just once, but up to ten times a day. She was obviously hanging up on him, so after each call he would be stressed and full of aggression. My bill went through the roof for months.

Tim was a leech. I was cooking and washing for him, driving him to and from work and so on. Why did I put up with all this? Well, I thought that when you like someone, that's what you are supposed to do. Tim started to become possessive and, before long, he was living at my house fulltime. Eventually I realised that he still wanted to hook up with his ex-girlfriend, despite her rejection of him. He was fanatically jealous of any man who came near her and he began taking out his aggression on me, especially when he was drinking.

It all came to a head on Valentine's Day in 2003. The previous week, Tim had seen his ex-girlfriend with another guy and was insanely jealous. He followed them into the GPO Club in the Valley and ended up in a fight with the guy. He not only lost the girl, he lost the fight. He came back with a cracked front tooth and a black eye. He turned up at my place at 2am, hopping mad, and said he was going to get the guy the next week.

Unbeknownst to me, that Valentine's Day Tim organised a couple of burly Maori mates to join us for dinner and clubbing. We went to dinner at an Italian restaurant in Bardon and had a nice bottle of Mateus Rosé, which was the only kind of wine I liked. I was content with one glass but, of course, Tim ordered another bottle, as well as a few beers. By the time we got to the Valley he was pretty drunk.

He was in a foul mood and kept talking about trying to find 'that guy'. I was really getting scared about what might happen. I wanted to hide. What am I doing here, I thought.

When we turned up at the GPO, the bouncers recognised Tim and wouldn't let him in. He objected, swearing loudly and making a scene. I moved away as I didn't want to get involved. Eventually he gave up and we walked around to another club, The Family. But we were rejected from there too, because one of the Maori guys had a floral Hawaiian shirt on. This made Tim even angrier and he caused another ugly scene. He swore at the bouncers but we managed to drag him off and went around the corner to another bar called the Press Club. By now Tim was in a really mean temper, so he turned his anger onto me.

'Go and get us a fuckin' drink,' he said.

I had already paid for dinner and was in no mood to continue the night. But I didn't want to upset him, so I went to the ATM to withdraw some money. Just as I was getting cash out, Tim approached.

'Where's our fuckin' drinks?'

I said nothing but went over to the bar and bought a round, including a Scotch for myself, and sat down alone, a distance away from the Maori mates. Tim came over and kept abusing me, spoiling for a fight. When I didn't retaliate, he grabbed my drink and threw it all over my lap. I was fuming but didn't say a word. I just picked up my bag, held it in front of my lap and walked out.

'Where the fuck are you goin'?' he yelled.

'Home.'

'You fuckin' slut, you fuckin' slag.' He abused me. He had such a foul mouth and would go off all the time. I hated it.

I jumped into the first cab I saw and, before I knew it, he had jumped in the other side. I wondered why he didn't stay with his mates but, on the trip home, I found out why. He was in the mood for a fight. I wasn't having any, so he was getting more and more abusive.

Finally, as we came to Ashgrove, the violence turned from verbal to physical. He punched me in the jaw, really hard. My teeth went through my tongue and I split my lip. I was so shocked I couldn't think. What could I do? The cab driver didn't want to get involved, so he stopped and told us to get out. We were near the Brisbane Broncos Leagues Club, about a kilometre from my home. After taking my shoes off I began walking home, ignoring the diatribe coming from Tim. He was insisting that I had spoiled his evening and kept up a torrent of abuse. I kept walking.

He eventually caught up to me and called me 'a fuckin' c—'. This is a word I hate. It's so degrading to women. Suddenly, he shoved me hard, sending me sprawling down a sloping concrete driveway. The blow to my head was bad enough but nothing compared to the excruciating pain in my knee. This was the knee that I had injured skiing in 1984 and had reconstructed. Another operation was required in

1992. But it felt worse than ever this time. I tried to stand but couldn't. I'd also twisted my ankle.

'What's wrong with you? Come on, you bitch, you can get up.' Tim was no help.

I needed to get home but was still about five blocks away and it was 2am. I couldn't straighten my leg at all and the right knee blew up like a balloon. Tim tried to get me to stand up, but I couldn't. He took my bag and my mobile, so I couldn't ring for help. He walked off, leaving me stranded. Even if I could, I probably wouldn't have rung anybody, because I was so embarrassed about the arsehole I was going out with.

Slowly and painfully I dragged myself by my hands, sliding along on my backside or else holding onto a fence and hopping. Each move was complete agony. Two hours later, I finally reached my front gate. Tim had let himself in and was already sleeping in my bed, so I crawled into Hannah's empty one. The kids were at their father's that weekend, which was just as well because Hannah would have gone crazy at Tim. She was so protective of me.

I woke about two hours later and rang the Mater Hospital and they said to come straight in. Tim heard me on the phone and said he would drive me. No word of apology or regret though. He still stank of alcohol and I said I would rather catch a cab. He warned me not to tell the hospital staff what he had done or he would 'get' me. I kept it a secret, even from Mum, until about a month later.

He did end up driving me to the Mater and a nurse came out with a wheelchair. Tim said I wouldn't need it, but the nurse could see the pain etched on my face and ignored him. They whizzed me straight into x-ray, where I was informed that I had a fractured tibia plateau. The surgeon said it was a mess and that the tibia plateau was 'smashed like a Violet Crumble'. They reconstructed my knee, inserting a 10-centimetre steel plate and five huge screws, as well as grafting bone from my hip onto the knee. Seven years later, it still aches. I was so angry. Fancy all this happening because an idiot broke up with his girlfriend.

The kids came to visit me in hospital and I concocted a story about how I had accidentally slipped and fallen down the internal stairs at my home. I may have fooled Daniel, who was only eleven, but I knew Hannah smelt a rat. Why I protected that cruel bastard, I'll never know.

***

I had bought three tickets for a Rolling Stones concert a week before the operation. Originally they were for me, Tim and a mate of his. They were supposed to repay me a hundred and fifty bucks each. Somehow, Tim had conned Mum into going in my place given that my knee prevented me from attending. He picked her up and arrived at my house with a big bunch of flowers. I suspected he was feeling guilty and was worried I would report him to the police. He was acting all lovey-dovey, saying, 'Are you okay, darling? Can I get you a coffee or something?'

Mum and I just looked at each other and I knew she saw through him, but at that stage I didn't tell her the full story. And I never got my hundred and fifty back.

Two weeks later, with my leg still in a splint, Tim came around again. He knocked on my door at 3am, pleading for me to open up. He was drunk and made such a racket I thought the neighbours would complain, so I let him in. The kids were staying with me and, coincidentally, that evening I had just told Hannah what really happened to my knee. She was angry and upset.

Tim made straight for my bedroom and saw Daniel asleep in my bed.

'Get him out. Make him go to his own room.'

'No. He's asleep and I don't want to wake him. Why should I?'

'Because I want to go to sleep and I can't with him there.'

'No. It's my house and I'll do what I want. Just get out, you drunken mongrel!'

At that moment, Hannah came racing upstairs. There I was in t-shirt and undies, hobbling on crutches with Tim abusing me. I crumpled onto the floor in a heap and in tears. She was irate, confronting him and yelling at him for the way he had treated me. Although only fourteen, she was smart and fiercely protective of me. She told Tim to pack up his things and get out of our house, once and for all.

When he refused, she rang 000 and told them what was happening. He made so much noise that the operator couldn't hear what Hannah was saying at first, but they managed to trace the call. When Tim heard the police were coming around, he fled. No more than five minutes later, four police cars and a paddy wagon arrived, their lights flashing. For some reason, Tim returned and started yelling about how Daniel had been in my bed and I'd been cruel to him. Me! On crutches! I was a blubbering mess, hysterical and in pain.

The police took him into my study for an interview and he apparently started bashing his fist onto the polished timber floor. Then he came back out to show me his bruised knuckles.

'Look what you've fucking done to me.'

What an idiot, I thought.

I just shook my head in amazement. After a couple of hours the police wound up their interviews and took Tim to the watch-house where he spent the night. A Domestic Violence Protection Order was placed against him and finally I had some peace. He was not allowed within 100 metres of my house and not allowed to contact me in any way, even by telephone. I thought I was finally rid of him.

A few months later, he showed up out of the blue. I had moved house out of sheer embarrassment at what the neighbours must think. I had no idea how he found the new address, but he had. Despite the DVP Order, he wanted to take me out to dinner. Of course I said no. I told him if he ever came around again, I would call the police. He left, for the last time.

Later I realised that the reason he had come over at all was to take a photo of the two of us together, in breach of the order. Tim wanted to get a gun licence, which was impossible if the order was still in place. If I was seen to be acquiescing, he would get a friend to take a photo and swear in an affidavit that we were going out again. He was tricky, that bastard Tim.

***

My leg has never been the same and probably never will be. After the abuse, I was in more pain than ever. The heavy cast placed a lot of strain on my back. I had suffered from a disc problem since my swimming days and this time it really flared up, aggravated by the use of crutches. I would get a migraine and back pain just from vacuuming the carpet.

One night, it was all just too much. I got Mum to drive me to the Mater Hospital, where I saw a doctor in the Emergency section. He put me on a very strong morphine-based painkiller, which was even more potent than the prescription I had become addicted to in the late 1990s.

I was supposed to take one or two a day, but they didn't seem to do any good and I was depressed and in excruciating pain. I began taking more and more and soon I was gulping them down like jelly beans. I was taking three or four times the recommended dosage and I grew really depressed. The pills helped with the physical pain and they dulled the emotional pain as well. Before long, I was addicted.

I blamed Tim, of course. I'd never heard of the pills before he bashed me and the doctors put me on them. I think the medical profession also has a lot to answer for when it comes to prescription medication addiction in patients. I felt I wasn't given any real warning as to how addictive what they had given me could be. Once you're in the grip of the pills, it's a horrible road to get off and your body keeps crying out for more. To this day, I have to watch what I'm taking and make sure it doesn't get out of hand.

Eventually, I had an operation on my back, a laminectomy, in which the painful disc was removed. But despite this, I was still in agony from my sciatic nerve. The pain would stab me in the lower back and shoot down my leg. I was depressed, with no job and no money and I became a virtual recluse, unable to get around properly because of my health problems.

My life seemed to go into a downward spiral and I became even more dependent on the painkillers. I lived in a dream world, sleeping fitfully, barely wanting to get up in the morning and was always alone. The only thing that kept me going was the thought of my children coming over each week.

My doctor finally put me into a hospital where I was weaned off the painkillers. And I was off men too. It would have to be a knight in shining armour before I ever went with a guy again. I just wanted my life to return to normal. But it was a catch-22 situation. I needed the painkillers for my back pain and the doctor would just pass out scripts without hesitation. I was in and out of hospital, constantly trying to recover. Surely things couldn't get any worse?

Little did I know that every mother's nightmare lay just around the corner.

PART 5

HANNAH

34

FROM THE DIARY OF HANNAH CIOBO 9 OCTOBER 2002

If you could tell the world just one thing it would be to live life to the fullest. Only because you never know what's coming around the corner! You don't know what's going to happen. One minute you could be fine; the next you could be in a critical condition. No one knows their future or how long they have. That's why you should live every day as if it were your last – because one day it will be.

You have to try all things new to you, things that you won't regret doing. You have to have fun, be loud and be yourself, so that you can be heard and be remembered for who you are. You have to tell people your feelings and thoughts about everything, so they know how you see life and what sort of person you really are.

Don't plan out your life too far ahead – live it on the edge. It's more fun that way coz you never know what's around the corner.

On 13 July 1988, I was blessed with the arrival of a beautiful girl with jet-black hair and blue eyes. We called her Hannah Lee. Lee is my second name, which I got from my dad's eldest brother, Uncle Lee. I never got to meet him because he died a few years before I was born in an accident, two weeks before his twenty-first birthday.

As she grew up, Hannah developed into a clever, happy, outgoing little girl. She was serious and cautious. She would prefer a colouring book to a merry-go-round and she adored animals. Her favourite creature was the butterfly. As she grew older she played soccer and tennis, learnt ballet and drums and, naturally, was a good swimmer. But her passion was art. She was a remarkable painter, but where she got that talent from, nobody knows. It certainly wasn't from me or Rob.

Of course I loved her to bits. She liked singing at the top of her voice in the car and, when she did her Donald Duck impersonation, she was better than the original. She had a great sense of humour.

She was a stunner. She became a model as a teenager and loved it. Tall and long-legged, with a mane of sandy blonde hair, beautiful oyster-blue eyes and full lips, she was a natural in front of the camera. Even behind the camera she was talented, with an unfulfilled ambition to become a professional photographer.

She loved parties and I loved organising them for the kids and their friends. Also, we'd host sleepovers nearly every weekend the kids were over, since it was the done thing, they'd tell me. When she was fifteen, Hannah had a school semi-formal afterparty at my place. It went from 11pm to 3am and about thirty of her friends attended and had a ball. She often came with me to functions and enjoyed meeting new people. She was a clever student and always got good grades. Her forte was fashion design. A glittering career lay ahead of her. And then it happened.

On 7 October 2004, Hannah was diagnosed with cancer. The week before, she called me into the bathroom where she was sitting in the bath, shaving her legs before going out that night with some friends.

'Mum, there's something here near my groin. It feels really gristly, can you feel it?'

I could.

The next day we went to the Kedron Park Medical Centre where the GP had a quick look and told us it was probably just swollen glands due to an infection. Hannah and I exchanged glances. No way is it an infection, we thought, it's more than that. Fortunately, we were able to get an ultrasound on the spot.

While the ultrasound operator was preparing the scan, Hannah told him how she had been kicked in the groin in a soccer match a few weeks earlier and thought the lump might be a deep bruise. As the operator began the ultrasound, he started to frown and went very quiet.

'There's definitely something there,' he said.

A few minutes went by and then Hannah pointed at the monitor. 'Is it that black area?'

That black area was a mass measuring 7x4x2 centimetres. I hoped it was only a cyst. We were referred to a specialist and made an appointment for two days' time. I rang Rob that night, and the three of us went together to see Dr Peter Stedman, the orthopaedic oncology specialist at Mater Private Hospital. Dr Stedman was kind and softly spoken. He examined the scans, flicking them over and upside down. Finally he spoke.

'Well, it's definitely a tumour of some sort.'

'A tumour!' I blurted out. I wanted to stay calm in front of Hannah but my mind was racing.

'It could be fifty-fifty. It's either malignant or benign, that's all I can say right now. We don't know how long it's been there.'

'So what happens from here?' Rob asked.

'We'll book a biopsy for two days' time.'

It was too much. Hannah was so overwhelmed she hardly said a word. Rob asked most of the questions because I was still dumbfounded. My stomach sank and I felt sick. All I could think was that this was so unfair. Hannah was just sixteen and had her whole life ahead of her. I kept reassuring myself: teenagers don't get cancer, only old people. But I didn't get much sleep over the next two nights.

Hannah was keen to get the biopsy done, so she could hear the words, 'All clear. It's benign.' If it was, they were going to take it out straightaway. If not? Well, Dr Stedman didn't say. We all had to be optimistic, of course, but when I think back, I know that the doctor would have seen these tumours in kids many times and he probably knew the outcome already. Still, he said nothing.

Both immediate families were waiting outside the theatre and a pathologist was on hand to diagnose immediately. As Rob and I sat in the waiting room, all the anger, frustration and hate we had built up between us evaporated. I was shocked when Dr Stedman came out of the theatre after only twenty minutes. I knew that if the lump was benign, he would have been in there longer for the operation to remove it. He dropped his face mask and, with a slight frown, said simply, 'Look, it is cancer, but...'

That's all I heard. I went numb, as if the world had stopped. I went ballistic.

'Not my baby, not cancer!' I screamed. 'Why Hannah? Please God, tell me this isn't happening. It's not cancer, it's all wrong!'

I let out a primal groan like an animal dying which lasted almost half an hour. I ran down the corridor and back again. I screamed and yelled so much, our family couldn't hear what the doctor was saying. I couldn't breathe and, hyperventilating, I collapsed. Doctors, nurses, a social worker and even a priest came to my aid. The nurse gave me a paper bag to breathe into, but it didn't help. With someone holding me on each side, I was given a sedative and taken down in a lift to a padded room, probably designed to reduce noise and stop people harming themselves.

Two hours later when I started to recover from the shock and horror of the word 'cancer', Rob and Mum told me the news. Hannah had a rare and nasty form of cancer called Ewing's synovial sarcoma and would need chemo and radiation therapy.

Sarcoma is a cancer of the connective tissue, attacking tendons, ligaments, fat and non-connective soft tissues like muscles and blood vessels. Synovial sarcoma in particular attacks the membranes in the joints and is usually found in the legs. It is much harder to treat than bone cancer and affects only four children in two million. The children are usually between the ages of five and twenty-five and Hannah had a fifty percent chance of surviving it. Most children diagnosed have approximately three to five years left to live.

I wanted to run into the theatre right then to cuddle my baby, but she was still under sedation.

'How does God do this to Hannah? What has she done to deserve this? Not my baby girl. She's an angel. Everyone loves her.'

I lay in a recliner chair in the padded room, my head buried in my hands. My eyes were so swollen from crying they were almost slits. All I could think was, 'God, help my baby. Why did he do this to her? Why? Why? God, I hate you!' How long had that tumour been there? From birth, for two months, two years, how long? No one will ever know. As one doctor said, 'These things just happen, out of the blue, for no reason.'

I wanted to curl up and die but I had to see Hannah first. They wouldn't allow me to, because of the state I was in. They wanted me to be strong, smiling and happy. HAPPY! How on earth was I going to do that? What an actress I would have to be.

Well, I did it eventually and, three hours later, I was allowed to see my daughter. I was calm and relaxed and sat with her for an hour with other family members. I kissed her forehead and acted positive as if this was just a little hiccup in our lives and would be all over in a few months. I wanted to believe this. Hannah was strong-willed, brave and determined. She was amazing. I wished I had her determination when I was swimming. God knows what I would have achieved.

Later that day, I went to Wesley Chapel to pray. Shouting and crying, I begged God to give the cancer to me rather than my daughter.

'She's not an axe murderer, or a rapist or even a thief. You've picked the wrong person, God. She's one of your angels.'

Little did I know that Mum had done the same thing an hour earlier.

At home that evening, I just wanted to be alone. I collapsed on the floor and curled up in the foetal position and cried and cried. I didn't sleep the whole night.

35

Before Hannah was due to start her first round of chemotherapy, the doctor advised her to have some of her eggs frozen, as the chemo could make her infertile. She agreed, thinking she might want children down the track. She asked me then and there if I would carry her baby for her, if it came to that. She wanted our genes to continue.

'Of course, darling.'

We both had tears in our eyes. It was our little secret. I would have done anything for her. I would have given her my heart if I could and died right there. I didn't care – at least I would have had a chance at half a life. I just wanted her to have one too.

Hannah began chemo and radiation therapy to reduce the tumour within the next few days. Her lump was the size of a squashed grapefruit and had to be down to the size of a plum before they could operate. Kind Dr John Bashford was her oncologist and guided Hannah through. He was very sympathetic to our family, having four little children himself. I was in awe of him having to do such a stressful job with such young victims.

Hannah was always so brave during her ordeal and only twice did I see her shed a tear: before her first biopsy to see if there was cancer and then when they started the chemo injections. She was scared of the unknown, but nothing else. I'll never forget the sight of her face as the reddish-coloured liquid was pumped into her arm, via a drip. A single tear rolled slowly down her cheek. The long battle had begun.

She was a fighter and was positive that no treatment would stop her from her normal life. But within two weeks of starting the chemo, she screamed for me to come into the bathroom where she was blow-drying her long, beautiful hair. There were large clumps of it in the sink. It had begun to fall out.

I tried to console her but she was angry and upset. She had been hoping that she would be in the minority of people who have chemo and don't lose their hair. She went to bed crying and I quietly saved some of her long hair in a plastic bag, hardly knowing what I was doing.

Within days it was all coming out in huge clumps all over her pillow and sheets. Rob's girlfriend at the time, a former hairdresser, cut it really short but it was itchy, so Hannah decided to have it all shaved off. She and Aunt Donnie, Rob's sister, went wig shopping and came back with some great wigs so that nobody could even tell.

After several months, the tumour was less than a third of its original size and the doctor was able to operate. Christmas came around and the tumour was removed. Hannah had a huge scar from the operation, running from her groin to just above her knee. Dr Stedman said it couldn't be avoided because he had to cut through a major nerve and some muscle. We were grateful that at least she still had her leg, as we knew some children with sarcoma could end up having part or the whole of the limb amputated.

Two months later, Hannah had her first scan to see whether the cancer was still there or not. It was a long and detailed process and she had to be sedated so she didn't move while every millimetre of her skin was being examined. It took three hours and I tried to sleep on a fold-out bed in her hospital room while we were waiting. I used to think I was nervous before a swim race, but that was nothing compared to what I was now going through. My daughter's life was at stake.

Suddenly, Rob came bursting into the ward, yelling, 'Tracey! Tracey!'

I bolted up, still half-drowsy, and ran to meet him.

'It's gone! It's gone! The cancer is gone!' Rob yelled.

'Thank God,' I said, with tears in my eyes.

Rob was also crying and I saw the nurses smiling, happy for us. Then one of them turned to the other with a strange look on her face, as if to say, 'We've seen this all before and it hasn't worked out, so don't get your hopes up too much.'

I was taken aback and it dampened my excitement. In that moment, I had an inkling that the nightmare wasn't over, although I had not yet realised just how deadly and rare synovial sarcoma was. What pathetic luck.

***

Rob was a huge support for all of us during Hannah's illness and bent over backwards to care for her. He put all his time, effort and money into finding the right doctors and searching for remedies.

After the diagnosis, Rob and I both realised that our fickle bickering for all those years was just stupid and unnecessary. More than ever, we began to stick together for Hannah's sake. There were no more fights or lawyers: our past just didn't matter anymore. Hannah was so glad that we had teamed up to help her, and was determined to fight on.

'I'm living with cancer, not dying from it,' she would say.

She never complained and was always busy. While recuperating, she did a magnificent painting, reflecting her battle against cancer and dubbed it, 'I'm Still Me'. That painting hangs on Mum's wall.

Even though we had been told that all was well after the major scan, I still felt the cancer lurking in the background, threatening to pounce. When the kids and I were out together I would sometimes grab their hands and start skipping, just like the Vita-Weats advertisement. Hannah would laugh but get angry and say, 'Stop it, Mum.' It was embarrassing for her, but I couldn't help myself. Daniel loved it, and all their friends thought I was a 'cool mum'. The three of us would laugh together over my 'silliness'.

I know most mums have been given instructions by their children not to kiss or hug them in public, but I didn't care who saw us and neither did they. We would always say 'I love you' whenever we said goodbye in front of friends, in a text or on the phone. They said it and I said it and we all meant it. Daniel and I still do, and he told me he would never want me to stop telling him how much I care. I believe that every parent should kiss and hug their children to give them a feeling of security. You never know when it can all be taken away from you. Every day is a gift, and should be treasured.

We tried to make life as normal as possible for Hannah, so she could be the teenage girl she was. In between hospital stays, which she hated, she would go to parties and do all the girly things: shopping, make-up, going to beaches and boys.

'So what that I've got a 40-centimetre scar on my skinny thigh? So what if I'm bald? I'm alive and I'm going to make the most of it.'

For Daniel, we made sure his life was still going smoothly, but he understood, even at the age of thirteen, that Hannah was a priority. As a mother, I felt terribly guilty that I couldn't spend as much time with Daniel as I should have, but when one of your children's life is at stake, you have blinkers on. I am still trying to make it up to him, and he understands that we had to do what we did.

***

Despite all the drama, Hannah still wanted to finish Year Twelve. When she was too unwell to attend school, she would bring her assignments home and Mum would often help her with them. All Hallows was fantastic to her and she responded by graduating with flying colours.

She still looked beautiful, as bald as a billiard ball. With her two new wigs, she continued her modelling undaunted. On the M1 freeway, in suburbs around the city and on the way to Brisbane airport, there were huge billboards with Hannah posing in a silver, strapless formal gown for a clothing company, looking stunning in her black wig.

Hannah taught us how to cope. She always acted her normal self. Every six weeks she had x-rays and scans and afterwards we would all relax. But the tension would build up again as the next x-ray session drew near. My anxiety was always there, every day. When Hannah looked tired or unwell, or had a slight cold, I would be worried sick thinking, 'Oh shit, it must be back again.' Somehow I just knew when it would be bad news for Hannah. A mother's intuition, I suppose.

As I walked into her ward, I would see other children who were there having lumps removed or chemotherapy. Even Hannah used to wonder whether the chemo would work on these poor little darlings. It used to break our hearts seeing the little ones there with their parents sleeping beside them, basically living with their children in their rooms for months at a time. Hannah used to hope that at least the kids would reach puberty but, with sarcoma, most of them didn't.

I take my hat off to the nurses and doctors who work in those wards, who have to see children losing their lives slowly over a two-to-five year period, if that. I know Hannah had so much love for everyone in her ward at the Wesley, all the nurses and even the cleaners, and they loved her too. She did a beautiful canvas painting that hangs on the wall there, in ward 2W.

In mid-2005, the Starlight Foundation contacted Hannah about whether she would like a wish to be granted. She didn't want anything dramatic, like going overseas to Disneyland, all she wanted was to buy some clothes in Melbourne. The foundation organised for us two to go down there in the summer.

We had a ball, spending two thousand dollars on the famous Bridge Road in Richmond. Boy, she loved that place ever since we'd been there for a charity function for the Alannah and Madeline Foundation. At the event she met the AFL player Cameron Cloke from the Collingwood Football Club and they were sweet on each other. They'd send each other text messages every few days, although they weren't boyfriend and girlfriend. That's why we'd even thought of moving down in 2004, before her diagnosis. I'd always wanted to live there so it was a great excuse.

***

One day in 2005, a nurse told Hannah there was a cute guy two doors down who she should meet. So Hannah, with her bald head and pyjamas, rocked up to his room, rolling her drip trolley with her. She gave a quick knock before walking straight in and saying, 'Hi, I'm Hannah, what's your name?'

The boy, Tom Driscoll, had been lying in his boxers and playing Playstation, so was a bit taken aback. But they hit it off straightaway and exchanged phone numbers. Tom was a year older than her and from Rockhampton. Over time they caught up, went out to dinner and talked about their highs and lows. His sarcoma was slightly different, in that it attacked the bones and was easier to find and treat than Hannah's. But soon, the two became inseparable.

I was rapt that my daughter had a partner who totally understood what she was going through. They were both fighting this deadly disease and leaned on each other for support. Only those two really knew what the other was experiencing.

***

Eight months after going into remission for the first time, Hannah went in for her regular check-up. She went with Rob because I couldn't bear waiting for the results in the hospital. She rang me at home and said only two words, 'It's back.'

It was enough to send me into hysterics after I hung up the phone. I collapsed on the ground in a foetal position and gave that primal groan again, then cried and cried, hyperventilating. I rang Mum and she didn't even know who was calling. I was screaming incoherently. She just said, 'Are you alone? Don't drive. Ashley and I will be right over.' From the pain in my voice, she knew exactly what had happened.

Not again, I thought. Why? Why? That fucking word 'cancer' is taking away the life that I was looking forward to sharing with my daughter. How much more can one person take?

This second time, the cancer had entered her lungs, which was what Dr Bashford warned us could happen. X-rays revealed eleven tiny tumours in both lobes. When the surgeon operated, he actually used his fingers to pluck out the tumours, like picking mushrooms.

After six weeks of chemo sessions and another two months' wait, the major scan results came back: clear once again. But how long would it last? A year? Ten years? I just knew that Hannah's life was going to be one big merry-goround forever: on, off, on, off.

Within eight months, the cancer returned for the third time. Again it was approximately thirteen small tumours in the lungs with the same plucking operation conducted by the excellent Dr Peter Wragg, a thoracic surgeon. Then another bout of chemo.

Hannah hated her stays in hospital and would bolt out the front gate of the Wesley on the Saturday morning following her week-long treatments. She was in a rush to get on with life.

Poor Daniel was taking it hard. He and Hannah used to fight like cat and dog when they were younger but this illness had brought about a closer bond. Three and a half years younger, he idolised her and listened to every word of advice she offered. At the age of fourteen, Daniel couldn't bear the thought of losing his only adored sibling, his big sister.

A week before Hannah turned eighteen, in July 2006, she was told she was in her third remission. Hallelujah! To celebrate, she went to Italy for two months with Aunt Donnie and her family. Hannah looked a vibrant picture of health and nothing would stop her going. It was hard to believe what was to come.

Around January 2007, she felt sore. She had a cough and found it painful to breathe. An x-ray revealed a massive tumour on one lung. The cancer was back for the fourth time. She was offered more chemotherapy by Dr Bashford, which she declined, knowing a new style of chemo would be available in a few months that might give her a better chance. I could see her slowly deteriorating.

During this time, Hannah told us that she wanted to move into her own place and be independent. She knew that, underneath it all, she was facing her own mortality. I know she just wanted to experience what it would be like to have her own place.

Rob found a cute cottage in Alderley, and Hannah settled in. Like any teenager, she enjoyed having friends around for barbecues and dinners. We all had keys and would take turns to cook and clean for her. She and Tom were getting along well and everyone had their fingers crossed. Everything seemed to be looking up. But sarcoma, once it takes hold, rarely lets go.

36

On 17 July 2007, Hannah was back in intensive care. Eventually Dr Wragg took her aside and quietly told her that this fourth bout of cancer was terminal. A huge tumour that had grown on one lung could not be removed because of the risk of Hannah dying on the operating table. She would only have a few months to live. The battle was coming to an end and Hannah seemed calm and resigned to her fate.

Rob, Mum and I were told together. I immediately ran out of the hospital and rang Lee and Stephen Goodall, my friend Julie Hayne and Stephen 'Fossil' Fry, my old training partner. A couple of nurses were with me as I made the calls. I was screaming: 'What else can we do? Can we take her somewhere else?' I panicked.

I collapsed on the grass near the entrance of the hospital and began hyperventilating. I had a cigarette in my hand but I shook so much I couldn't put it in my mouth. 'I want my Hannah! I want my Hannah! No! No!' I screamed continually. I had been officially told that my baby was dying and I could not take it anymore.

I started pill-popping painkillers to numb the emotional agony. I couldn't drive, so 'Fossil' called up our mate, Michael Bohl, who left his training squad to come down to the hospital with 'Fossil' and take me home. I was totally inconsolable.

That same day, after learning the cancer was terminal, Tom asked Rob for Hannah's hand in marriage and proposed to her in intensive care. They kept the engagement secret and only they knew for almost a month. They made the big announcement at a party a few weeks later, although Hannah told me on the quiet about an hour earlier. I was moved to tears.

Hannah and Tom were determined to be married and set a date of October 14 for a beach-themed wedding at Twin Waters on the Sunshine Coast. October 14 was the day they had first begun 'officially' going out in 2006, after texting each other constantly while Hannah was overseas with Donnie. I understood it was special for them. Nevertheless, I was anxious about my daughter's health and urged them to make the wedding sooner. But they were adamant.

As often happens with cancer, Hannah seemed to recover for a time and was allowed to go home. She was so excited about planning her dream wedding for three months' time. Nevertheless, she was looking very pale and weak and didn't even want to risk driving her car – which she adored – a little black Holden Barina will alloy mag wheels.

***

In late September, Hannah was taken to hospital with a high fever. Ironically, her tumour was shrinking thanks to the new type of chemo, but there was an infection in her good lung. It took the doctors a week to find exactly where it was and to work out what antibiotics to give her. Despite the treatment, the lung was well and truly infected.

Outside Hannah's room, I confided in Tom: 'Gee, I wish the wedding had been a couple of weeks ago, when she wasn't as sick as she is now.'

He shocked me with his reply. 'It's our wedding not yours. If we want it on the fourteenth, we'll have it then. It's none of your business,' he snapped.

I bit my lip in anger and frustration. I only wanted the best for my daughter, I just wanted her to enjoy the most exciting day of her life.

On Monday, 1 October 2007, eleven days after she was admitted, I made my early morning visit to the Wesley Hospital and was shocked to see Hannah's condition. Overnight, she had lost more weight and had even more trouble breathing. Only twenty-four percent of her infected lung was functioning. The other lung with the massive tumour hadn't been functioning all year.

Hannah's skin had a grey pallor and she was so doped up with morphine that she was in a dream world. The nurses did a wonderful job but Sue, the head nurse, told me to expect the worst. During that final day, I kept asking two of the nurses, 'Will she make it?'

They wouldn't say, 'Yes', they simply put their arms around me. That meant, 'No, she won't make it.'

I was so desperate for positive reinforcement that I just lost it. I went to the head nurse's office and hurled anything I could find onto the ground – papers, glasses, books – nearly a whole bookcase. And I was screaming that primal groan again.

I was taken downstairs for a cigarette and a glass of water. As I was sitting there, I was amazed to get a text message from Hannah. She always sent one on the first day of the month: 'Pinch and a punch ha ha! Where are you? H xx'.

I raced back up the stairs to her room and tried to bring myself under control. She couldn't talk. She was concentrating on every breath and her frail little chest was heaving in and out. I held her hand and she asked me if I could take her pyjamas home to wash. I talked to her a little but she just wanted me to be there.

There was nothing I could do so, in the late afternoon, I went home for a few hours. At 6.30pm, my old school friend, Heather, a nurse in Hannah's ward, rang to see how I was. I told her what had happened and she dropped everything to come and sit with me before her hospital shift. While she was making her way over, Heather was afraid I would do something to myself so she had her mother call and talk with me to keep me calm. Heather stayed for half an hour before she had to leave for work.

Twenty minutes later, at about 8pm, I got the dreaded official call from the doctor.

'Hannah won't last the night. You had better come in now.'

I was crying and panicking. I screamed at myself, 'Where's my keys? Where's my keys?'

I couldn't stop shaking and was petrified that Hannah would pass away before I could see her. Sure enough, the keys were right in front of me, on the coffee table the whole time. I grabbed them and sprinted out to my car. I must have run about five red lights en route to the hospital, but fortunately there wasn't much traffic. It was pouring rain and tears were streaming down my face as I yelled out to God, 'Please don't take my Hannah, please. Why are you doing this?'

I could hardly see the road in front of me, but somehow I made it to the hospital and screeched into the parking spot in front of the main entrance. As I raced inside a nurse greeted me with a caution from Tom to act normally, as Hannah didn't know that she would not make it through the night. I didn't need anyone telling me how to act, I was Hannah's mother. I wasn't going to go in there screaming. I knew I had to be the bravest mum in the whole world at this point.

I went into her room with a gentle smile and kissed her forehead. She was struggling for breath and looked so thin, but she was pleased to see me. Tom was sitting next to her and saying that the priest would be there shortly. I was shocked, thinking it was for the last rites, but Tom told me that he had hastily arranged a bedside ceremony.

There were nearly twenty of us there by 9pm: the whole of the Ciobo family, Mum and Ashley and half a dozen of Hannah's school friends. It was bizarre. I felt it was like people gawking at animals in the zoo. No offence, but I felt this was a time only for parents, grandparents and Tom.

The priest arrived at 9.45pm and fifteen minutes later they were man and wife. I remember Hannah being worried about her hair looking a mess and she tried to make it look better but she was shuddering so much from the morphine that it was pointless. When she signed the marriage certificate her hand shook so that her signature was barely legible.

Then the priest said to Hannah that he would like to say a prayer for her, for sick people. I knew it was the last rites, but whether Hannah knew I'll never find out. Tears were streaming down my face and the last two hours were terrible for everyone. I really wished for her sake that she had passed a few hours before, because now she was in terrible pain and struggling to breathe.

Tom stayed with her and occasionally I would go in. An hour before she passed, I popped in through the door and said, 'I love you, baby.'

'Love you too.'

The end came quickly. I had been waiting outside when Heather, the nurse who was a school friend from All Hallows, came to fetch me. 'Quick, quick!'

When I went inside there were people gathered all around her. Her friends, who had been outside having a cigarette, had rushed inside, not wanting to miss the last moments. I was suddenly angry.

'This isn't a zoo. She's not on show, just get out.'

I was upset because my baby was about to go to heaven. I wanted to be with her, with Tom, Mum and Rob, and no one else. It was private. My angel was taking her last few breaths. Every-one bar immediate family filed out.

Hannah had been contorted with pain but the nurses rearranged her and placed her arms in her lap. She looked like a beautiful angel. It was 1.15am on Tuesday, 2 October 2007. Hannah was still a teenager, just nineteen. I whispered into her ear. 'I love you, darling. I'll see you in heaven.'

With her little chest heaving, she swallowed her last breath, then she was gone.

I was numb, crying, but relieved to know Hannah wasn't going to go through any more pain. After ten minutes of holding her, I bolted out the door. I couldn't bear it anymore.

I hung around the hospital and then drove home at 3am. I stared through the television, trying to take in what had happened. I stayed awake for days. I was a zombie.

***

Hannah's funeral was held on Sunday, October 7, at All Hallows Chapel and she was placed in her tomb at Nudgee Cemetery the same day. Hundreds of people were there, many of whom I didn't know. Even Cameron Cloke flew up from Melbourne with his brother, Travis. Hannah had spoken to Cameron just a week before. No one could believe she was gone.

It was the ceremony that her wedding was supposed to be. The groomsmen became pallbearers, her best friends wore bridesmaid's dresses but she rode in a hearse, not a limousine. I felt numb with grief. I managed to get through a eulogy and, as I kissed her casket, thirteen butterflies were released. Her body was laid to rest in the Ciobo family crypt, but her spirit was free.

***

I will never get over Hannah's passing but I've slowly learnt to live with the pain. I feel cheated as a mother. I was naturally looking forward to grandchildren. It's not supposed to be this way. No one should bury their child. I still have the pyjamas Hannah gave me to wash on her last day and I know I will never wash them. They smell like her.

There were still the eggs that Hannah had frozen before her first round of chemotherapy, but a year later the doctor wrote to tell me that legally they would have to be destroyed since Hannah had passed. I wanted so badly to keep them frozen, since they were the only part of Hannah that was still alive. Nevertheless, they were discarded. I had a lot of tears in my eyes that day. Deep inside I had dreamed of having IVF with them for her, even though I knew it could never happen.

In the aftermath of Hannah's death, I would often find Daniel in his bedroom or the study with the music blaring, bawling his eyes out because he missed her so much. He feels lost without his sister, and I felt so guilty I couldn't give him another sibling. I have had four pregnancies in my life and I've lost the first three babies: the miscarriages and Hannah. Daniel is the world to me.

After she had gone through her third remission, Hannah had an idea to launch an anti-cancer foundation for teenage sufferers, which she and Tom called 'Hannah's Chance'. She was still deciding on the name the week that she died. She was passionate about making people more aware of sarcoma, and when she was alive we went on Bert Newton's television show *Good Morning Australia* a few times to talk about her ordeal. She even took her wig off live on the air. She wasn't ashamed or embarrassed about her condition.

Since her passing, our family have planned and attended many fundraising functions, in conjunction with the Wesley Research Institute, raising awareness of the disease. Hannah wanted to fundraise for research and wanted to build a special teenage wing in the hospital, since she and Tom had to stay in a children's ward.

I feel that the reason I was given the gift of swimming fast and becoming famous was to be able to be Hannah's voice. That was what Hannah wanted from me. Ten days before she died, she asked me to be the patron of 'Hannah's Chance'. I know I can help create awareness of this revolting cancer and continue the foundation. Her legacy will live on. As an ambassador I do a lot of promotion work and so far we have raised over three hundred thousand dollars for research into sarcoma.

In 2007, Hannah wrote a poem to read during her motivational talks, when she was a guest speaker. She recited it twice, and these days I read it on her behalf, to keep her memory alive.

Tiger's Daughter

I was born with Mother's tog mark branded on my back In swimming, Tracey Wickham was Australian for 'attack' Regarded by Dawn Fraser though her reign was sweet and short As having the best killer instinct known in water sport.

A nation shared her ecstasy
But few would share her agony
She empowered the psyche of our national
 spine
As she churned up and down that thin black
 line.

She got the tag of 'Tiger' from her lethal will
  to win
When she creamed her first state title at the
  tender age of ten
World records tumbled in her early teens,
'Slashed', then smashed to smithereens.

Tough as teak but tiny by qualified critique
In middle-distance swimming's description of
  physique
And in the twilight I was left to grow
In a super athlete's afterglow.

Although a fish's daughter, I never followed her
  into water
I was a semi-Italian sprog, my dad a nut
  roasting bloody wog
Happy times gave way to sadder days,
Mum and Dad went separate ways.

Tit for tat, points to score,
Peace talks fail, they went to war
I never bask in reflected glory,
It's there simply to tell my story.

I was sixteen, bulletproof, sort of easy on the
  eye
And there were a million things I wanted to try
Then came the conclusion that cut like a knife
The tumour in my leg was a threat to life.

The audition's over, you've got the part and
  fear packs ice around your heart
Painful biopsies, scans and screens, your life's
  attached to giant machines
The swimmer and the wog agree they'll fight
  their greatest fight for me.

Philosophies are fielded, some of them fit
Like, 'You're not dying, Hannah, you're living
 with it.'
The chemo clicks in and your hair falls out
There's a traffic jam on life's roundabout
Not a good look, whatever which way
And you reckon you're having a bad hair day!

A tumour the size of a grapefruit's gone
Just an apple now – operation's on.
Daybreak, doped ... you've come off the wall
You hope to God they've got it all
And there in the gloom on the flat of my back
Comes ...'You're Tiger's daughter ... it's time
 to attack.'

Chemo clicks in combination
With the branding irons of radiation
I'm going great – a girl on a mission
In the glorious eighth straight month of
 remission.

Then I stepped on a mine and my world
 imploded
As the lines on a CT scan exploded

There on the phone I heard Mother's heart
 crack
When through blinding tears I screamed: 'It's
 back!'

My lust for life had popped its bungs
Eleven tumours had attached to my lungs
I freaked out, broke down, dropped to the
 floor
The 'my way' princess couldn't take any more.

No ... no ... no ... the chemo and pain
I just couldn't lose my hair again.
I'd been there, done that, this just can't be
Sweet Jesus God. Why me, why me?

When I'd got beyond the scope of crying
I felt that I might just be dying
Then I thought ... stuff this, I'm far too young
There's more to life than cancer of the lung.

Now – loose rein, tight grip, laser in
Think powerfully, take up the slack
'You're Tiger's daughter – it's time to attack.'

A couple of times I know Hannah has visited me. About six months after her death my mobile phone lit up at about 1am, the time that she passed. I couldn't sleep anyway so I answered. It was Hannah. We had a nice little chat, just like the old days, while I looked outside into the dark and up at the sky.

In January 2010, I was in Melbourne staying for a few days at a friend's place. I was in bed at about midnight when someone blew air into my ear. I froze and was about to cry, when I suddenly relaxed. I'm not scared anymore when she visits. It's just Hannah popping in to say, 'I love you, Mum.'

My mother also had a similar experience. She placed a pink mobile phone she'd given Hannah as a present inside her coffin. The number was disconnected but about two months after she passed, it came up on Mum's mobile!

I just know she's here with us.

I love you, my little Hanni □.

PART 6

NEVER GIVING UP

37

'The road to success is always under construction.'

All my life I've considered myself to be a strong person, physically and mentally. I was lucky to have been born with a strong body that enabled me to swim as far and as fast as I did. However, mental strength is something else. It's not a Godgiven gift, in my opinion. You can work on it and get stronger as you get older. When it came to swimming, I always had an unshakeable belief in myself, based on my disciplined training regime and natural ability.

But out of the pool, and after all I had been through, psychologically I was completely shot. In the wake of Hannah's diagnosis, my old bad habit of prescription medication addiction regained control of my life. The only way I could cope over those next three years, watching my beautiful girl die in front of my eyes, was by using the emotional crutch of painkillers.

I was not going out, avoided seeing people and became a virtual recluse. I was so angry at God and would stick my finger up at the church whenever I drove past. At night I would curl up into a ball and cry myself to sleep. In the morning, my back pain was worse, so I'd take a few pills to enable me to get out of bed. I was so lonely after cutting myself off from my friends, I even contemplated suicide, but I knew I had my son Daniel to look after. And so it continued.

Since Hannah's passing in 2007, I have steadily improved. Unfortunately, my back pain has worsened and I have spent the last few years in and out of hospital in order to fix my physical affliction. I have direct injections in my spine and use a wire lumbar support when driving the car. I try to be careful not to put stress on my back and I work on core strength with Pilates, which strengthens the back and stomach muscles.

I feel a bit lost in Brisbane, and don't feel like there's much for me here. I'm just part of the furniture in my home town. I did spend seven months down in Melbourne in 2009, living with dear friend Tracey Weideman. She's been my saviour over the past few years.

It felt so bittersweet to be in the city that Hannah adored so much. I lived a block from the hub of all the shops she loved going to every time I took her there for a function. I wandered the streets, window shopping and pretending I was with Hannah. I would sit in our favourite coffee shops and cry. If she was still here, I know she would have moved down with me had she not got cancer.

I returned to Brisbane soon after, as it all proved too much and the weather was awful. Due to my back problems and my depression, I have been on Centrelink benefits for a few years now. I don't own a home and can't afford to rent at the moment so, for the past two years, I've been living at Mum's. I'm struggling to get back on my feet.

Just after Hannah's passing, Alan Jones, the 2GB talkback presenter, read about how I was in a bad way. He sent me a personal cheque from his own pocket for five thousand dollars, with a beautiful bunch of roses and a card telling me what a true champ I was and encouraging me to power ahead. He said that Australia should look after its legends. What a kind and generous man.

***

Like a reformed alcoholic, I realise the danger of drug addiction and try to avoid temptation. The struggle is ongoing, but I am determined to overcome it. Writing this book has been a cathartic experience for me and I hope it helps others in a similar predicament. My advice to anyone struggling with an addiction is that they need to realise there are other ways of coping with physical and emotional pain.

If you feel lost and overcome by your reliance on medication, see your GP and tell them your story. Remember, you're not alone. I thought I was, but after meeting other people in hospital with the same problem, I soon learned I wasn't the only one suffering out there. We can all fight this.

When times are tough, one of the best ways to cheer myself up is with a spontaneous act of kindness. I always find that giving is better than receiving. One example that springs to mind is from a few years back when I was shopping at Brookside, in Brisbane's northern suburbs, and popped into the bank. Standing in the queue, I noticed a little old lady with a large bag of groceries. She was clutching an asthma puffer and shaking and was obviously in trouble. She went up to the counter, ignoring the line-up of customers and said to the young teller, 'I need to get some money out to pay my rent but I'm shaking too much from the Ventolin. I'll miss my bus. Can you help me?'

Several customers were grumbling impatiently but I joined her.

'Would you like a lift? Here, let me take that bag.'

She didn't have a clue who I was, but was very appreciative and off we went. She lived at Bardon, not far from me. When we got to her home, her husband came out to greet us.

'What have we got here, darling? Well, look who it is. Hello, Tracey.'

The old lady suddenly recognised me and was embarrassed to have taken me out of my way.

'Can I give you some money?' she inquired.

'No way! I enjoyed our chat.'

A week later I saw her again in the same bank and she recognised me straightaway.

'Hi, Tracey. How are you? We're off on a train trip to Cairns.'

'How lovely. Have a good trip,' I said to my new friend.

Another time, I picked up three pensioners at a cab rank. It was pouring rain and they all had groceries, so I pulled up and asked where they lived. The answer was Bardon, Ashgrove and Red Hill, all within a few kilometres radius.

'Okay, hop in. It's a bit of a squeeze but it's better than standing here getting drenched with no cabs about.'

We had a great chat and I dropped them all off. Then I went back and picked up two more pensioners and took them home. You know why? It made me feel so good. I never accept money. I get a buzz out of it and I know that I could be in their shoes one day. I only tell them, 'My name is Tracey.' Some recognise me, some don't, but it makes me feel good.

I have done this for many years. I just love the 'pay it forward' thing. We are all human beings and we should all help one another in some small way, whether it be opening a door, dropping someone off, helping people cross the road with their groceries or even just giving someone a smile. It all does make a difference in this world.

I also really get a kick out of performing in front of an audience, which may seem strange for someone who used to be as timid as a mouse. As I've become older, I've learned how to overcome my nerves and I really have a passion for my usual topics, swimming and fundraising for research into sarcoma. I love to throw in a few good stories and funny incidents and I get quite animated on stage.

About five months after Hannah passed away, I spoke at a Breast Cancer Ladies Luncheon at Royal Pines on the Gold Coast. My best friend Lee Goodall was there with a table of her friends. I was very nervous beforehand, wondering if I would be able to talk about my daughter without breaking down. The wounds were still raw and I hadn't spoken publicly for several years.

I planned to make it easy for myself. I showed a DVD of my greatest race, the 400-metre world record in Berlin, which got everyone going. Then I spoke jokingly about living with my sixteen-year-old son, Daniel. Everyone could identify with the same old problems – toilet seats up, towels on the floor and so on – and there were hoots of laughter. I finished with some memories of Hannah and read out one of her poems. There wasn't a dry eye in the house.

I was so proud of myself. I had kept it all together. I walked down the stairs from the stage and looked up to see that everyone was standing and applauding. Lee came over and, in the middle of the room, gave me a big hug which lasted a few minutes. When I sat down, people kept coming up for an autograph, patting me on the back and saying, 'What a fantastic talk. The best I ever heard!' I was rapt. To me, it was undoubtedly the best speech of my life.

I did another talk recently in Melbourne for the Collingwood Football Club. This was the opposite really, a room full of men, but they seemed to like what I had to say. I got a warm reception and, afterwards, the host Eddie McGuire came up to thank me. I noticed he had tears in his eyes. I really enjoy being on stage and talking to a crowded room. I love the adrenalin rush!

Another thing that always makes me feel good is my Mal tese terrier, Daisy. Even after the worst day, when she jumps into my lap it makes me feel good. Talk about unconditional love. Our little family has always had at least one dog, usually white Maltese terriers, and they've been great company.

Daisy used to have a sister, Lily, who died at seven years of age, two years before Hannah passed away. They both used to sleep on my bed from when they were just eight weeks old. I've now had Daisy for twelve years and I just adore her. Like me, she's been through a lot, losing Hannah and Lily, and I spoil her rotten.

In bed at night, Daisy will curl up behind me in the small of my back and go to sleep. I love it and it makes her feel secure to know that I'm there. I can sit on the couch watching television and have Daisy lying on her back beside me and I'll be patting and kissing her. I just love her to bits. She knows when I'm upset and she will come and lie next to me and look at me with those beautiful big brown eyes. I know she has only about four or five years left and I will have to say goodbye eventually.

Now I also have Jedda, a four-year-old black miniature poodle rescued by the RSPCA. She was from a puppy mill that was raided in 2009 and my neighbours fostered her for a while. She's totally blind, but you wouldn't know it. When my neighbours were forced to give her up, I rang the boss of the RSPCA and said I wanted to adopt her straightaway. I just can't stand to see animals in pain. Jedda was with me within forty-eight hours. She and Daisy both get treated like princesses and sleep on my bed, and always will.

Another source from which I can draw hope is Michael Jackson. He was a genius and a very humble human being. The more people put him down, the more love he would give back to them. Michael felt a lot for humanity and actually cared about people and our earth, long before 'caring for the planet' was trendy. I think we can all learn something from him.

I've always been a huge Michael Jackson fan ever since I was a child, but more so since *Thriller* came out. I bought the cassette and VHS movie and know the words off by heart. Since his passing, I have bought every CD and DVD of his, about fifteen titles in total, and I have the boxed set of all his international concerts and movies. When *This Is It,* the final film made before his death, was released on DVD in March 2010, I bought two copies: one to use and one to 'keep', in case I wear one out. I can't get enough of MJ and I have to watch at least one of his DVDs every day.

There's a particular line Michael says in *This Is It* that really speaks to me. He says that we need to be humble, or else God will take our gifts away: 'We have to use our gifts together to help others figure out what their gifts are.'

He was such a beautiful human being and has taught me how important it is to be grateful for what we have been given and to give back to others. We should all take a leaf out of his book. Hannah knew how much I loved MJ. I know she'd be telling him how crazy I am about him up in heaven. I cry for him too.

38

My swimming past will always be with me. I often like to think back on my happy days at the Valley Pool, hanging around with my mates Michael Bohl, Adam Sambrook, Gary Watson, Lionel Hogg Jnr, Stephen 'Fossil' Fry and others. As Michael remembers:

We used to socialise a lot in those days: barbecues, movies and surfing at the coast on weekends. Tracey was always 'one of the boys' and she and I were as close as you can be without being boyfriend/girlfriend. We have reunions from time to time, often organised by Tracey. She always gets a bit teary recalling the 'good old days'.

Tracey's a lovely, warm-hearted person and one of the greatest swimmers Australia has seen. She broke world records and won gold medals and gave so much to the sport, which really gave nothing back to her. I know she's suffered a lot of hardship personally. A few people got together a couple of years ago and organised a testimonial for her, sponsored by Carlton & United Breweries' Roy Prosser [a huge fan of Tracey's who passed away in August 2008]. Her dad was there and a lot of her old swimming mates. Her father's speech was excellent and Laurie Lawrence stole the show, as always. We raised a bit of money for her. We all want the best for Tracey.

Personally, I think she'd be a great coach. She's got all the attributes: experience, a deep knowledge of the sport and a wonderful ability to communicate. She's done plenty of clinics and loves working with kids. She's a natural.

I love Michael and I am so proud of his success in coaching. One of his squad members is the Olympic triple gold medallist Stephanie Rice. When asked by Peter Meares if she knows anything about Tracey Wickham, she replied, 'Do I? Of course. She's an absolute legend.'

My proudest achievement throughout my career was my 400-metre freestyle world record, 4:06.28, set in Berlin at the 1978 World Championships. It was also the Commonwealth and Australian record. While Janet Evans knocked off the world mark in 1987, the Commonwealth record lasted almost thirty years, until it was eventually broken by another Brisbane girl, Bronte Barratt, in 2007 in Chiba, Japan. The eighteen-year-old university student did something that the greats of the past had not been able to do. She clocked 4:05.93, just 0.35 seconds faster than my time twenty-nine years earlier, albeit in a supersuit in a wet-deck pool with anti-splash lane ropes. I had presented Bronte with a bronze medal at the Melbourne Commonwealth Games in 2006 and my record could not have gone to a nicer girl. Sometimes I wonder though, if it weren't for the supersuit, would my records still stand?

When I first swam in a race my costume was made of nylon, with a skirt in front of the hips. It took quite a while to dry, but at least it was an improvement on the itchy woollen costumes worn by my ancestor, Alick Wickham. In the late 1970s, lycra was introduced as the new wonder textile. It fitted like a second skin, as if you were competing naked like athletes in the ancient Olympics. I loved those togs because I didn't have to use a hair ribbon to hold the straps together to stop them falling off my shoulders.

In the late 1990s, swimmers began wearing full-body lycra swimsuits which covered most of their skin and reduced the drag in the water. By the late 2000s, these had become even more hi-tech as polyurethane panels were added and they became known as supersuits. Polyurethane squeezes the swimmer in to make them more aerodynamic and also provides a thick layer of foam full of tiny gas bubbles, giving more buoyancy to the wearer. It's a subtle form of cheating really, like wearing fins.

Polyurethane suits can cost up to fifteen hundred dollars a pop. As Kieren Perkins, the legendary Queensland distance swimmer, has said, hi-tech swimsuits should only be allowed if they are available to everyone, and that's never going to happen. Poor African nations can hardly afford swimming pools, let alone ridiculously expensive swimsuits that last only a few months.

At the 2009 Rome World Championships, thirty-one world marks were broken, some by relatively unknown swimmers, thanks to the unfair advantages of the supersuits. A classic example came in the men's 200-metre freestyle where American superstar, Michael Phelps, wearing a normal costume, was beaten by a little-known German, Paul Biedemann, wearing the controversial full polyurethane suit. Biedemann also wore the suit to win the 400 metres, breaking Ian Thorpe's world record. I think Thorpey's record should still stand as he swam it in his old full-length black suit.

In all, one hundred and eight world records were broken in 2008 and thirty in 2009, thanks to the advent of the new technology. In the old days, my world records in the 400-metre and 800-metre freestyle lasted almost a decade. (Personally, I wish they had lasted the whole decade rather than the nine-and-a-half years, but 'nearly a decade' is good enough!) Now it's not unusual for new records to last less than a week. I didn't begrudge Janet Evans for breaking my marks. I was proud and rather surprised that they stood for so long, especially during the turbulent period of the 1980s when drug-taking was rife among Eastern European nations.

FINA, the governing body of world swimming, finally decided enough was enough and banned polyurethane from 1 January 2010. From now on, suits cannot cover the arms or lower legs and the playing field will be level again. To me, that's fair. I also think it would be fair if all records made using a polyurethane suit were wiped and the records reverted to only those swum in the standard lycra.

***

Despite what could have been or should have been, I know that swimming has given me so much. I was incredibly lucky growing up that my parents, especially Mum, gave me their support to follow my dream in whichever field I wanted to.

I knew I was born to achieve great things, even at a very young age. We are all born with a natural talent and then it's a matter of finding your niche in life. You might discover that talent at the age of five, or the age of fifty, but when you do, you just know.

I loved to train, and train hard, which I couldn't have done without my swim mates. That's the key: you have to love the sport and not be forced into it, like I've seen happen so many times. I swam hard every time I dived into the pool. All I wanted to do was win and if that was a personal best then great, bonus.

But to accomplish what I did, it wasn't enough that I was dedicated. I needed the whole team behind me: Mum (the taxi driver, masseuse, psychologist, etc.), Dad with his 'you can do it' attitude, my loving Grampa and, of course, my coaches. How many Ian Thorpes or Susie O'Neills or Stephanie Rices are there that could have been but never were because their parents couldn't be bothered taking them to training every day? Like I say, it's a team effort.

My only regret in my career would be not having an Olympic gold medal. Swimming is all about timing and I peaked in the wrong years. As Mum puts it:

> Lady luck rarely smiled on Tracey. In 1976, she went to the Montreal Olympics but, at thirteen, she was far too young. She just played with her yo-yo and cried herself to sleep at night, she was so homesick. Four years later, she was too sick to go Moscow and in 1984 she watched the Los Angeles Olympics on television, two years retired.

I know I never did achieve my personal best and I retired too young. But even now when I look back, there was no incentive for me to stay in the sport.

If I had my time over again, I would have swum for another five years. I know I would have reached peak fitness in my mid-twenties. I was only a baby at fifteen years of age, breaking all those world records and winning gold medals. At nineteen, I had enough financially and emotionally, but these days a nineteen-year-old is the 'baby' of the Australian team.

Nearly thirty years into retirement, I can say that sport left me physically broken. Not only did I suffer scoliosis of the lumbar region in my back since the age of twelve, but I have been left with arthritis and shoulder pain. Every kilometre I swam during my career was approximately one thousand arm strokes, and I would swim up to 20 kilometres a day, multiplied over months and years. This led to the rotary cuffs in my shoulders becoming so degenerated I had to have two operations on them in 2005. I suffer arthritis in my knee, my wrists and fingers. The bones between my thumb and forefinger on my right hand fused together in 2006. There are major problems with all my joints, but it's the price you pay. It's all worth it.

I wouldn't swap my life the way it has gone so far. Sure there were a lot of ups and downs and probably more downs than ups, but it's made me all the stronger as a person. Mum often says, 'Had anyone else been through what you have in your life, Tracey, they would probably be six feet under.'

Swimming meant I got to see many countries a few times over and meet wonderful people. It wasn't just the celebrities I loved meeting, but also the everyday person on the street. I know I'm a human being like everyone else, the only difference is I could swim faster than others. People often say, 'I thought you would be a lot taller and bigger in real life.' I'm actually quite small. They are also often surprised by my personality. 'Tracey, you are just so normal and down-to-earth.'

Dad always taught me to be humble and that's how I want to be remembered. I hope people remember me as a kind person, a great mother, 'And the bonus was, she swam fast.'

39

There are still those times when the clinical depression I have struggled with for ten years gets me low. There have been mornings when I felt I simply couldn't get out of bed, when the blackness threatened to engulf me. I even felt like jumping off the Story Bridge, to put an end to the pain. But I know that if I did jump, I'd probably only break my ankle and swim a world record to the riverbank (just joking, of course). But when I get these black thoughts, I remember that I've got Daniel to look after, that Mum and Dad still love me and that, perhaps after all, life is worth living.

Mum has been my rock over all these years and words can't express how grateful I am for everything she's done for me. She has always wanted the best for me:

Tracey deserves to be lauded as one of the legends of her sport, she epitomised the little Aussie battler, yet she has been dogged by misfortune all her life. Her luck with men has been as bad as her luck with the Olympics.

Tracey has led a tumultuous life. She has found fame but not happiness. I found a perfect partner in my current husband, Ashley, the second time around. I hope Tracey can too. She deserves a better fate.

I miss having a partner and I don't think I've ever known what it's like to be in love. Maybe I never will, because I've been too hurt in the past to really trust in a relationship again. Still, I would like to experience it, even just for a month, to know what it's like before I'm gone.

I am so glad Mum has found so much happiness with Ashley. He's been a great help to all of us. He shares the family love of animals and he and Mum have three poodles and plenty of budgies and chooks that are cuddled and fed every day. He and Mum never had any kids, but they have their ten grandchildren (including Hannah) to keep them going.

My father is also doing well. He is still one of my biggest fans:

> How many other middle-distance and distance swimmers, male or female, ever thrashed a hot field of sprinters in a sprint event at national level? Murray Rose never did. Lorraine Crapp never did. Jon Konrads never did. Ilsa Konrads never did. Brian Goodell never did. Stephen Holland never did. Jenny Turrall never did and Kieren Perkins never did. Tracey's hero, the incredible Shane Gould did, and Tracey Wickham did, even unprepared.
>
> The fact that people thought Tracey was not a sprinter was because people categorise swimmers into boxes. Stroke boxes and distance boxes. Tracey could fit in any and all boxes. So could Shane Gould. For them it was a matter of choice.

They were swimmers. Stroke didn't matter and distance didn't matter. It's a very, very select club. Pound-for-pound, those two were as good as any Australia ever produced and their records attest to that.

I know Dad and I have had some good and bad times but the bottom line is he's my dad and I love him dearly. We have had a great relationship for quite a number of years now. He adores his children and he adores the grandkids and even though he's often in the States, I know we are never far from his mind.

We email each other just about daily. We have our own private joke, which is that I'm 'Roger Wickham's daughter' and he's not 'Tracey Wickham's father'. Just a little in-house giggle we like to have. That's also what he says if people ask him if we're related and if he's the dad of Tracey Wickham. 'No, she's Roger Wickham's daughter!' People have a good laugh.

I also have my sisters for support and I love them dearly. Kelly is a Qantas International air hostess and has been flying for twenty-two years. She has been married to her husband Ian for fifteen years and they have three children, so Kelly flies part-time now. My other sister Julie is married to Jim and they have five kids. Julie was a nurse in a cancer ward for ten years before also becoming a Qantas hostess for a time. Now she is a full-time mum. I am so lucky to have my eight nieces and nephews and I really enjoy being Aunty Tracey.

Rob and I have reconciled and are on good terms. The turning point was undoubtedly Hannah's illness, which linked us through a common bond of suffering, and these days we're the best of friends. Gone are all the fights, courts, faxes and the 'Whose turn is it to have the kids at Easter or Christmas this year?'

We have laughs about the good old days and remember our awesome honeymoon, amongst other things. We often chat about what we could have done differently in our lives. Hindsight is a great thing, isn't it? Rob's also had a few sad break-ups and failed relationships, like I have. It's amazing how the world keeps turning without you even realising.

Rob is a great guy. I know if I hadn't met him, we wouldn't have had our beautiful Hannah and Daniel. Now we are better friends than we have ever been. We will always have our children in common and will always be parents together.

Rob is a smart businessman and financially secure and he helps me out with advice on investments. He has been a firm influence on Daniel, who is deeply affected by his sister's death. I respect both Rob and his family, despite what we've been through. The pain we've been able to overcome just makes us respect each other more.

***

As I write, Daniel is nearly nineteen. He's grown into a burly boy with the same looks as his grandfather, Roger. In many ways he's the spitting image of me as well, with the same nose, skin tone and thick auburn hair.

Daniel has no trouble finding girlfriends and loves the grunge look. His undies show out of the top of his pants, which I can't stand, but I still love him for it. He is a talented swimmer and soccer player and toured overseas with a Brisbane City junior side, but he doesn't have the passion for sport I had. In his own words:

I still live at Dad's place at Hamilton, after living with Mum for a few years before she moved to Melbourne for a bit. I still see a lot of Mum though. She's been through a great deal and sometimes I've had to look after her emotionally. Even though it's been years, I still have days when I grieve over Hannah. We were really close.

Daniel misses his big sister so much and I know her passing has affected him greatly. It hasn't been easy for him over the past six years or so. Even though he and Hannah had the usual fights as kids do in the early days, it changed when they both became teenagers. When his sister got sick, he became even closer to her and any word of advice she gave him, he would take it all in. They used to hug each other all the time.

Daniel has a tattoo under his right bicep: the name Hannah in old English script. There's another on his chest which is a quote from something Hannah wrote. He and I both wear the same blue plastic band on our wrists, in support of Hannah's Chance Foundation. We both cherish the paintings Hannah made, and hang them on our walls. Daniel has strong plans for the future:

> Dad sold the nut business a few years ago and now he's in property development. I'd like to get my real estate licence and go into business with Dad in Brisbane. At the moment I'm looking at setting up my own coffee shop.

I still feel a lot of guilt over what Daniel went through during my abusive relationships but, as he says:

> If I was the size I am today and they did that to my mother, I'd smash them. I warn her about guys she meets now but there's no need. She just doesn't seem interested. She just wants a good job and a nice home. She's been a fantastic mother and deserves to be happy, after what she's been through. I love her so much. I really do have the best mother in the world.

My children were and are the most important people in my life. I tell them that I love them every single day, many times over, even though Hannah is only here in spirit. I would do anything for my kids.

I am so grateful to have my little man Daniel, but of course he is an adult now and beginning to live his own life. With a son, you have them until they're in a relationship, although they will always love their mothers. But with a daughter, you have them for life. The mother/daughter bond is different, that's what my mother says. She's lucky, she has three daughters, and even though they are married, they are always there for her.

I just love kids. The only regret that I have in life is not having more, and I can't believe that Daniel is now an only child. I never imagined it would be that way. Four children at the least would have been fantastic and was my goal, but it wasn't meant to be. When I separated at the age of thirty-two, I thought I would meet someone and have another couple of kids. Now, at forty-seven, I know it will never happen.

I always wanted to adopt, even when I was separated and single. The kids and I spoke about it a lot and they were keen. Even just before Hannah was diagnosed we were still talking about it, but of course that idea went out the window. We did sponsor a little girl through World Vision though, for a long time.

***

Hannah often visits me via her spirit. I just know when she's here: my mobile lights up in the middle of the night and I often feel a breeze in my ear. She's happy now, no more pain. What a brave, tough girl she was, not only when she was sick but when she was younger. I have a small tattoo of her name with a butterfly, which symbolises freedom, on the inside of my left wrist so I can put it close to my heart. It's not for show to anyone, but for me to look at and remember the beautiful girl that she was and still is.

I've only been to her gravesite about six times. It's emotionally draining when I go and it takes me days to get over it. I get so nervous and anxious on the way to the Nudgee Cemetery and have to gee myself up to go. Then I get very upset when I leave, knowing that she's there all alone. I get worried about how the weather is affecting her, especially when it's raining or boiling, even though she is a metre above ground in a little chapel in the Ciobo crypt, with a wrought-iron gate and a hibiscus flower leadlight. We all leave notes and flowers in the drawer inside. I found out recently that her crypt is vacuum-sealed so she won't decay. I am so relieved that she is still my little Hanni, the way I last saw her.

It has been three years now since her passing. Even though I will never get over it, I'm managing to get through each day a whole lot better than when it all started. I don't know what is going to happen in my life in the future, but I know one thing: I'm going to take a leaf out of Hannah's diary.

> No one knows their future or how long they have. That's why you should live every day as if it were your last – because one day it will be.

When Hannah was diagnosed, I hated God, but now I appreciate the blessing he gave me: two beautiful children. It is a gift that surpasses anything I have ever done in the pool, all the gold medals. Nothing compares to being a mum and all mums know that. I was one of the fortunate ones to be able to be a great mum and I know that to be true.

My 'Hannah Banana' and my little 'Dan the Man'.
My two adorable gifts I will treasure for life.
I love them to bits!

WHY WORRY?

BY UNKNOWN

There are only two reasons to worry.
Whether you are sick or you are well.
If you're well there is really nothing to worry
 about.
And if you are sick, there are only two things to
 worry about
—whether you will get better or worse.
If you get better, there is really nothing to worry
 about
And if you get worse, there are only two things
 to worry about
—whether you will live or die.
Now if you live there is nothing really to worry
 about
And if you die there are only two things to worry
 about
—whether you go to heaven or to hell.
If you go to heaven there will be nothing to worry
 about
And if you go to hell you will be so busy catching
 up with all your old mates you won't have time
 to worry.
So why worry?

AFTERWORD

WRITING TREADING WATER

I have always wanted to write my story, to show people the real Tracey Wickham. It frustrates me when people assume that because someone is famous, life must be easy. If only they knew the truth and that, due to my financial situation, I have been living out of a suitcase amongst my storage boxes in a room under my mum's house since July 2008.

The title of the book came to me twelve years ago in the middle of the night. I bolted upright and wrote it down: 'Treading Water'. This idea encapsulates me as a person and what I have had to go through in life. I've had to keep my head above water to survive. Somehow, I've managed to face adversity and I am getting stronger each day: emotionally and physically.

After Hannah's passing, I needed time to heal inside – not that I will ever fully recover from the tragedy. So I put off writing the book I'd dreamed of, knowing that it would bring up the dirt and hurt and pain in my life and would be emotionally draining.

About two years ago, Peter Meares came into the picture. We bumped into each other at our local post office and had a coffee. I asked him to help me write and he accepted immediately. We have known each other for well over thirty years and I have a huge amount of respect for him: he is a sports encyclopaedia. I wrote a fair amount of my story down and we began by discussing my life in recorded sessions, the first one in February 2009 and then Peter and I met many times, sitting in coffee shops and out on his deck. There were plenty of shared laughs and tears. And a bit of anger, from me of course.

I told Peter I had a few newspaper clippings he might find useful. Now, I'm not one to have anything in chronological order, but Peter nearly did a backflip when he saw how many boxes there were, dating right back to the mid-1970s. He sifted through the lot and returned them in monthly and yearly order for me. I was thrilled. I can't thank him enough for his dedication and 'putting up' with me for all these months. I thank him for all his patience, support, eagerness and for bringing out the best (and worst) in my life. He has really put in the hard yards. It must have been like going a round with Mike Tyson sometimes!

The section of *Treading Water* where I relive Hannah's passing was the hardest to write. I needed to do it myself. I wanted to write every emotion and put the reader in my shoes. I sat up in bed for five hours, crying and crying while writing her horrific story. Each time I re-read and revised my words, I wept again.

In mid-May this year, I spent five weeks in hospital, purely to cleanse myself of all the stuff I'd been depending on. I promised Hannah that I was doing this for her. I want to be 'right' emotionally for the launch of *Treading Water,* which I have dedicated to my daughter.

There were times I thought writing this book would be an impossible task and I'm grateful to the support I received from Random House – Maisie and Alison – who urged me to keep going and convinced me that it was a story that could inspire others who are struggling with their demons. I also want to thank Mum and Dad for contributing and researching things from the early days that I was too young to remember.

I hope you enjoyed reading about the real Tracey Wickham and please, if you know anyone struggling with addiction, pass my book on to them. If I can help just a handful of people, I will know it has all been worthwhile.

This book is my story, warts-and-all.

STATISTICAL RECORD

AWARDS

1978 Australian Sportsperson of the Year
Queensland Sportsperson of the Year

1979 Member of the Order of the British Empire (MBE)
Inaugural Australian Sportswoman of the Year
ABC Sportsperson of the Year
Queensland Sportswoman of the Year

1982 Queensland Sportswoman of the Year

1986 Inducted into the Sport Australia Hall of Fame

1992 Inducted into the World Swimming
Hall of Fame, Fort Lauderdale, Florida, USA

2000 Australian Sports Medal, for outstanding
contribution as a competitor in swimming

2005 Order of Australia Medal (OAM),
for community service to children in rural Australia
and for the development of young swimmers through
motivational speaking and swim clinics

SWIM RECORD

1976 Montreal Olympic Games

- Team member

1978 Edmonton Commonwealth Games

- Gold: 400-metre freestyle (Commonwealth record)
- Gold: 800-metre freestyle (world record standing for nearly ten years, a record in itself)
- Silver: 200-metre freestyle
- Silver: 4x100-metre medley relay (butterfly leg)
- Bronze: 4x100-metre freestyle relay

1978 Berlin World Championships

- Gold: 400-metre freestyle (world record standing for nearly ten years, a record in itself)
- Gold: 800-metre freestyle

1982 Brisbane Commonwealth Games

- Gold: 400-metre freestyle
- Gold: 800-metre freestyle
- Silver: 200-metre freestyle

1976–1982, 23 Australian Championship Victories

- 200-metre, 400-metre, 800-metre, 1500-metre freestyle
- 100-metre butterfly

1990 Magnetic Island to Townsville Swim

- First place

1990 Italian Gran Fondo Marathon Lake Swim

- First place

Total Records

- 365 Queensland records
- 275 Australian records
- 12 Commonwealth records
- 5 world records (400 metres, 800 metres x2, 1500 metres x2)

ACKNOWLEDGEMENTS

TRACEY WICKHAM

I would like to thank the following people in my life:

My beautiful children Hannah and Daniel, you both are my everything. Daniel, you are my rock and with you, life is still worth living. Mum, who has loved and supported me always: my chef, driver, masseuse, psychologist and shoulder to cry on. My love for you is precious and unconditional. Dad, for your wonderful support, love and guidance over the years. I love you with all my heart and I'm so proud to be Roger Wickham's daughter.

Ashley, I thank you for your loving support over the years and your love for my dear mum. You have been there for her through all the rough times. Thank you for supporting Hannah, Daniel and me during our tragedy. You are a part of our family and we all love you. Kelly and Julie, thank you both so much for being my little 'big' sisters and for giving me eight beautiful nieces and nephews. I'm very lucky to have you both in my life. I love you dearly.

To my aunties Denise and Narelle, and uncles Graham and Terry, I will always be thankful for your help and love over the years. Uncle Jon, you are very special to me. You have borne your blindness for forty-three years and I would give every single cent I own for you to be able to see your children and grandchildren. You are the greatest, Uncle Jon. I love you heaps.

Rob, thank you for our happy times and for giving me our two gorgeous children. I thank you for your tireless work to keep our beautiful Hannah alive. It hasn't gone unnoticed and I will never forget it.

Thank you to my coaches Peter Diamond, John Rigby, Mark Schubert (US), Bill Sweetenham and Laurie Lawrence. Without all of you my swimming career would not have taken the path that it did. You are all experts in your field and have been with me right from the start. I salute you all for being the greatest coaches and I'm thankful to all of you that I had the opportunity to be your student. To all my training mates whom I love dearly, thank you for your friendship, encouragement and support during the countless hours we spent together looking at the black line every day. And the laughs we had, without which training would have been unbearably boring! Bohly, Fossil, Jillian, Adam, Gary, Noel, Jo, Justin, Jono, Russell, Lionel and the rest of you guys (you know who you are). Love you all heaps!

PETER MEARES

Peter Meares is a leading Australian sports journalist and commentator based in Queensland. He has written several books on sport and hosted the ABC coverage of the 1982 Brisbane Commonwealth Games.

The first time I became aware of Tracey Wickham was in February 1978 when, as a fifteen-year-old, she broke the world record for the 1500-metre freestyle at Brisbane's Valley Pool. We go back a long way. I always admired her as a competitor – talented and tough – but I liked her as a person: warm and down-to-earth. When she asked me to help write a book on her life, I was delighted to accept.

First and foremost, I want to thank Tracey for her assistance in writing the book. Honest, fearless and trusting, she has applied the same tireless work ethic she had as a swimmer. Newspaper and magazine clippings, photos and even old schoolbooks have been made available and, most importantly, her time in recording interviews.

I would also like to thank all the others who contributed through their memories of Tracey's career. Swimming officials, coaches, competitors, journalists and family members have all been unfailingly generous.

Finally, my thanks to Alison Urquhart and Maisie Dubosarsky of Random House for their patience and passion for the project.

Donations to Hannah's Chance Foundation can be made by visiting the website: www.hannahschancefoundation.org.au

Back Cover Material

INSPIRATIONAL

'Tracey Wickham has he most devastating iller instinct in Australian sport'

Dawn Fraser

In the water, Tracey Wickham was a marvel. Out of it, she was a mess. As a teenager in the 1970s, she was the brightest star of Australian swimming, held the 400, 800 and 1500-metre freestyle world records concurrently and mixed with celebrities. But, after withdrawing from the Moscow Olympics and staging a triumphant comeback for the 1982 Brisbane Commonwealth Games, Tracey retired at the age of nineteen.

From that time on, Lady Luck didn't smile on Tracey. Her marriage ended in divorce and her new partner bashed her so savagely she was hospitalised. In line at Centrelink, Tracey thought she'd hit rock bottom. Worse was to come. Her beautiful daughter, Hannah, was diagnosed with terminal cancer and passed away, aged nineteen, three hours after a deathbed marriage.

Tracey's life spiralled out of control. Broke and alone, she struggled with depression and prescription-drug addiction. But our world champion would never give up without a fight and, with humour and determination, this little Aussie battler is winning the toughest race of all: life.

TREADING WATER *reveals the lows and soaring highs of a much-loved Australian sports star, candidly and fearlessly.*

Books For ALL Kinds of Readers

At ReadHowYouWant we understand that one size does not fit all types of readers. Our innovative, patent pending technology allows us to design new formats to make reading easier and more enjoyable for you. This helps improve your speed of reading and your comprehension. Our EasyRead printed books have been optimized to improve word recognition, ease eye tracking by adjusting word and line spacing as well as minimizing hyphenation. Our EasyRead SuperLarge editions have been developed to make reading easier and more accessible for vision-impaired readers. We offer Braille and DAISY formats of our books and all popular E-Book formats.

We are continually introducing new formats based upon research and reader preferences. Visit our web-site to see all of our formats and learn how you can Personalize our books for yourself or as gifts. Sign up to Become A (RHYW) Registered Reader.

www.readhowyouwant.com

Printed in Great Britain
by Amazon

47237631R00219